JOINDER OF CLAIMS

1. Joinder of claims is generally permissive.
2. Party asserting original claim, counterclaim, cross-claim, or third-party claim may join as many extant claims. (FRCP 18(a)). *M.K. v. Tenet*, 216 F.R.D. 133 (D.Cl. 2002).
   a. Counterclaims. *Plant v. Blazer Financial Services*, 598 F.2d 1357 (5th Cir. 1979).
      i. Compulsory. (FRCP 13(a))
         a. Must arise from same transaction/occurrence.
         b. If omitted, waived.
      ii. Permissive. (FRCP 13(b))
         a. Does not arise from same transaction/occurrence.
         b. Asserted at party's option.
   b. Cross-claims. (FRCP 13(g)). *Lasa per l'industria del Marmo Societa per Azioni v. Alexander*, 414 F. 2d 153 (1969).
      i. Asserted by co-parties.
      ii. Must arise from same transaction/occurrence as:
         a. Original claim;
         b. Counterclaim; or
         c. Property in issue.

JOINDER OF PARTIES – INTERPLEADER

Owner of property subject to multiple claims may invoke to require parties to litigate in single proceeding; *Cohen v. The Republic of the Philippines*, 146 F.R.D. 90 (S.D.N.Y. 1993).
1. Statutory interpleader. *State Farm Fire & Casualty Co. v. Tashire*, 386 U.S. 532 (1967).
   a. Minimal diversity.
   b. Jurisdictional amount minimum: $500.
2. Rule interpleader.
   a. Complete diversity or federal question.
   b. If diversity, jurisdictional amount: $75,000.

JOINDER OF PARTIES – INTERVENTION

Third party initiates joinder to action already in progress.
1. As of right (FRCP 24(a)(2)), requires:
   a. Risk of impairment of interest.
   b. Timely application.
   c. Lack of adequate representation. *Natural Resources Defense Council v. United States Nuclear Regulatory Commission*, 578 F.2d 1341 (10th Cir. 1978).
2. Permissive (FRCP 24(b)(1)-(2)) requires:
   a. Conditional right under federal statute.
   b. Claim or defense and main action have common question of law or fact.

JOINDER OF PARTIES – COMPULSORY
FRCP 19

Applies to a party needed for just adjudication. *Temple v. Synthes Corp.*, 498 U.S. 5 (1990); *Helzberg's Diamond Shops v. Valley West Des Moines Shopping Center*, 564 F.2d 816 (8th Cir. 1977).
1. Complete relief not available in its absence.
2. Absence of party would impair ability to protect interests. *Provident Tradesmens Bank & Trust Co. v. Patterson*, 390 U.S. 102 (1968).
3. Absence of party would expose other parties to substantial risk of inconsistent or multiple obligations.

JOINDER OF PARTIES – CLASS ACTION
Hansberry v. Lee, 311 U.S. 32 (1940); *Communities for Equity v. Michigan High School Athletic Assn.*, 1999 U.S. Dist. LEXIS 5780 (W.D. Mich. 1999).
1. Numerosity: too many class members to join individually.
2. Commonality: common question of law or fact.
3. Typicality: claims of named representatives must match those of the class.
4. Adequacy: named representatives must provide adequate representation.

JOINDER OF PARTIES – IMPLEADER
FRCP 18(a)

1. Joinder of additional party who may be liable to indemnify existing party.
2. Once joined, joinder of additional claims is also allowed.

JOINDER OF PARTIES – PERMISSIVE
Amchem Products v. Windsor, 521 U.S. 591 (1997).
1. Same transaction or occurrence.
2. Common question of law or fact.
3. Complete diversity and jurisdictional amount requirements apply.

PRECLUSION DOCTRINES

MUTUALITY DOCTRINE

Common law doctrine requiring the parties to the second action to be the same or in privity to the parties to the first action.
1. Preclusion cannot be used against person not a party to first action.
2. Exception: Collateral estoppel generally available by party not bound by first litigation. *Parklane Hosiery Co., Inc. v. Shore*, 439 U.S. 322 (1979).

COLLATERAL ESTOPPEL (ISSUE PRECLUSION)

1. Relitigating an issue of law or fact prohibited if issue was
   a. actually litigated and necessarily determined; and
   b. essential to a valid and final judgment.
2. Entered previously in litigation to which that person was a party, provided estopped party had incentive and opportunity to litigate issue conclusively. *Parklane Hosiery Co., Inc. v. Shore*, 439 U.S. 322 (1979).
3. Subject to additional fairness constraints when asserting party not party to prior litigation.
4. Subject to additional fairness constraints when issue was litigated in companion cases that reached inconsistent outcomes. *State Farm Fire & Casualty Co. v. Century Home Components*, 275 Or. 97 (1976).

RES JUDICAT[A]

A valid, final judg[ment] constitutes an ab[...] action between th[e...] privity, upon sam[e...]

1. Same parties to first and second suits. *Searle Brothers v. Searle*, 588 P.2d 689 (Utah 1978).
2. Final judgment on all parties' claims.
3. Final judgment on the merits.

INTERSYSTEM PRECLUSION

1. State court judgments in state court: the Full Faith and Credit Clause (Art. IV, §1) requires states to give preclusive effect to valid judgments in other states. *Durfee v. Duke*, 375 U.S. 106 (1963).
2. State court judgments in federal court: the Full Faith and Credit Act (28 U.S.C.§1738) requires federal courts to give preclusive effect to valid judgments rendered by state courts. *Gargallo v. Merrill Lynch, Pierce, Fenner & Smith*, 918 F.2d 658 (6th Cir. 1990).

DISCOVERY

BASIC DEVICES

1. Oral and written depositions. (FRCP 30 & 31)
2. Interrogatories. (FRCP 33). *In re Convergent Technologies Securities Litigation*, 108 F.R.D. 328 (1985).
3. Request for production of documents and orders for inspection. (FRCP 34). *Kozlowski v. Sears, Roebuck & Co.*, 73 F.R.D. 73 (1976).
4. Physical and mental examinations. (FRCP 35)
5. Requests for admission (FRCP 36):
   a. admission of truthfulness of facts; or
   b. admission of genuineness of documents.

SCOPE OF DISCOVERY

1. Inclusive – discovery is available for any matter: *Davis v. Precoat Metals*, 2002 WL 1759828 (N.D. Ill. 2002).
   a. Relevant to subject matter of action (FRCP 26(b)(1)),
   b. which appears reasonably calculated to lead to admissible evidence.
2. Exceptions:
   a. Privileged matter (attorney-client, self-incrimination, spousal, physician-patient). *Upjohn Co. v. United States*, 449 U.S. 383 (1981); *Butler v. Rigsby*, 1998 U.S. Dist. LEXIS 4618 (E.D. La. 1998).
   b. Attorney work-product. (FRCP 26(b)(3))
3. Experts. (FRCP 26(b)(4)). *Thompson v. The Haskell Co.*, 65 F. Empl. Prac. Cas. (BNA) 1088 (M.D. Fla. 1994); *Chiquita International Ltd. v. M/V Bolero Reefer*, 1994 U.S. Dist. LEXIS 5820 (S.D.N.Y. 1994).
4. Abuse and sanctions. (FRCP 26 & 27) *Zubulake v. UBS Warburg LLP*, 220 F.R.D. 212 (S.D.N.Y. 2003).
   a. Unreasonable/excessive use of discovery.
   b. Unreasonable compliance or refusal.
5. Duty to supplement responses (FRCP 26(e)):
   a. General rule: no duty to supplement to include later-acquired information or for correction.
   b. Exceptions:
      i. Disclosure materially incomplete or incorrect, if not made known to other parties. (FRCP 26 (e)(1))
      [...] obtaining information that response [...] was incorrect or failure to correct [...] would constitute concealment.
      [...] required by agreement among court [...] nd parties.

D1289946

REMOVAL JURISDICTION

28 U.S.C. §1441. *Caterpillar Inc. v. Lewis*, 519 U.S. 61 (1996).

Any civil action that was filed in state court may be removed to federal court for the district in which the case was pending, if the case is within the original jurisdiction of the federal court.

1. Original jurisdiction in federal court.
2. Only defendants may remove, all must agree.
3. Judicial district in which action was pending.

PLEADING

GENERAL TYPES OF PLEADINGS

1. Code-pleading – complaint requires a statement of fact that constitutes a cause of action. *Gillespie v. Goodyear Service Stores*, 258 N.C. 487 (1963).
2. Notice pleading – (FRCP 8) merges law and equity. Complaint merely requires (a) jurisdictional statement, (b) "short and plain" statement of the claim showing pleader is entitled to relief, and (c) demand for judgment. *Bell Atlantic v. Twombly*, 127 S. Ct. 1955 (2007).

ATTACKING THE PLEADINGS (OBJECTIONS)

1. Preliminary Objections. *Haddle v. Garrison*, no. 96-00029-CV-1 (S.D. 1996); *Haddle v. Garrison*, 525 U.S. 121 (1998).
   a. May be raised by motion or in responsive pleading.
   b. Objections to the manner in which action was initiated:
      i. lack of subject-matter jurisdiction;
      ii. lack of personal jurisdiction;
      iii. improper venue;
      iv. insufficient process;
      v. insufficient service of process; and
      vi. failure to join an indispensable party.
2. Formal pleading objections.
   a. Procedural errors.
   b. Motions to strike or motions for more definitive statement.
3. Substantive pleading objections.
   a. Attack legal theory of claim.
4. Federal pleading objections: Pleadings may be attacked by responsive pleadings or by motion.
5. Code pleading objections, e.g., demurrer.
6. Motions to dismiss.

THE ANSWER

1. Admissions and denials of allegations in complaint. (FRCP 8(b)). *Zielinski v. Philadelphia Piers, Inc.*, 139 F. Supp. 408 (E.D. Pa. 1956).
2. Affirmative defenses available.
3. Other defenses of a preliminary nature. (FRCP 12(b)). *Huddle v. Garrison*, 525 U.S. 121 (1958).
4. Counterclaim or cross-claim making allegations of liability owed the answering party (federal practice only).

SPECIAL PLEADING REQUIREMENTS
FRCP 9

1. Allegations of fraud or mistake.
2. Special damages.
3. Complex proceedings.
4. Alternative/inconsistent allegations are permitted.

TRUTHFULNESS IN PLEADING

Requires that all parties be candid and proceed in good faith.

1. Verification. Party who files pleading must:
   a. do so under oath; and
   b. sign her name attesting that matters therein are true to best information and belief.
2. Lawyers' certification. (FRCP 11)
3. Courts retain power to sanction bad-faith conduct. *Christian v. Mattel*, 286 F.3d 1118 (2003).

AMENDMENTS TO PLEADINGS
FRCP 15

1. Before trial. *Beeck v. The Aquaslide 'n' Dive Corp.*, 562 F.2d 537 (1977).
   a. After any responsive pleading is served.
   b. Within 20 days after served, if pleading itself does not permit responsive pleading, and action not yet on trial calendar. (FRCP 15)
2. Any time during/after trial with consent of all adverse parties.
3. Relatng back. *Bonerb v. Richard J. Caron Foundation*, 159 F.R.D. 16 (W.D.N.Y. 1994).
   a. Amendments relate back automatically if permitted by applicable statute of limitations.
   b. Amendments relate back to original pleading if claim or defense arose out of the same conduct, transactions, or occurrence.
4. Changing a party. *Moore v. Baker*, 989 F.2d 1129 (1993).
   a. Relates back if:
      i. Same conduct, transaction or occurrence.
      ii. Party received sufficient notice.
      iii. Party knew or should have known, but for a mistake, that the action would have been brought against him.
      iv. Notice for (ii) and (iii) must be provided within 120 days after filing complaint.

VALIDITY AND ENFORCEMENT OF THE JUDGMENT

THE THREE ELEMENTS OF VALIDITY

1. Valid subject-matter jurisdiction. *See above*
2. Valid territorial jurisdiction. *See above*
3. Proper notice. See **Due Process Requirements**.

THE SIX STEP APPROACH [DETERMINING VALIDITY]

1. Local law of trial court subject-matter jurisdiction.
2. Federal constitutional limits on subject-matter jurisdiction. *Kalb v. Feurstein*, 308 U.S. 433 (1940).

3. Local law of trial court territorial jurisdiction.
   a. State courts:
      i. *In personam* jurisdiction: against persons personally served within state.
      ii. *In rem* jurisdiction: against property subject to attachment within state.
      iii. State long-arm statutes authorize service on absent defendant. *Gibbons v. Brown*, 716 So. 2d 868 (Fla. Dist. Ct. App. 1998).
   b. Federal courts:
      i. Have jurisdiction over any served party (FRCP 4) while that person present in the state.
      ii. *In rem* jursidction: may exercise only in accordance with local law.
      iii. *In personam* jurisdiction: may generally exercise against person served outside state, as authorized by local state law.
      iv. Nationwide service is specifically authorized by FRCP 4(k)(1)(C)–(D) under Federal Interpleader Act and other federal statutes.
4. Federal constitutional limits on territorial jurisdiction. *Baldwin v. Iowa State Traveling Men's Assoc.*, 283 U.S. 522 (1931).
5. Local law of proper notice.
   a. State court service of process:
      i. Careful compliance with technical details.
      ii. Process includes summons and complaint.
      iii. Service requirements.
      Personal:
      a. Delivery in hand to named defendant.
      b. To entity: delivery to person appointed to accept.
      Substituted:
      a. Delivery to person of suitable age and discretion, who lives with defendant.
      b. Service by mail may require acknowledgment.
      Constructive:
      a. Newspaper publication.
      b. Posting at designated location.
      iv. federal court service of process (FRCP 4).
6. Federal constitutional standards for proper notice. *Mullane v. Central Hanover Bank & Trust Co.*, 339 U.S. 306 (1950).

ENFORCEMENT OF JUDGMENTS (PROVISIONAL REMEDIES)

1. Attachment – holding asset when defendant not available. *Connecticut v. Doehr*, 501 U.S. 1 (1991).
2. Garnishment – attachment of wages or other income.
3. Preliminary injunctions / Temporary Restraining Orders (TROs) (FRCP 65) – available ex parte when defendant acting in way that would render the judgment ineffectual. *William Inglis & Sons Baking Co. v. ITT Continental Baking Co.*, 526 F.2d 86 (9th Cir. 1976).
4. Receivership – appointment of overseer to manage assets pendente lite, generally in cases of insolvency. (FRCP 66)
5. Civil arrest – functional equivalent of imprisonment for debt and severely restricted.
6. Notice of Pendency – not strictly a remedy, but notice to third parties concerning property in dispute, etc.

PRE-TRIAL PROCEDURE/ DISPOSITIONS

VOLUNTARY AND INVOLUNTARY DISMISSALS

1. Voluntary dismissal. (FRCP 41(a)). *McCants v. Ford Motor Co.*, 781 F. 2d 855 (1986).
   a. Without prejudice: plaintiff may reinstate action, within limitations period.
   b. With prejudice:
      i. Court order required.
      ii. Second voluntary dismissal.
      iii. Court or parties do not specify otherwise.
2. Involuntary dismissal. (FRCP 41(b)). *Link v. Wabash R.R.*, 370 U.S. 626 (1962).
   a. Defendant may seek for action or any claim, alleging:
      i. Failure to prosecute.
      ii. Failure to comply with federal rules.
      iii. Failure to comply with court order.
   b. Presumptively, with prejudice:
      i. Constitutes adjudication on merits.
      ii. Bars plaintiff, triggers *res judicata*.
   c. Exceptions:
      i. Lack of jurisdiction.
      ii. Improper venue.
      iii. Failure to join party. (FRCP 19)

PRETRIAL CONFERENCES OR ORDERS

Judge brings parties together to do the following:
1. Resolve procedural and discovery matters.
2. Schedule pretrial matters and conferences.
3. Consider settlement or other early disposition.
4. Simplify legal and factual issues for trial. *Sanders v. Union Pacific RR. Co.*, 154 F. 3d 1037 (9th Cir. 1998); *McKey v. Fairbairn*, 345 F. 2d 739 (D.C. Cir. 1965).
   a. Pretrial conferences (FRCP 16) to:
      i. expedite litigation;
      ii. control the case;
      iii. streamline pretrial activities;
      iv. encourage preparation for trial; and
      v. encourage settlement
   b. Discovery planning meeting (FRCP 26(f)) must be held and discovery plan submitted. District court then issues scheduling order that limits time in which:
      i. pleadings may be amended;
      ii. parties may be joined;
      iii. motions may be filed; and
      iv. discovery may be completed.
   c. Scheduling order must be issued within 120 days of service of complaint upon defendant.
   d. Court enters pretrial order (FRCP 16(d)).
   e. Sanctions available on motion or *sua sponte*:
      i. failure to obey scheduling order;
      ii. failure to make an appearance;
      iii. substantial lack of preparedness; or
      iv. failure to participate in good faith.

SUMMARY JUDGMENT
FRCP 56

1. Absence of a genuine issue of material fact. *Anderson v. Liberty Lobby, Inc.*, 477 U.S. 242 (1986).
2. Moving party entitled to judgment as matter of law and establishes:
   a. Nonexistence of a critical fact.

---

   b. That nonmoving party lacks sufficient evidence to prove critial fact. *Celotex Corp. v. Catrett*, 477 U.S. 317 (1986).
   c. Burden then shifts to nonmoving party to show that there is a genuine issue of material fact. *Bias v. Advantage International Inc.*, 905 F.2d 1558 (1990).
3. Procedure:
   a. Plaintiff may move any time after 20 days from commencement of action. (FRCP 56(a))
   b. Defendant may move immediately. (FRCP 56(b))
   c. Motion must be served at least 10 days before hearing date. (FRCP 56(c))
4. Required evidence (*Adickes v. S. H. Kress & Co.*, 378 U.S. 144 (1970)):
   a. Affidavits:
      i. based on personal knowledge;
      ii. containing facts admissible in evidence;
      iii. demonstrating witness competency.
   b. All products of discovery.
5. Partial summary judgment also available. (FRCP 56 (d))

DEFAULT JUDGMENT
FRCP 55. *Peralta v. Heights Medical Center*, 485 U.S. 80 (1980).

1. Entry of party's default:
   a. Answering party fails to plead or defend.
   b. Default secured by filing affidavit with clerk.
2. Clerk of court enters judgment.

TRIAL/RIGHT TO TRIAL

STAGES OF TRIAL PROCESS

1. Pre-trial conference.
2. Motions in limine.
3. Voir dire.
4. Opening statement.
5. Plaintiff's case-in-chief.
6. Motion (JMOL).
7. Defendant's case-in-chief.
8. Rebuttal evidence.
9. Motions (JMOL).
10. Closing arguments.
11. Jury instructions.
12. Jury deliberations.

RIGHT TO TRIAL

1. Constitution-based (Seventh Amendment). *Teamsters Local No. 391 v. Terry*, 494 U.S. 558 (1990).
2. Applies to cases that mix law and equity. *Ross v. Bernhard*, 396 U.S. 531 (1970).
3. Exceptions:
   a. Bankruptcy cases. *Katchen v. Landy*, 383 U.S. 323 (1966).
   b. Section 1981 cases.

JURY INSTRUCTIONS

Three types:
1. General verdict: finding in favor of one party without explanation.
2. Special verdict: specific written findings on some/all factual issues.
3. Mixture of general/special: See FRCP 49(b).

TRIAL/POST-TRIAL MOTIONS

JUDGMENT AS A MATTER OF LAW (JMOL) (DIRECTED VERDICT)
Pennsylvania R.R. v. Chamberlain, 288 U.S. 333 (1933).

Judge may grant a JMOL or directed verdict if opposing party fails to produce evidence sufficient to support a finding in its favor. (FRCP 50)
1. Timing: generally at close of opposing party's evidence, but may be made at end of opening statements.
2. If renewed at conclusion of all evidence in case, party retains right to move later for post-verdict JMOL.

POST-VERDICT MOTIONS

1. Post-verdict or renewed JMOL (JNOV) requires:
   a. Evidence insufficient to make a case for the jury.
   b. Timeliness: motion must be made within 10 days after judgment or jury dismissal.
2. Motion for a new trial (FRCP 59) requires (*Lind v. Schenley Industries*, 278 F.2d 79 (3d Cir. 1960)):
   a. Verdict against great weight of the evidence. *Peterson v. Wilson*, 141 F.3d 573 (5th Cir. 1998).
   b. Timeliness: must be made within 10 days of entry of judgment.
3. Extraordinary Postjudgment Relief (FRCP 60):
   a. "clerical mistakes."
   b. "mistake, inadvertence or excusable neglect."
   c. "fraud, misrepresentation, misconduct."

APPEAL

REQUIREMENT OF FINALITY

1. Final judgment rule: No appeal may be taken until a final judgment has been issued. *Cohen v. Beneficial Industrial Loan Corp.*, 337 U.S. 541 (1949); *Liberty Mutual Insurance Co. v. Wetzel*, 424 U.S. 737 (1976).
2. Exception – the collateral order doctrine for orders that:
   a. conclusively determine the disputed question;
   b. resolve important issue not related to merits;
   c. are unreviewable by appeal.
3. Partial exception – right to appeal certain interlocutory orders. (28 U.S.C. §1292(a)). *Gulfstream Aerospace Corp. v. Mayacamas Corp.*, 485 U.S. 271 (1988).
4. Partial exception – extraordinary writs (Mandamus). *Kerr v. United States District Court*, 426 U.S. 394 (1976).

STANDARDS OF REVIEW

1. Errors of law ("abuse of discretion"). *Salve Regina College v. Russell*, 499 U.S. 225 (1999).
2. Errors of fact ("clearly erroneous"). *Anderson v. City of Bessemer*, 479 U.S. 564 (1985).
3. Harmless error. *Harnden v. Jayco, Inc.*, 496 F.3d 579 (6th Cir. 2007).

CIVIL PROCEDURE

TERRITORIAL JURISDICTION

Territorial jurisdiction is the authority of the court to exercise jurisdiction over a defendant or property.

TYPES OF JURISDICTION

1. *In personam:* Whether the court has the power to adjudicate claims against a particular person depends on whether the person over whom jurisdiction is sought has a sufficient territorial connection to the forum state.
   a. Defendant is present in state and process is physically served.
   b. Domicile.
   c. Consent. *Carnival Cruise Lines v. Shute*, 499 U.S. 585 (1991); *Hess v. Pawloski*, 274 U.S. 352 (1927).
   d. State long-arm statute grants personal jurisdiction over defendant or property. *Gray v. American Radiator & Standard Sanitary Corp.*, 22 Ill.2d 432 (1961).
2. *In rem:* Jurisdiction over a particular item of property. *Shaffer v. Heitner*, 433 U.S. 186 (1977).
   a. Determines who owns certain property in territorial control of the forum.
   b. Adjudicates ownership interests of world at large to the property.
3. *Quasi in rem:* Rights of particular person to certain property. *McGee v. International Life Insurance Co.*, 355 U.S. 220 (1957).
   a. Suit in which dispute arises out of parties' interests in the property.
   b. Attachment jurisdiction.
      i. Suit in which dispute between the parties has nothing to do with the presence of the property within the forum state.
      ii. Property can be attached by court as "hostage" to a suit against the owner of the property.

DUE PROCESS REQUIREMENTS
Pennoyer v. Neff, 95 U.S. 714 (1877).

1. Fair and adequate notice. *Mullane v. Central Hanover Bank & Trust Co.*, 339 U.S. 306 (1950).
2. Minimum contacts with forum state. *International Shoe Co. v. Washington*, 326 U.S. 310 (1945).

MINIMUM CONTACTS ANALYSIS

International Shoe Co., v. Washington, 326 U.S. 310 (1945).

Defined – The minimal connection with the forum state necessary to justify general jurisdiction.
1. Does the defendant have any contacts within the forum state?
2. Are the contacts purposeful? *Burger King Corp. v. Rudzewicz*, 471 U.S. 462 (1985).
   a. Foreseeability of litigation? *World-Wide Volkswagen Corp. v. Woodson*, 444 U.S. 286 (1980).

   b. "Stream of commerce." *Asahi Metal Industry Co. v. Superior Ct.*, 480 U.S. 102 (1987).
   c. "Purposeful availment." *Hanson v. Deckla*, 357 U.S. 235 (1958).
3. Are the contacts continuous, systematic and substantial enough to justify general jurisdiction?
4. If there is no general jurisdiction, are the defendant's purposeful contacts with the forum sufficiently related to the litigation or do they constitute minimum contacts conferring the power to exercise specific jurisdiction?
5. Is the exercise of jurisdiction reasonable? *Burger King Corp. v. Rudzewicz*, 471 U.S. 462 (1985).

FEDERAL SUBJECT MATTER JURISDICTION

DIVERSITY JURISDICTION
28 U.S.C. §1332

1. Complete diversity of citizenship: No plaintiff may be a citizen of the same state as any defendant.
   a. Refers to suits between:
      i. Citizens of different states.
      ii. Citizens of a state and citizens of a foreign state. *Redner v. Sanders*, 2000 WL 1161080 (S.D.N.Y. 2000).
      iii. Citizens of different states and in which citizens of a foreign state are additional parties.
      iv. Plaintiff in a foreign state and citizens of a state or different states.
   b. An individual is a citizen of the state in which he is domiciled (place of fixed residence). *Saadeh v. Farouki*, 107 F.3d 52 (D.C. Cir. 1997).
   c. A corporation is a citizen of any state in which it is incorporated or in which it has its principal place of business. (28 U.S.C. §1332(c)(1))
2. Jurisdictional amount requirement.
   a. In excess of $75,000.
   b. Good-faith allegations of the amount.
   c. Exclusive of interest and costs.

THE ERIE DOCTRINE
Erie R.R. v. Tompkins, 304 U.S. 64 (1938).

In a diversity case, a federal court must apply state substantive law; however, even in diversity cases the federal courts may follow their own express procedural rules & statutes. *Hanna v. Plummer*, 380 U.S. 460 (1965).
1. Is the issue clearly substantive and not even arguably procedural?
2. If not, is federal law specified by federal legislation or an express federal rule?
3. If not, has the state conditioned the enjoyment of a state-created right in issue on enforcement of it according to state law?
4. If not, is the foreseeable impact on outcome of conforming to state law substantially likely to encourage forum shopping and the inequitable administration of the laws? *Byrd v. Blue Ridge Electrical Coop*, 356 U.S. 525 (1958).

5. If yes, are there countervailing considerations of federal policy that outweigh application of state law in diversity cases?
   Note: In general *Guaranty Trust Co. v. York*, 326 U.S. 99 (1945), requires state law to apply if a different outcome would result under federal law. *Byrd* & *Hanna* are exceptions.

FEDERAL VENUE 28 U.S.C. §1391

1. District in which any defendant resides, if all reside in same state.
2. District in which substantial part of the events / omissions occurred or in which property is located.
3. "Fallback venue" applies only if otherwise there is no district in which venue is proper.
   a. In diversity cases, where defendants are subject to personal jurisdiction when action commenced.
   b. If no diversity, where any defendant is found. *"Forum non conveniens:"* State or federal court may refuse to exercise jurisdiction because forum has no interest, and controversy may be litigated more conveniently elsewhere. Transfer permitted between federal district courts. (28 U.S.C. §§1404 and 1406). *Piper Aircraft Co. v. Gaynell Reyno, et al.*, 454 U.S. 235 (1981).

SUPPLEMENTAL JURISDICTION
28 U.S.C. §1367. *In re Ameriquest Mortgage Co. Mortgage Lending Practices Litigation*, 2007 U.S. Dist. LEXIS 70805 (N.D. Ill. 2007); *Szendrey-Ramos v. First Bancorp*, 2007 U.S. Dist. LEXIS 74896 (D.P.R. 2007).

In any action in which the federal court has original jurisdiction, it also has supplemental jurisdiction over any other claims in the action that may form part of the same case or controversy. This includes claims involving the joinder or intervention of additional parties. Supplemental jurisdiction is limited in diversity cases. Courts may decline to exercise supplemental jurisdiction if:
1. novel or complex state-law issue;
2. the supplemental claim substantially predominates over the main claim(s);
3. the district court has dismissed all claims; or
4. there are other compelling reasons for declining.

FEDERAL QUESTION JURISDICTION
28 U.S.C. §1331. *Louisville & Nashville R.R. v. Mottley*, 211 U.S. 149 (1908).

1. Confers subject-matter jurisdiction over all suits to enforce federally created rights to relief.
2. In rare instances may also confer federal jurisdiction over suits to enforce state-created rights to relief that necessarily turn on substantial and disputed issues of federal law.

Federal Subject-Matter Judiction continues on page 2 ▶

Casenote® Legal Briefs

CIVIL PROCEDURE

Keyed to Courses Using

Yeazell's

Civil Procedure

Eighth Edition

Wolters Kluwer
Law & Business

Copyright © 2012 CCH Incorporated. All Rights Reserved.

Published by Wolters Kluwer Law & Business in New York.

Wolters Kluwer Law & Business serves customers worldwide with CCH, Aspen Publishers, and Kluwer Law International products. (www.wolterskluwerlb.com)

No part of this publication may be reproduced or transmitted in any form or by any means, electronic or mechanical, including photocopy, recording, or utilized by any information storage and retrieval system, without written permission from the publisher. For information about permissions or to request permission online, visit us at www.wolterskluwerlb.com, or a written request may be faxed to our permissions department at 212-771-0803.

To contact Customer Service, e-mail customer.service@wolterskluwer.com, call 1-800-234-1660, fax 1-800-901-9075, or mail correspondence to:

Wolters Kluwer Law & Business
Attn: Order Department
P.O. Box 990
Frederick, MD 21705

Printed in the United States of America.

1 2 3 4 5 6 7 8 9 0

ISBN 978-1-4548-0799-5

About Wolters Kluwer Law & Business

Wolters Kluwer Law & Business is a leading global provider of intelligent information and digital solutions for legal and business professionals in key specialty areas, and respected educational resources for professors and law students. Wolters Kluwer Law & Business connects legal and business professionals as well as those in the education market with timely, specialized authoritative content and information-enabled solutions to support success through productivity, accuracy and mobility.

Serving customers worldwide, Wolters Kluwer Law & Business products include those under the Aspen Publishers, CCH, Kluwer Law International, Loislaw, Best Case, ftwilliam.com and MediRegs family of products.

CCH products have been a trusted resource since 1913, and are highly regarded resources for legal, securities, antitrust and trade regulation, government contracting, banking, pension, payroll, employment and labor, and healthcare reimbursement and compliance professionals.

Aspen Publishers products provide essential information to attorneys, business professionals and law students. Written by preeminent authorities, the product line offers analytical and practical information in a range of specialty practice areas from securities law and intellectual property to mergers and acquisitions and pension/benefits. Aspen's trusted legal education resources provide professors and students with high-quality, up-to-date and effective resources for successful instruction and study in all areas of the law.

Kluwer Law International products provide the global business community with reliable international legal information in English. Legal practitioners, corporate counsel and business executives around the world rely on Kluwer Law journals, looseleafs, books, and electronic products for comprehensive information in many areas of international legal practice.

Loislaw is a comprehensive online legal research product providing legal content to law firm practitioners of various specializations. Loislaw provides attorneys with the ability to quickly and efficiently find the necessary legal information they need, when and where they need it, by facilitating access to primary law as well as state-specific law, records, forms and treatises.

Best Case Solutions is the leading bankruptcy software product to the bankruptcy industry. It provides software and workflow tools to flawlessly streamline petition preparation and the electronic filing process, while timely incorporating ever-changing court requirements.

ftwilliam.com offers employee benefits professionals the highest quality plan documents (retirement, welfare and non-qualified) and government forms (5500/PBGC, 1099 and IRS) software at highly competitive prices.

MediRegs products provide integrated health care compliance content and software solutions for professionals in healthcare, higher education and life sciences, including professionals in accounting, law and consulting.

Wolters Kluwer Law & Business, a division of Wolters Kluwer, is headquartered in New York. Wolters Kluwer is a market-leading global information services company focused on professionals.

Format for the Casenote® Legal Brief

Nature of Case: This section identifies the form of action (e.g., breach of contract, negligence, battery), the type of proceeding (e.g., demurrer, appeal from trial court's jury instructions), or the relief sought (e.g., damages, injunction, criminal sanctions).

Fact Summary: This is included to refresh your memory and can be used as a quick reminder of the facts.

Rule of Law: Summarizes the general principle of law that the case illustrates. It may be used for instant recall of the court's holding and for classroom discussion or home review.

Facts: This section contains all relevant facts of the case, including the contentions of the parties and the lower court holdings. It is written in a logical order to give the student a clear understanding of the case. The plaintiff and defendant are identified by their proper names throughout and are always labeled with a (P) or (D).

Palsgraf v. Long Island R.R. Co.

Injured bystander (P) v. Railroad company (D)

N.Y. Ct. App., 248 N.Y. 339, 162 N.E. 99 (1928).

NATURE OF CASE: Appeal from judgment affirming verdict for plaintiff seeking damages for personal injury.

FACT SUMMARY: Helen Palsgraf (P) was injured on R.R.'s (D) train platform when R.R.'s (D) guard helped a passenger aboard a moving train, causing his package to fall on the tracks. The package contained fireworks which exploded, creating a shock that tipped a scale onto Palsgraf (P).

🏛 RULE OF LAW
The risk reasonably to be perceived defines the duty to be obeyed.

FACTS: Helen Palsgraf (P) purchased a ticket to Rockaway Beach from R.R. (D) and was waiting on the train platform. As she waited, two men ran to catch a train that was pulling out from the platform. The first man jumped aboard, but the second man, who appeared as if he might fall, was helped aboard by the guard on the train who had kept the door open so they could jump aboard. A guard on the platform also helped by pushing him onto the train. The man was carrying a package wrapped in newspaper. In the process, the man dropped his package, which fell on the tracks. The package contained fireworks and exploded. The shock of the explosion was apparently of great enough strength to tip over some scales at the other end of the platform, which fell on Palsgraf (P) and injured her. A jury awarded her damages, and R.R. (D) appealed.

ISSUE: Does the risk reasonably to be perceived define the duty to be obeyed?

HOLDING AND DECISION: (Cardozo, C.J.) Yes. The risk reasonably to be perceived defines the duty to be obeyed. If there is no foreseeable hazard to the injured party as the result of a seemingly innocent act, the act does not become a tort because it happened to be a wrong as to another. If the wrong was not willful, the plaintiff must show that the act as to her had such great and apparent possibilities of danger as to entitle her to protection. Negligence in the abstract is not enough upon which to base liability. Negligence is a relative concept, evolving out of the common law doctrine of trespass on the case. To establish liability, the defendant must owe a legal duty of reasonable care to the injured party. A cause of action in tort will lie where harm,

though unintended, could have been averted or avoided by observance of such a duty. The scope of the duty is limited by the range of danger that a reasonable person could foresee. In this case, there was nothing to suggest from the appearance of the parcel or otherwise that the parcel contained fireworks. The guard could not reasonably have had any warning of a threat to Palsgraf (P), and R.R. (D) therefore cannot be held liable. Judgment is reversed in favor of R.R. (D).

DISSENT: (Andrews, J.) The concept that there is no negligence unless R.R. (D) owes a legal duty to take care as to Palsgraf (P) herself is too narrow. Everyone owes to the world at large the duty of refraining from those acts that may unreasonably threaten the safety of others. If the guard's action was negligent as to those nearby, it was also negligent as to those outside what might be termed the "danger zone." For Palsgraf (P) to recover, R.R.'s (D) negligence must have been the proximate cause of her injury, a question of fact for the jury.

▶ ANALYSIS
The majority defined the limit of the defendant's liability in terms of the danger that a reasonable person in defendant's situation would have perceived. The dissent argued that the limitation should not be placed on liability, but rather on damages. Judge Andrews suggested that only injuries that would not have happened but for R.R.'s (D) negligence should be compensable. Both the majority and dissent recognized the policy-driven need to limit liability for negligent acts, seeking, in the words of Judge Andrews, to define a framework "that will be practical and in keeping with the general understanding of mankind." The Restatement (Second) of Torts has accepted Judge Cardozo's view.

━━

Quicknotes
FORESEEABILITY A reasonable expectation that change is the probable result of certain acts or omissions.

NEGLIGENCE Conduct falling below the standard of care that a reasonable person would demonstrate under similar conditions.

PROXIMATE CAUSE The natural sequence of events without which an injury would not have been sustained.

━━

Party ID: Quick identification of the relationship between the parties.

Concurrence/Dissent: All concurrences and dissents are briefed whenever they are included by the casebook editor.

Analysis: This last paragraph gives you a broad understanding of where the case "fits in" with other cases in the section of the book and with the entire course. It is a hornbook-style discussion indicating whether the case is a majority or minority opinion and comparing the principal case with other cases in the casebook. It may also provide analysis from restatements, uniform codes, and law review articles. The analysis will prove to be invaluable to classroom discussion.

Issue: The issue is a concise question that brings out the essence of the opinion as it relates to the section of the casebook in which the case appears. Both substantive and procedural issues are included if relevant to the decision.

Holding and Decision: This section offers a clear and in-depth discussion of the rule of the case and the court's rationale. It is written in easy-to-understand language and answers the issue presented by applying the law to the facts of the case. When relevant, it includes a thorough discussion of the exceptions to the case as listed by the court, any major cites to the other cases on point, and the names of the judges who wrote the decisions.

Quicknotes: Conveniently defines legal terms found in the case and summarizes the nature of any statutes, codes, or rules referred to in the text.

Note to Students

Wolters Kluwer Law & Business is proud to offer *Casenote® Legal Briefs*—continuing thirty years of publishing America's best-selling legal briefs.

Casenote® Legal Briefs are designed to help you save time when briefing assigned cases. Organized under convenient headings, they show you how to abstract the basic facts and holdings from the text of the actual opinions handed down by the courts. Used as part of a rigorous study regimen, they can help you spend more time analyzing and critiquing points of law than on copying bits and pieces of judicial opinions into your notebook or outline.

Casenote® Legal Briefs should never be used as a substitute for assigned casebook readings. They work best when read as a follow-up to reviewing the underlying opinions themselves. Students who try to avoid reading and digesting the judicial opinions in their casebooks or online sources will end up shortchanging themselves in the long run. The ability to absorb, critique, and restate the dynamic and complex elements of case law decisions is crucial to your success in law school and beyond. It cannot be developed vicariously.

Casenote® Legal Briefs represents but one of the many offerings in Legal Education's Study Aid Timeline, which includes:

- *Casenote® Legal Briefs*
- *Emanuel Law Outlines*
- *Examples & Explanations* Series
- *Introduction to Law* Series
- *Emanuel Law in a Flash* Flash Cards
- *Emanuel CrunchTime* Series

Each of these series is designed to provide you with easy-to-understand explanations of complex points of law. Each volume offers guidance on the principles of legal analysis and, consulted regularly, will hone your ability to spot relevant issues. We have titles that will help you prepare for class, prepare for your exams, and enhance your general comprehension of the law along the way.

To find out more about Wolters Kluwer Law & Business's study aid publications, visit us online at *www.wolterskluwerlb.com* or email us at *legaledu@ wolterskluwer.com*. We'll be happy to assist you.

A. Decide on a Format and Stick to It

Structure is essential to a good brief. It enables you to arrange systematically the related parts that are scattered throughout most cases, thus making manageable and understandable what might otherwise seem to be an endless and unfathomable sea of information. There are, of course, an unlimited number of formats that can be utilized. However, it is best to find one that suits your needs and stick to it. Consistency breeds both efficiency and the security that when called upon you will know where to look in your brief for the information you are asked to give.

Any format, as long as it presents the essential elements of a case in an organized fashion, can be used. Experience, however, has led *Casenotes® Legal Briefs* to develop and utilize the following format because of its logical flow and universal applicability.

NATURE OF CASE: This is a brief statement of the legal character and procedural status of the case (e.g., "Appeal of a burglary conviction").

There are many different alternatives open to a litigant dissatisfied with a court ruling. The key to determining which one has been used is to discover *who is asking this court for what.*

This first entry in the brief should be kept as *short as possible.* Use the court's terminology if you understand it. But since jurisdictions vary as to the titles of pleadings, the best entry is the one that addresses who wants what in this proceeding, not the one that sounds most like the court's language.

RULE OF LAW: A statement of the general principle of law that the case illustrates (e.g., "An acceptance that varies any term of the offer is considered a rejection and counteroffer").

Determining the rule of law of a case is a procedure similar to determining the issue of the case. Avoid being fooled by red herrings; there may be a few rules of law mentioned in the case excerpt, but usually only one is the rule with which the casebook editor is concerned. The techniques used to locate the issue, described below, may also be utilized to find the rule of law. Generally, your best guide is simply the chapter heading. It is a clue to the point the casebook editor seeks to make and should be kept in mind when reading every case in the respective section.

FACTS: A synopsis of only the essential facts of the case, i.e., those bearing upon or leading up to the issue.

The facts entry should be a short statement of the events and transactions that led one party to initiate legal proceedings against another in the first place. While some cases conveniently state the salient facts at the beginning of the decision, in other instances they will have to be culled from hiding places throughout the text, even from concurring and dissenting opinions. Some of the "facts" will often be in dispute and should be so noted. Conflicting evidence may be briefly pointed up. "Hard" facts must be included. Both must be *relevant* in order to be listed in the facts entry. It is impossible to tell what is relevant until the entire case is read, as the ultimate determination of the rights and liabilities of the parties may turn on something buried deep in the opinion.

Generally, the facts entry should not be longer than three to five *short* sentences.

It is often helpful to identify the role played by a party in a given context. For example, in a construction contract case the identification of a party as the "contractor" or "builder" alleviates the need to tell that that party was the one who was supposed to have built the house.

It is always helpful, and a good general practice, to identify the "plaintiff" and the "defendant." This may seem elementary and uncomplicated, but, especially in view of the creative editing practiced by some casebook editors, it is sometimes a difficult or even impossible task. Bear in mind that the *party presently* seeking something from this court may not be the plaintiff, and that sometimes only the cross-claim of a defendant is treated in the excerpt. Confusing or misaligning the parties can ruin your analysis and understanding of the case.

ISSUE: A statement of the general legal question answered by or illustrated in the case. For clarity, the issue is best put in the form of a question capable of a "yes" or "no" answer. In reality, the issue is simply the Rule of Law put in the form of a question (e.g., "May an offer be accepted by performance?").

The major problem presented in discerning what is the issue in the case is that an opinion usually purports to raise and answer several questions. However, except for rare cases, only one such question is really the issue in the case. Collateral issues not necessary to the resolution of the matter in controversy are handled by the court by language known as *"obiter dictum"* or merely *"dictum."* While dicta may be included later in the brief, they have no place under the issue heading.

To find the issue, ask who wants what and then go on to ask *why did that party succeed or fail in getting it.* Once this is determined, the "why" should be turned into a question.

The complexity of the issues in the cases will vary, but in all cases a single-sentence question should sum up the issue. *In a few cases,* there will be two, or even more rarely, three issues of equal importance to the resolution of the case. Each should be expressed in a single-sentence question.

Since many issues are resolved by a court in coming to a final disposition of a case, the casebook editor will reproduce the portion of the opinion containing the issue or issues most relevant to the area of law under scrutiny. A noted law professor gave this advice: "Close the book; look at the title on the cover." Chances are, if it is Property, you need not concern yourself with whether, for example, the federal government's treatment of the plaintiff's land really raises a federal question sufficient to support jurisdiction on this ground in federal court.

The same rule applies to chapter headings designating sub-areas within the subjects. They tip you off as to what the text is designed to teach. The cases are arranged in a casebook to show a progression or development of the law, so that the preceding cases may also help.

It is also most important to remember to *read the notes and questions* at the end of a case to determine what the editors wanted you to have gleaned from it.

HOLDING AND DECISION: This section should succinctly explain the rationale of the court in arriving at its decision. In capsulizing the "reasoning" of the court, it should always include an application of the general rule or rules of law to the specific facts of the case. Hidden justifications come to light in this entry: the reasons for the state of the law, the public policies, the biases and prejudices, those considerations that influence the justices' thinking and, ultimately, the outcome of the case. At the end, there should be a short indication of the disposition or procedural resolution of the case (e.g., "Decision of the trial court for Mr. Smith (P) reversed").

The foregoing format is designed to help you "digest" the reams of case material with which you will be faced in your law school career. Once mastered by practice, it will place at your fingertips the information the authors of your casebooks have sought to impart to you in case-by-case illustration and analysis.

B. Be as Economical as Possible in Briefing Cases

Once armed with a format that encourages succinctness, it is as important to be economical with regard to the time spent on the actual reading of the case as it is to be economical in the writing of the brief itself. This does not mean "skimming" a case. Rather, it means reading the case with an "eye" trained to recognize into which "section" of your brief a particular passage or line fits and having a system for quickly and precisely marking the case so that

the passages fitting any one particular part of the brief can be easily identified and brought together in a concise and accurate manner when the brief is actually written.

It is of no use to simply repeat everything in the opinion of the court; record only enough information to trigger your recollection of what the court said. Nevertheless, an accurate statement of the "law of the case," i.e., the legal principle applied to the facts, is absolutely essential to class preparation and to learning the law under the case method.

To that end, it is important to develop a "shorthand" that you can use to make marginal notations. These notations will tell you at a glance in which section of the brief you will be placing that particular passage or portion of the opinion.

Some students prefer to underline all the salient portions of the opinion (with a pencil or colored underliner marker), making marginal notations as they go along. Others prefer the color-coded method of underlining, utilizing different colors of markers to underline the salient portions of the case, each separate color being used to represent a different section of the brief. For example, blue underlining could be used for passages relating to the rule of law, yellow for those relating to the issue, and green for those relating to the holding and decision, etc. While it has its advocates, the color-coded method can be confusing and time-consuming (all that time spent on changing colored markers). Furthermore, it can interfere with the continuity and concentration many students deem essential to the reading of a case for maximum comprehension. In the end, however, it is a matter of personal preference and style. Just remember, whatever method you use, underlining must be used sparingly or its value is lost.

If you take the marginal notation route, an efficient and easy method is to go along underlining the key portions of the case and placing in the margin alongside them the following "markers" to indicate where a particular passage or line "belongs" in the brief you will write:

N (NATURE OF CASE)
RL (RULE OF LAW)
I (ISSUE)
HL (HOLDING AND DECISION, relates to the RULE OF LAW behind the decision)
HR (HOLDING AND DECISION, gives the RATIONALE or reasoning behind the decision)
HA (HOLDING AND DECISION, APPLIES the general principle(s) of law to the facts of the case to arrive at the decision)

Remember that a particular passage may well contain information necessary to more than one part of your brief, in which case you simply note that in the margin. If you are using the color-coded underlining method instead of marginal notation, simply make asterisks or checks in the margin next to the passage in question in the colors that indicate the additional sections of the brief where it might be utilized.

The economy of utilizing "shorthand" in marking cases for briefing can be maintained in the actual brief writing process itself by utilizing "law student shorthand" within the brief. There are many commonly used words and phrases for which abbreviations can be substituted in your briefs (and in your class notes also). You can develop abbreviations that are personal to you and which will save you a lot of time. A reference list of briefing abbreviations can be found on page xii of this book.

C. Use Both the Briefing Process and the Brief as a Learning Tool

Now that you have a format and the tools for briefing cases efficiently, the most important thing is to make the time spent in briefing profitable to you and to make the most advantageous use of the briefs you create. Of course, the briefs are invaluable for classroom reference when you are called upon to explain or analyze a particular case.

However, they are also useful in reviewing for exams. A quick glance at the fact summary should bring the case to mind, and a rereading of the rule of law should enable you to go over the underlying legal concept in your mind, how it was applied in that particular case, and how it might apply in other factual settings.

As to the value to be derived from engaging in the briefing process itself, there is an immediate benefit that arises from being forced to sift through the essential facts and reasoning from the court's opinion and to succinctly express them in your own words in your brief. The process ensures that you understand the case and the point that it illustrates, and that means you will be ready to absorb further analysis and information brought forth in class. It also ensures you will have something to say when called upon in class. The briefing process helps develop a mental agility for getting to the gist of a case and for identifying, expounding on, and applying the legal concepts and issues found there. The briefing process is the mental process on which you must rely in taking law school examinations; it is also the mental process upon which a lawyer relies in serving his clients and in making his living.

Abbreviations for Briefs

acceptance	acp	offer	O
affirmed	aff	offeree	OE
answer	ans	offeror	OR
assumption of risk	a/r	ordinance	ord
attorney	atty	pain and suffering	p/s
beyond a reasonable doubt	b/r/d	parol evidence	p/e
bona fide purchaser	BFP	plaintiff	P
breach of contract	br/k	prima facie	p/f
cause of action	c/a	probable cause	p/c
common law	c/l	proximate cause	px/c
Constitution	Con	real property	r/p
constitutional	con	reasonable doubt	r/d
contract	K	reasonable man	r/m
contributory negligence	c/n	rebuttable presumption	rb/p
cross	x	remanded	rem
cross-complaint	x/c	res ipsa loquitur	RIL
cross-examination	x/ex	respondeat superior	r/s
cruel and unusual punishment	c/u/p	Restatement	RS
defendant	D	reversed	rev
dismissed	dis	Rule Against Perpetuities	RAP
double jeopardy	d/j	search and seizure	s/s
due process	d/p	search warrant	s/w
equal protection	e/p	self-defense	s/d
equity	eq	specific performance	s/p
evidence	ev	statute	S
exclude	exc	statute of frauds	S/F
exclusionary rule	exc/r	statute of limitations	S/L
felony	f/n	summary judgment	s/j
freedom of speech	f/s	tenancy at will	t/w
good faith	g/f	tenancy in common	t/c
habeas corpus	h/c	tenant	t
hearsay	hr	third party	TP
husband	H	third party beneficiary	TPB
injunction	inj	transferred intent	TI
in loco parentis	ILP	unconscionable	uncon
inter vivos	I/v	unconstitutional	unconst
joint tenancy	j/t	undue influence	u/e
judgment	judgt	Uniform Commercial Code	UCC
jurisdiction	jur	unilateral	uni
last clear chance	LCC	vendee	VE
long-arm statute	LAS	vendor	VR
majority view	maj	versus	v
meeting of minds	MOM	void for vagueness	VFV
minority view	min	weight of authority	w/a
Miranda rule	Mir/r	weight of the evidence	w/e
Miranda warnings	Mir/w	wife	W
negligence	neg	with	w/
notice	ntc	within	w/i
nuisance	nus	without	w/o
obligation	ob	without prejudice	w/o/p
obscene	obs	wrongful death	wr/d

Table of Cases

Overview

Quick Reference Rules of Law

Hawkins v. Masters Farms, Inc.

Representative of estate (P) v. Tractor driver (D)

2003 WL 21555767 (D. Kan. 2003).

NATURE OF CASE: Motion to dismiss for lack of subject matter jurisdiction.

FACT SUMMARY: James Creal was killed when his automobile was struck by a tractor owned by Masters Farms, Inc. (D). Creal's estate (P) brought suit against Masters Farms, Inc. (D) in federal court alleging diversity subject matter jurisdiction. Masters Farms, Inc. (D) moved to dismiss on grounds of incomplete diversity among the parties.

> ## RULE OF LAW
> For purposes of determining diversity juris-diction, a person is a "citizen" of the state in which he or she is "domiciled," which for adults is estab-lished by physical presence in a place in connection with the intent to remain there.

FACTS: On December 8, 2000, James Creal (P) was killed in an automobile accident just south of Troy, Kansas, when his car was struck by a tractor driven by Masters (D), a citizen of Kansas. At the time of his death, James Creal (P) was living in Kansas with his wife and her children. James Creal (P) had lived in Missouri most of his life, while Mrs. Creal had resided in Kansas the majority of her life. When Mrs. Creal moved into an apartment in Troy, Kansas, in March 2000, James Creal brought his clothes, furniture and many other items and moved to the new apartment. The Creals were mar-ried in July 2000. In November, the Creals moved into a house in Troy, Kansas. His death certificate listed Kansas as his residence. The representatives of James Creal (P) brought suit against Masters (D) in the federal district court for Kansas, alleging the existence of diversity ju-risdiction under 28 U.S.C. § 1332. Masters (D) moved to dismiss, disputing that there was complete diversity among the parties.

ISSUE: For purposes of determining diversity juris-diction, is a person a "citizen" of the state in which he or she is "domiciled," which for adults is established by physical presence in a place in connection with the in-tent to remain there?

HOLDING AND DECISION: (Van Bebber, J.) Yes. For purposes of determining diversity jurisdiction, a person is a "citizen" of the state in which he or she is "domiciled," which for adults is established by physi-cal presence in a place in connection with the intent to remain there. Here, at the time of his death, Creal (P) had not only established a physical presence in the State of Kansas, but also displayed an intent to remain there. Although he lived the majority of his life in Missouri, he had been living in Kansas with his wife of five months for nearly one year at the time he died. Among other things, he had moved household items into the Kansas home; he contributed to household costs; and he purchased a new bedroom set with his wife. Any non-specific so-called "floating intention" of Creal (P) to return to his former Missouri domicile would be insufficient to overcome the evidence that he was domiciled in Kansas at the time of his death. Masters's (D) motion to dismiss is granted.

▶ ANALYSIS

In *Hawkins*, the court noted that the party seeking to invoke federal jurisdiction bears the burden of prov-ing that jurisdiction is proper. Because federal courts are courts of limited jurisdiction, the presumption is against federal jurisdiction.

■=■

Quicknotes

DIVERSITY JURISDICTION The authority of a federal court to hear and determine cases involving $10,000 or more and in which the parties are citizens of different states, or in which one party is an alien.

FEDERAL JURISDICTION The authority of federal courts to hear and determine cases of a particular nature derived from the United States Constitution and rules promul-gated by Congress pursuant thereto.

■=■

Bridges v. Diesel Service, Inc.

Disabled employee (P) v. Employer (D)

1994 U.S. Dist. LEXIS 9429 (E.D. Pa. 1994).

NATURE OF CASE: Motion for sanctions pursuant to Fed. R. Civ. P. 11.

FACT SUMMARY: Bridges (P) commenced this action against Diesel Service Inc. (D) under the Americans with Disabilities Act (ADA) alleging that his employer dismissed him from his job as a result of a disability.

🏛 RULE OF LAW
Fed. R. Civ. P. 11 imposes an obligation on counsel and client to stop, think, investigate and research before filing papers either to initiate the suit or to conduct the litigation.

FACTS: Bridges (P) commenced this action against Diesel Service Inc. (D) under the Americans with Disabilities Act (ADA) alleging that his employer dismissed him from his job as a result of a disability. By an order dated June 29, 1994, the court dismissed Bridges's (P) complaint without prejudice for failure to exhaust administrative remedies. In particular, Bridges (P) did not file a charge with the Equal Employment Opportunity Commission (EEOC) until after commencement of this action. Diesel Service, Inc. (D) then moved for sanctions pursuant to Fed. R. Civ. P. 11.

ISSUE: Does Fed. R. Civ. P. 11 impose an obligation on counsel and client to stop, think, investigate and research before filing papers either to initiate the suit or to conduct the litigation?

HOLDING AND DECISION: (Huyett, J.) Yes. Fed. R. Civ. P. 11 imposes an obligation on counsel and client to stop, think, investigate and research before filing papers either to initiate the suit or to conduct the litigation. The court is not convinced that Plaintiff's lawyer displayed a competent level of legal research. A brief review of case law would have revealed the EEOC filing requirement. Further, an award of sanctions for failure to exhaust administrative remedies is not unprecedented. However, the court will not grant sanctions. The prime goal of Rule 11 sanctions is deterrence of improper conduct. In this case, monetary sanctions are not necessary to deter future misconduct, since plaintiff's counsel immediately acknowledged his error and attempted to rectify the situation. Motion is denied.

▶ ANALYSIS

It is possible that the court treated plaintiff's counsel with lenience in this case, since the action was brought under the Americans with Disabilities Act. As the court states in its decision, "The Court is aware of the need to avoid 'chilling' Title VII litigation." Generally, Rule 11 sanctions are awarded where the complaint filed asserts patently unmeritorious or frivolous allegations.

Quicknotes

ADMINISTRATIVE REMEDIES Relief that is sought before an administrative body as opposed to a court.

FED. R. CIV. P. 11 Sets forth the requirement that every pleading or written paper be signed by at least one attorney of record; the representations made by the attorney to the court upon the signing of such document; and the sanctions for violation of the provision.

Bell v. Novick Transfer Co.

Automobile passenger (P) v. Trucking company (D)

17 F.R.D. 279 (D. Md. 1955).

NATURE OF CASE: Motion to dismiss for failure to state a claim.

FACT SUMMARY: Bell (P) filed a tort complaint in federal court after removal that stated only that Novick Transfer Co.'s (D) agent drove a truck that negligently collided with the car in which Bell (P) was riding, causing injury to Bell (P).

🏛 **RULE OF LAW**
A complaint that alleges only that a defendant negligently drove a motor vehicle and thereby injured the plaintiff is sufficient under Fed. R. Civ. P. 8.

FACTS: After Bell's (P) tort action arising out of an automobile-truck accident was removed to federal court, Bell (P) filed a complaint there that alleged only that an agent of Novick Transfer Co. (Novick) (D) drove a truck negligently so as to collide with a car in which Bell (P) was riding, causing injury to Bell (P). Novick (D) moved to dismiss the complaint for failure to state a cause of action.

ISSUE: Is a complaint that alleges only that defendant negligently drove a motor vehicle and thereby injured the plaintiff sufficient under Fed. R. Civ. P. 8?

HOLDING AND DECISION: (Thompsen, J.) Yes. This tort action was originally filed in Court of Common Pleas of Baltimore City but was removed to federal court. After such a removal, the Federal Rules of Civil Procedure apply rather than the laws of the State of Maryland. Thus, while Maryland law might regard the complaint here as insufficient for failure to state a cause of action, the inquiry here is to be made in light of the Federal Rules of Civil Procedure. Rule 8 controls the sufficiency of complaints, and requires only "a short and plain statement of the claim showing the pleader is entitled to relief." The complaint in this case contains such a statement and sufficiently states a cause of action under Rule 8. A complaint that alleges only that a defendant negligently drove a motor vehicle and thereby injured the plaintiff is sufficient under Rule 8. Motion is overruled.

▶ *ANALYSIS*

A complaint is designed to apprise the defendant of the claim against which he is to defend. The argument against sufficiency in this case is that the defendant is not told what negligent acts he has allegedly committed, other than the general allegation of "negligence," giving rise to liability. However, the policy of granting everyone access to the courts militates toward permitting generalized allegations and forcing the defendant to move for a more particularized statement under Fed. R. Civ. P. 12(e).

■■■

Quicknotes

FED. R. CIV. P. 8 Sets forth the general rules of pleading a claim for relief.

MOTION TO DISMISS Motion to terminate a trial based on the adequacy of the pleadings.

REMOVAL Petition by a defendant to move the case to another court.

■■■

Larson v. American Family Mutual Ins. Co.

Insured (P) v. Insurance company and lawyer (D)

2007 U.S. Dist. LEXIS 41864 (D. Colo. 2007).

NATURE OF CASE: Motion to amend complaint to add party.

FACT SUMMARY: The Larsons (P) sought to add their former lawyer to a complaint they filed against their insurance company, which failed to pay a house-fire claim. Their lawyer at the time was in private discussions with the insurance company about the possibility of representing the company.

🏛 RULE OF LAW
(1) An amendment to a complaint seeking to join a party to a lawsuit that is filed one month after complainant confirms the party's involvement in the lawsuit is timely filed under the Federal Rules of Civil Procedure.
(2) All persons may be joined in one action as defendants if claims against them arise out of the same transaction or occurrence as the other claims.

FACTS: The Larsons (P) retained an attorney, Brad Ross-Shannon (D) to sue American Family Mutual Insurance Company (American Family) (D), which held their homeowners' policy, after the company (D) failed to pay a house-fire claim. Ross-Shannon (D) did not pursue their claim because he was trying to be hired by American Family (D) in other matters. The Larsons (P) fired Ross-Shannon (D) and hired another attorney, who initially filed a complaint in April 2006 against only American Family (D), in state court. American Family (D) removed the case to federal court on the basis of diversity jurisdiction. After the insurance company (D) provided discovery in January 2007, the Larsons (P) learned that Ross-Shannon (D) was in talks with the company (D) while he was representing the Larsons (P). The Larsons (P) attorney then sought to amend their complaint to add Ross-Shannon (D) as an additional defendant, based on breach of fiduciary duty, legal malpractice, and conspiracy, claims that would destroy diversity and force a remand to state court. Ross-Shannon (D) and American Family (D) objected, arguing that the amendment was not timely filed, since they knew of the purported claims against Ross-Shannon (D) in February 2006, but waited until February 2007 to filed the amendment, and that joinder of new parties should not be allowed, because the new claims do not arise out of the same transaction or occurrence as the other claims.

ISSUE:
(1) Is an amendment to a complaint seeking to join a party to a lawsuit that is filed one month after complainant confirms the party's involvement in the lawsuit timely filed under the Federal Rules of Civil Procedure?
(2) May all persons be joined in one action as defendants if claims against them arise out of the same transaction or occurrence as the other claims?

HOLDING AND DECISION: (Figa, J.)
(1) Yes. An amendment to a complaint seeking to join a party to a lawsuit that is filed one month after complainant confirms the party's involvement in the lawsuit is timely filed under the Federal Rules of Civil Procedure. The Larsons (P) may have suspected that Ross-Shannon (D) was negotiating with American Family (D) before February 2006, but could not confirm that it was so until American Family (D) provided discovery in January 2007. In addition, they would be prejudiced if they were denied the opportunity to amend their complaint to add these claims in this case, because they would then be required to bring the claims in a separate and somewhat duplicative lawsuit in state court.
(2) Yes. All persons may be joined in one action as defendants if claims against them arise out of the same transaction or occurrence as the other claims. One theory proposed in the amended complaint is that the delay by Ross-Shannon (D) in the filing of a lawsuit against American Family (D) and American Family's (D) denial of payment of the claim was due in part to the fact that the lawyer (D) and insurer (D) were discussing the possibility of joining forces. The breach of their respective duties arise out of the same occurrence or transaction, or series of occurrences or transactions, and it would be inefficient to have one set of claims tried against American Family (D) in federal court and another set tried against the lawyer (D) in state court. Joinder is therefore proper. Remanded to state court.

▶ ANALYSIS

Note that the court looked for evidence that the plaintiffs tried to join the lawyer to the case in order to cause the cause to be remanded to state court, but did not find any such evidence. But even if the court did find such evidence, the plaintiffs were within their rights to amend the complaint.

■=■

Continued on next page.

Quicknotes

BREACH OF FIDUCIARY DUTY The failure of a fiduciary to observe the standard of care exercised by professionals of similar education and experience.

FIDUCIARY DUTY A legal obligation to act for the benefit of another, including subordinating one's personal interests to that of the other person.

JOINDER The joining of claims or parties in one lawsuit.

■━━■

Butler v. Rigby

[Parties not identified.]

1998 U.S. Dist. LEXIS 4618 (E.D. La. 1998).

NATURE OF CASE: Appeal from denial of protective order in personal-injury action.

FACT SUMMARY: American Medical Group and Midtown Health Care, two groups of doctors, sought a protective order against having to produce certain documents for a lawsuit in which they were not a party.

RULE OF LAW

Lists of past and current patients are privileged from discovery.

FACTS: After an automobile accident, the plaintiffs hired attorneys who may have had some connection to American Medical Group (AMG) and Midtown Health Care (MHC), two medical care providers. The defendants filed identical notices of depositions on AMG and MHC and sought past and current patient lists, as well as the total number of patients treated over a significant period of time. AMG and MHC moved for a protective order on the grounds that the information was not relevant, was protected by the health care provider-patient privilege and was overly burdensome. However, the magistrate judge disagreed and ordered that most of the information was discoverable. AMG and MHC appealed.

ISSUE: Are lists of past and current patients privileged from discovery?

HOLDING AND DECISION: (Vance, J.) Yes. Lists of past and current patients are privileged from discovery. The Federal Rules provide for liberal discovery and broad treatment of relevance. The discovery sought need not be admissible at trial if the information appears reasonably calculated to lead to the discovery of admissible evidence. However, discovery may be limited by the court if it determines that the discovery sought is unreasonably cumulative or duplicative or if the burden and expense outweighs its likely benefit. Privileged information also is not discoverable. In the present case, the number of total patients treated by AMG and MHC could be relevant in demonstrating that their connection with the plaintiff's attorneys shows bias. Thus, the magistrate was not clearly wrong in ordering this information discoverable despite the significant expense and burden of compiling the information. However, as to the patient lists sought, Louisiana law construes the health care provider-patient privilege broadly. Thus, the lists are not discoverable and an order should have been granted to AMG and MHC on that issue. Affirmed in part, reversed in part.

ANALYSIS

The court also made two related points in this case. Acknowledging that there was some expense involved in compiling the number of patients, the court ordered that the defendants pay half the cost. Also, the court noted that the patient lists sought were probably not relevant even if they hadn't been privileged.

Quicknotes

FED. R. CIV. P. 26(B)(1) Provides for a broad scope of discovery.

Houchens v. American Home Assurance Co.

Spouse of decedent (P) v. Life insurance company (D)

927 F.2d 163 (4th Cir. 1991).

NATURE OF CASE: Appeal of dismissal of action for damages for breach of contract.

FACT SUMMARY: On American Home Assurance Co.'s (D) summary judgment motion, the court dismissed Houchens's (P) suit for payment on two accidental death policies because of insufficient evidence that Houchens's (P) husband died accidentally.

🏛 RULE OF LAW
Under Fed. R. Civ. P. 56, a federal court must enter summary judgment if after complete discovery a party fails to show that the evidence, viewed in the light most favorable to that party, is sufficient to establish the existence of an essential element on which that party has the burden of proof.

FACTS: Houchens's (P) husband disappeared in Thailand in August, 1980, and was not heard from since. Under Virginia law, a person who is missing for seven years is presumed dead. In 1988, Houchens (P) had her husband declared legally dead. Houchens (P) attempted to collect on two life insurance policies issued by American (D), under which the proceeds would only be paid upon proof that the insured's death was accidental. American Home Assurance Co. (American) (D) refused to pay and Houchens (P) sued in federal court for breach of contract. American (D) moved for summary judgment, arguing there was no evidence that the insured had died or that he had died accidentally. The district court granted the motion and dismissed the case, and Houchens (P) appealed.

ISSUE: Under Fed. R. Civ. P. 56, must a federal court enter summary judgment if a party fails to show that the evidence, viewed in the light most favorable to that party, is sufficient to establish the existence of an essential element on which that party has the burden of proof?

HOLDING AND DECISION: (Ervin, C.J.) Yes. Under Fed. R. Civ. P. 56, a federal court must enter summary judgment if a party fails to show that the evidence, viewed in the light most favorable to that party, is sufficient to establish the existence of an essential element on which that party has the burden of proof. Under Rule 56(c), a summary judgment motion must be granted where there is "no genuine issue as to any material fact." Here, Houchens (P) is entitled to the Virginia presumption that her husband is dead. However, for recovery on the policy it still must be shown that her husband's death was accidental. The meager circumstances surrounding

his disappearance do not provide sufficient evidence to allow a reasonable jury to conclude that he died accidentally. Under Virginia law, Houchens (D) had the burden of proof as to accident, a necessary element of her case. She had insufficient evidence to meet this burden. Thus, as there was no genuine issue as to a material fact, the summary judgment motion was properly granted. Affirmed.

▶ ANALYSIS

Houchens (P) cited two cases where the issue was the same and a summary judgment motion by the insurance company defendant was denied. In *Valley National Bank of Arizona v. J.C. Penney Ins. Co.*, Ariz. Ct. App., 129 Ariz. 108, 628 P.2d 991 (1981), the insured disappeared, and his skeletal remains were later found with bullet casings nearby. In *Martin v. Insurance Co. of America*, 1 Wash. App. 218, 460 P.2d 682 (1969), the insured disappeared in fog and snow on a steep and wooded mountainside after having last been seen, asking for directions, without a compass at the 3,000-foot level. In each of these cases, the court found that there was a genuine issue of material fact because there was sufficient evidence, unlike in the *Houchens* case, for a jury to find that the insured died accidentally.

■=■

Quicknotes

BURDEN OF PROOF The duty of a party to introduce evidence to support a fact that is in dispute in an action.

FED. R. CIV. P. 56(C) Provides that a court arrive at a pre-verdict disposition on the case at bar when one party fails to prove an essential element of its case.

SUMMARY JUDGMENT Judgment rendered by a court in response to a motion by one of the parties, claiming that the lack of a question of material fact in respect to an issue warrants disposition of the issue without consideration by the jury.

■=■

Norton v. Snapper Power Equipment

Gardener (P) v. Lawn mower manufacturer (D)

806 F.2d 1545 (11th Cir. 1987).

NATURE OF CASE: Appeal from judgment notwithstanding the verdict denying damages for personal injuries.

FACT SUMMARY: In Norton's (P) suit for damages against Snapper Power Equipment (Snapper) (D), Snapper (D) moved for and was granted a judgment notwithstanding the verdict, contending that since a reconstruction of Norton's (P) accident with a Snapper (D) riding mower was impossible, the jury could not determine whether a blade-stopping device would have eliminated or lessened Norton's (P) injury.

RULE OF LAW
A judgment notwithstanding the verdict should be granted only where the evidence so strongly points in favor of a moving party that reasonable people could not arrive at a contrary verdict.

FACTS: Norton (P), a commercial gardener, was injured while riding a lawn mower manufactured by Snapper Power Equipment (Snapper) (D). Norton (P) sued Snapper (D) for damages based on strict liability. At the close of Norton's (P) case, and against the close of all evidence, Snapper (D) moved for a directed verdict. The court left the strict liability claim for the jury, and the jury returned a verdict for Norton (P), holding Snapper (D) liable for 80 percent of the injuries. After dismissing the jury, the court indicated that it would enter a judgment notwithstanding the verdict based on Snapper's (D) contention that since a reconstruction of Norton's (P) accident with the mower was impossible, the jury could not determine whether a blade-stopping device would have eliminated or lessened Norton's (P) injury. Norton (P) appealed.

ISSUE: Should a judgment notwithstanding the verdict be granted only where the evidence so strongly points in favor of a moving party that reasonable people could not arrive at a contrary verdict?

HOLDING AND DECISION: (Clark, J.) Yes. A judgment notwithstanding the verdict should be granted only where the evidence so strongly points in favor of a moving party that reasonable people could not arrive at a contrary verdict. The issues here were whether the failure to install "dead man" devices rendered the mower defective, and if the mower was defective, whether the lack of a "dead man" control caused the injury. Snapper (D) claims that there was little or no evidence to support the jury's verdict. The jury is, however, permitted to reconstruct the series of events by drawing an inference upon an inference. The causation evidence here, although circumstantial, was far more impressive than Snapper (D) contends, and Snapper (D) was given every opportunity to point out the weaknesses in Norton's (P) proof, but was unpersuasive to the jury. Reversed and remanded.

▶ ANALYSIS

Within ten days of an adverse verdict, the loser may move for a judgment notwithstanding the verdict. This motion asserts that even if all of the winner's evidence is true, the loser is entitled to a verdict as a matter of law. A motion for a new trial may be based either on an error of law or an erroneous charge.

Quicknotes

DIRECTED VERDICT A verdict ordered by the court in a jury trial.

JUDGMENT N.O.V. A judgment entered by the trial judge reversing a jury verdict if the jury's determination has no basis in law or fact.

STRICT LIABILITY Liability for all injuries proximately caused by a party's conducting of certain inherently dangerous activities without regard to negligence or fault.

Rush v. City of Maple Heights

Motorcycle passenger (P) v. Municipality (D)

Ohio Ct. App., 147 N.E.2d 599, *cert. denied*, 358 U.S. 814 (1958).

NATURE OF CASE: Action for damages for personal injuries.

FACT SUMMARY: In Rush's (P) action against the City of Maple Heights (D) to recover damages for personal injuries suffered in a motorcycle accident, Rush (P) claimed that she should be permitted to split her cause of action, filing a claim for property damage in one court and a separate action for personal injuries in another court.

> 🏛 **RULE OF LAW**
> Where a person suffers both personal injuries and property damage as a result of the same wrongful act, only a single cause for action arises, the different injuries occasioned thereby being separate items of damages from such act.

FACTS: Rush (P) was riding on a motorcycle operated by her husband and was injured when the cycle ran into a hole in the road, throwing her to the ground. Rush (P) brought suit against the City of Maple Heights ("the City") (D) for damage to the cycle. The lower court found that the City (D) was negligent in not repairing the road and awarded Rush (P) $100. That judgment was affirmed by the court of appeals and the Ohio Supreme Court. Then, Rush (P) brought the present suit to recover damages for personal injuries suffered in the same accident, contending that she should be permitted to split her cause of action and file separate claims for property damage and personal injuries in separate courts. The trial court held that the issues of negligence and proximate cause had been determined in the prior action against the City (D) and were binding. The jury awarded Rush (P) $12,000 solely on the question of damages, and the court of appeals affirmed this judgment. The City (D) appealed.

ISSUE: Where a person suffers both personal injuries and property damage as a result of the same wrongful act, does only a single cause of action arise, the different injuries occasioned thereby being separate items of damage from such act?

HOLDING AND DECISION: (Herbert, J.) Yes. Where a person suffers both personal injuries and property damage as a result of the same wrongful act, only a single cause of action arises, the different injuries occasioned thereby being separate items of damage from such act. This is the majority rule in this country, and the reasoning behind it is that a single tort can be the basis of but one action. It is not improper to declare in different counts for damages to the person and property when both result from the same tort; it is the better practice to do so where there is any difference in the measure of damages, and all damages must be sued for in one suit. This is necessary to prevent multiplicity of suits, burdensome expense, delay, and vexatious litigation. Here, Rush (P) suffered both personal injuries and property damage as a result of the same wrongful act—nonrepair of the road. The different injuries occasioned by the wrongful act were separate items of damage from such act, but the actions of the City (D) constituted but one tort. A single tort can be the basis of but one suit. Reversed.

CONCURRENCE: (Stewart, J.) The rule at common law and in a majority of the states of the union is that damages resulting from a single wrongful act, even though they include both property and personal injury damages, are, when suffered by the same person, the subject of only one action against the wrongdoer.

DISSENT: (Zimmerman, J.) Established law should remain undisturbed in order to insure a stability on which the lower courts and the legal profession generally may rely with some degree of confidence.

▶ ANALYSIS

Former adjudication can be divided into claim preclusion and issue preclusion. Two requirements must be met before the rules of claim preclusion apply: (1) the claim must be the same in the first and second action; and (2) the first decision must be "on the merits." Issue preclusion prevents a litigant from basing a claim, in a second suit, on the same events as those in the first suit if the same issues were determined in the first litigation between the parties.

■■■

Quicknotes

CAUSE OF ACTION A fact or set of facts the occurrence of which entitle a party to seek judicial relief.

COLLATERAL ESTOPPEL A doctrine whereby issues litigated and determined in a prior proceeding are binding upon all subsequent litigation between the parties regarding that issue.

RES JUDICATA The rule of law that a final judgment by a court precludes subsequent litigation between the parties regarding the same cause of action.

■■■

Apex Hosiery Co. v. Leader

Hosiery company (P) v. Appellant (D)

102 F.2d 702 (3d Cir. 1939).

NATURE OF CASE: Appeal from a court order to produce, for inspection, documents for trial in antitrust action.

FACT SUMMARY: Leader (D) appealed from an order of the court for the discovery and production of documents for inspection, copying, and photographing by Apex Hosiery Co. (P) for use at trial.

🏛 RULE OF LAW
An order of the court made under Fed. R. Civ. P. 34 for discovery and production of documents is interlocutory and therefore not appealable.

FACTS: Leader (D), in an action for treble damages under the Sherman Anti-Trust Act, appealed from an order of the district court made under Fed. R. Civ. P. 34 for the discovery and production by it of documents for inspection, copying, and photographing by Apex Hosiery (D) for use at the trial of the action.

ISSUE: Is an order of the court made under Fed. R. Civ. P. 34 for discovery and production of documents interlocutory and therefore not appealable?

HOLDING AND DECISION: (Per curiam) Yes. An order of the court made under Fed. R. Civ. P. 34 for discovery and production of documents is interlocutory and therefore not appealable. In this case, the disposition made of the motion will necessarily determine the conduct of the trial and may vitally affect the result. In essence, the motion resembles others made before or during a trial to secure or to suppress evidence, such as applications to suppress a deposition, to compel the production of books or documents, or to physically examine a plaintiff. The orders made upon such applications, so far as they affect the rights only of parties to the litigation, are interlocutory. Appeal dismissed.

▶ ANALYSIS

The above doctrine is known as the "final judgment" rule. Its application prevents endless litigation of interim rulings that may ultimately be mooted anyway by resolution or settlement of a case. However, some jurisdictions permit appeal of nonfinal rulings at the trial court level, provided they are judged to be sufficiently "significant."

Quicknotes

FED. R. CIV. P. 34 Governs discovery and the production of documents at trial.

FINAL JUDGMENT A decision by the court settling a dispute between the parties on its merits and which is appealable to a higher court.

INTERLOCUTORY (ORDER) An order entered by the court determining an issue that does not resolve the disposition of the case, but is essential to a proper adjudication of the action.

Quick Reference Rules of Law

Pennoyer v. Neff

Purchaser of property (D) v. Real property owner (P)

95 U.S. 714 (1877).

NATURE OF CASE: Action to recover possession of land.

FACT SUMMARY: Neff (P) attacked the validity of a sheriff's sale of his property to satisfy a personal judgment obtained against him where service was by publication.

RULE OF LAW
Where the object of an action is to determine the personal rights and obligations of the parties, service by publication against a nonresident is ineffective to confer jurisdiction upon the court.

FACTS: Neff (P) owned real property in Oregon. Mitchell brought suit in Oregon to recover legal fees allegedly owed him by Neff (P). Neff (P), a nonresident, was served by publication and Mitchell obtained a default judgment. The court ordered Neff's (P) land sold at a sheriff's sale to satisfy the judgment. Pennoyer (D) purchased the property. Neff (P) subsequently learned of the sale and brought suit in Oregon to recover possession of the property. Neff (P) alleged that the court ordering the sale had never acquired in personam jurisdiction over him. Therefore, the court could not adjudicate the personal rights between Neff (P) and Mitchell and the default judgment had been improperly entered.

ISSUE: Where an action involves the adjudication of personal rights and obligations of the parties, is service by publication against a nonresident sufficient to confer jurisdiction?

HOLDING AND DECISION: (Field, J.) No. Substituted service of process in actions against nonresidents of a state is effective only in proceedings in rem. Where an action involves the determination of personal rights and obligations of the parties, service by publication is ineffective to confer jurisdiction over the nonresident defendant. No state can exercise direct jurisdiction and authority over persons or property outside of its boundaries. The validity of every judgment depends upon the jurisdiction of the court rendering judgment. Thus, Mitchell could not obtain a personal judgment against Neff (P) without first obtaining in personam jurisdiction. Substituted service by publication is ineffective to confer personal jurisdiction over a nonresident. The sale was therefore void. A different result could have been reached if Mitchell had first obtained in rem jurisdiction by seizing the property at the time suit was commenced. Affirmed.

► ANALYSIS

Although no state can exercise direct jurisdiction and authority over people or property outside the state, the state may exercise jurisdiction over persons and property inside the state in ways that will affect persons and property outside the state. *Pennoyer v. Neff* established that every state had the power to regulate the way in which property within the state is acquired, enjoyed, and transferred. But a state cannot bring a person or property outside the state into its jurisdiction simply by using substituted service.

Quicknotes

IN PERSONAM JURISDICTION The jurisdiction of a court over a person as opposed to his interest in property.

IN REM JURISDICTION A court's authority over a thing so that its judgment is binding in respect to the rights and interests of all parties in that thing.

SERVICE OF PROCESS The communication of reasonable notice of a court proceeding to a defendant in order to provide him with an opportunity to be heard.

International Shoe Co. v. Washington

Delaware corporation (D) v. State (P)

326 U.S. 310 (1945).

NATURE OF CASE: Proceedings to recover unemployment contributions.

FACT SUMMARY: A state statute authorized the mailing of notice of assessment of delinquent contributions for unemployment compensation to nonresident employers. International Shoe Co. (International) (D) was a nonresident corporation. Notice of assessment was served on one of its salespersons within the state and was mailed to International's (D) office.

🏛 RULE OF LAW
For a state to subject a nonresident defendant to in personam jurisdiction, due process requires that the nonresident defendant have certain minimum contacts with the state such that the maintenance of the suit does not offend traditional notions of fair play and substantial justice.

FACTS: A Washington statute set up a scheme of unemployment compensation, which required contributions by employers. The statute authorized the commissioner, Washington (P), to issue an order and notice of assessment of delinquent contributions by mailing the notice to nonresident employers. International Shoe Co. (International) (D) was a Delaware corporation having its principal place of business in Missouri. International (D) employed 11 to 13 salespersons under the supervision of managers in Missouri. These salespeople resided in Washington, did most of their work there, and had no authority to enter into contracts or make collections. International (D) did not have an office in Washington and made no contracts there. Notice of assessment was served upon one of International's (D) Washington salespersons and a copy of the notice was sent by registered mail to International's (D) Missouri address.

ISSUE: For a state to subject a nonresident defendant to in personam jurisdiction, does due process require that the nonresident have certain minimum contacts with the state, such that the maintenance of the suit does not offend notions of fair play and substantial justice?

HOLDING AND DECISION: (Stone, C.J.) Yes. Historically the jurisdiction of courts to render judgment in personam is grounded on their power over the defendant's person, and the defendant's presence within the territorial jurisdiction of a court was necessary to a valid judgment. But now, due process requires only that in order to subject a defendant to a judgment in personam, if he is not present within the territorial

jurisdiction, he has certain minimum contacts with the territory such that the maintenance of the suit does not offend traditional notions of fair play and substantial justice. The contacts must be such as to make it reasonable, in the context of our federal system, to require a defendant corporation to defend the suit brought there. An estimate of the inconveniences that would result to the corporation from a trial away from its "home" is relevant. To require a corporation to defend a suit away from home where its contact has been casual or its activities isolated has been thought to lay too unreasonable a burden on the corporation. However, even single or occasional acts may, because of their nature, quality, and circumstances, be deemed sufficient to render a corporation liable to suit. Hence, the criteria to determine whether jurisdiction is justified are not simply mechanical or quantitative. Satisfaction of due process depends on the quality and nature of the activity in relation to the fair and orderly administration of the laws. In this case International's (D) activities were neither irregular nor casual. Rather, they were systematic and continuous. The obligation sued upon here arose out of these activities. They were sufficient to establish sufficient contacts or ties to make it reasonable to permit Washington (P) to enforce the obligations International (D) incurred there. Affirmed.

DISSENT: (Black, J.) The U.S. Constitution leaves to each state the power to tax and to open the doors of its courts for its citizens to sue corporations who do business in the state. It is a judicial deprivation to condition the exercise of this power on this court's notion of "fair play."

▶ ANALYSIS

Before this decision three theories had evolved to provide for suits by and against foreign corporations. The first was the consent theory. It rested on the proposition that since a foreign corporation could not carry on its business within a state without the permission of that state, the state could require a corporation to appoint an agent to receive service of process within the state. However, it soon became established law that a foreign corporation could not be prevented by a state from carrying on interstate commerce within its borders. The presence doctrine required that the corporation was "doing business" and "present" in the state. The third theory used either the present or consent doctrine, and it was necessary to determine whether the corporation was doing business within the state

Continued on next page.

either to decide whether its consent could properly be implied or to discover whether the corporation was present.

■≡■

Quicknotes

CONSENT JURISDICTION The forum having jurisdiction over a lawsuit as agreed upon by the parties prior to litigation.

IN PERSONAM JURISDICTION The jurisdiction of a court over a person as opposed to his interest in property.

MINIMUM CONTACTS The minimum degree of contact necessary in order to sustain a cause of action within a particular forum, consistent with the requirements of due process.

■≡■

McGee v. International Life Insurance Co.

Beneficiary (P) v. Insurance company (D)

355 U.S. 220 (1957).

NATURE OF CASE: Suit to enforce payment of life insurance proceeds.

FACT SUMMARY: McGee (P) was the beneficiary of a life insurance policy on a California resident who had purchased the policy from an insurer who was subsequently bought by International Life Insurance Co. (D). McGee obtained a judgment for the proceeds in California and attempted to enforce the judgment in Texas.

🏛 RULE OF LAW
Due process requires only that in order to subject a nonresident defendant to the personal jurisdiction of the forum, the suit be based on a contract that has substantial connection with the forum.

FACTS: Lowell Franklin, a resident of California, purchased a life insurance policy from an insurer. The reinsurer, International Life Insurance Co. (D), mailed a reinsurance certificate to the California resident offering to insure him. Franklin accepted this offer and paid all premiums by mail from his California home to the reinsurer's Texas office. The insured died, and the beneficiary, McGee (P), notified the insurer (D) of the death. The insurer (D) refused to make payment, and McGee (P) sued the insurer in California, obtaining a judgment.

ISSUE: Does due process require only that in order to subject a nonresident defendant to the personal jurisdiction of the forum, the suit be based on a contract that has substantial connection with the forum?

HOLDING AND DECISION: (Black, J.) Yes. Due process requires only that in order to subject a nonresident defendant to the personal jurisdiction of the forum, the suit be based on a contract that has substantial connection with the forum. Here, the insurance contract was delivered to California, and the premiums were payable there. The beneficiary and policyholders are California residents. It cannot be denied that California has a manifest interest in providing effective means of redress for its residents when their insurers refuse to pay claims. These residents would be at a severe disadvantage if forced to follow the insurance company to a distant state in order to hold it legally accountable.

▶ ANALYSIS

The fact of solicitation of the policy in California was a key element of this decision. That solicitation, albeit a single incident, could reasonably be thought to have put International Life Insurance Co. (D) on notice that it might be sued in California. If, on the other hand, the insured had taken out the policy in Texas and then moved to California, where he was the sole policyholder, this foreseeability argument would be greatly diluted. However, if the insured was one of a number of California policyholders, the exercise of personal jurisdiction there could be expected.

■━■

Quicknotes

FULL FAITH AND CREDIT Doctrine that a judgment by a court of one state shall be given the same effect in another state.

MINIMUM CONTACTS The minimum degree of contact necessary in order to sustain a cause of action within a particular forum, consistent with the requirements of due process.

■━■

Hanson v. Denckla

Will legatees (P) v. Trust beneficiaries (D)

357 U.S. 235 (1958).

NATURE OF CASE: Appeal from disposition of property in a trust.

FACT SUMMARY: Mrs. Donner, mother of three daughters, established a trust in Delaware and later moved to Florida where she died.

🏛 RULE OF LAW
For there to be "minimal contacts" sufficient to support in personam jurisdiction, it is essential that there be some act by which the defendant purposefully avails itself of the privilege of conducting activities within the forum state, thus invoking the benefits and protections of its laws.

FACTS: Mrs. Donner established a trust in Delaware and later moved to Florida where she died. A will contest ensued among her three daughters: if Florida could acquire jurisdiction over the Delaware trust, two daughters would get the entire estate; if the Delaware courts had jurisdiction, all three daughters would share equally.

ISSUE: For there to be "minimal contacts" sufficient to support in personam jurisdiction, is it essential that there be some act by which the defendant purposefully avails itself of the privilege of conducting activities within the forum state, thus invoking the benefits and protections of its laws?

HOLDING AND DECISION: (Warren, C.J.) Yes. For there to be "minimal contacts" sufficient to support in personam jurisdiction, it is essential that there be some act by which the defendant purposefully avails itself of the privilege of conducting activities with the forum state, thus invoking the benefits and protections of its laws. In this case, no such contacts could be found. The Delaware trustee had no office in Florida and conducted no business there. No trust assets were ever held in Florida or administered there, and there was no solicitation of business in that state either in person or by mail. Consequently, this suit was not one to enforce an obligation that arose from a privilege exercised in Florida. However minimal the burden of defending in a foreign tribunal, a defendant may not be called upon to do so unless he has had the minimum contacts with that state, that are a prerequisite to its exercise of power over him.

▶ ANALYSIS

The case really revolves around the validity of the inter vivos trust. The trust was created in Delaware, and the corpus remains there. The fact that some Florida residents are beneficiaries thereunder, or that they wish to defeat the trust, is not a compelling state interest. It certainly is not a more substantial interest than is Delaware's right to construe the validity of a trust created under its laws and the corpus of which is within its jurisdiction. The fact that the settlor was a Florida resident is immaterial. She was not a resident when the trust was created, nor was she attempting to have the trust set aside.

Quicknotes

IN PERSONAM JURISDICTION The jurisdiction of a court over a person as opposed to his interest in property.

INTER VIVOS TRUST Property that is held by one person for the benefit of another and which is created by an instrument that takes effect during the life of the grantor.

MINIMUM CONTACTS The minimum degree of contact necessary in order to sustain a cause of action within a particular forum, consistent with the requirements of due process.

RESIDUARY CLAUSE (OF WILL) A clause contained in a will disposing of the assets remaining following distribution of the estate.

Shaffer v. Heitner

Corporation (D) v. Shareholder (P)

433 U.S. 186 (1977).

NATURE OF CASE: Appeal from a finding of state jurisdiction.

FACT SUMMARY: Heitner (P) brought a derivative suit against Greyhound (D) directors for antitrust losses it had sustained in Oregon. The suit was brought in Delaware, Greyhound's (D) state of incorporation.

RULE OF LAW
Jurisdiction cannot be founded on property within a state unless there are sufficient contacts within the meaning of the test developed in *International Shoe Co. v. Washington*.

FACTS: Heitner (P) owned one share of Greyhound (D) stock. Greyhound (D) had been subjected to a large antitrust judgment in Oregon. Heitner (P), a nonresident of Delaware, brought a derivative suit in Delaware, the state of Greyhound's (D) incorporation. Jurisdiction was based on sequestration of Greyhound (D) stock that was deemed to be located within the state of incorporation. The Delaware sequestration statute allowed property within the state to be seized ex parte to compel the owner to submit to the in personam jurisdiction of the court. None of the stock was actually in Delaware, but a freeze order was placed on the corporate books. Greyhound (D) made a special appearance to challenge the court's jurisdiction to hear the matter. Greyhound (D) argued that the sequestration statute was unconstitutional under the line of case's beginning with *Snidatch v. Family Finance Corp.*, 395 U.S. 337 (1969), Greyhound (D) also argued that there were insufficient contacts with Delaware to justify an exercise of jurisdiction. The Delaware courts found that the sequestration statute was valid since it was not a per se seizure of the property and was merely invoked to compel out-of-state residents to defend actions within the state. Little or no consideration was given to the "contact" argument based on a finding that the presence of the stock within the state conferred quasi in rem jurisdiction.

ISSUE: May a state assume jurisdiction over an issue merely because defendant's property happens to be within the state?

HOLDING AND DECISION: (Marshall, J.) No. Mere presence of property within a state is insufficient to confer jurisdiction on a court absent independent contacts within the meaning of *International Shoe Co. v. Washington*, 326 U.S. 310 (1945), which would make acceptance constitutional. We expressly disapprove that line of cases represented by *Harris v. Balk*, 198 U.S. 215 (1905), which permits jurisdiction merely because the property happens to be within the state. If sufficient contacts do not exist to assume jurisdiction absent the presence of property within the state, it cannot be invoked on the basis of property within the court's jurisdiction. We base this decision on the fundamental concepts of justice and fair play required under the Due Process and Equal Protection Clauses of the Fourteenth Amendment. Here, the stock is not the subject of the controversy. There is no claim to ownership of it or injury caused by it. The defendants do not reside in Delaware or have any contacts there. The injury occurred in Oregon. No activities complained of were done within the forum. Finally, Heitner (P) is not even a Delaware resident. Jurisdiction was improperly granted. Reversed.

CONCURRENCE: (Powell, J.) I would only disagree as to cases involving property permanently within the state, e.g., real property. Such property should confer jurisdiction.

CONCURRENCE: (Stevens, J.) I concur in the result since purchase of stock in the marketplace should not confer in rem jurisdiction in the state of incorporation. I also concur with Mr. Justice Powell's statements.

CONCURRENCE AND DISSENT: (Brennan, J.) A state may exercise jurisdiction over a party only on the basis of the minimum contacts among the parties, the contested transaction and the forum state. In this case, however, the assertion of jurisdiction was based on the presence of property, in the form of capital stock, in Delaware. This is quasi in rem jurisdiction and is not based upon minimum contacts. However, even under the minimum contacts analysis that the majority requires today, jurisdiction should not be denied in this case. The State of Delaware has a strong interest in adjudicating claims as to corporations chartered by it. It must provide restitution for its corporations, it has a regulatory interest, and an interest in providing a convenient forum for the entity that is a creature of its law. Thus, jurisdiction should attach.

ANALYSIS

While the corporation could be sued in its state of incorporation under the dissent's theory, the suit is against the directors and neither the site of the wrong nor the residence of a defendant is in Delaware. The decision will have a major impact only in cases such as

Continued on next page.

this one, where the state really has no reason to want to adjudicate the issue. Of course, real property would still be treated as an exception.

■■━━■

Quicknotes

EX PARTE A proceeding commenced by one party without providing any opposing parties with notice or which is uncontested by an adverse party.

IN REM JURISDICTION A court's authority over a thing so that its judgment is binding in respect to the rights and interests of all parties in that thing.

QUASI IN REM JURISDICTION A court's authority over the defendant's property within a specified geographical area.

■■━━■

World-Wide Volkswagen Corp. v. Woodson

Automobile distributor (P) v. Court (D)

444 U.S. 286 (1980).

NATURE OF CASE: Petition for a writ prohibiting the exercise of in personam jurisdiction.

FACT SUMMARY: World-Wide Volkswagen Corp. (P) sought a writ of prohibition to keep district court Judge Woodson (D) from exercising in personam jurisdiction over it, alleging it did not have sufficient "contacts" with the forum state of Oklahoma to render it subject to such jurisdiction.

> ## 🏛 RULE OF LAW
> A state court may exercise personal jurisdiction over a nonresident defendant only so long as there exist sufficient "minimum contacts" between him and the forum state such that maintenance of the suit does not offend "traditional notions of fair play and substantial justice."

FACTS: World-Wide Volkswagen Corp. (World-Wide) (P) was the regional distributor of Audi automobile for the tri-state area of New York, New Jersey, and Connecticut. It was the distributor of the particular Audi that the Robinsons purchased from a New York dealer and drove to Oklahoma, where three family members were severely burned when another car struck their Audi in the rear. The Robinsons brought a products-liability action in an Oklahoma district court, suing the New York dealership and World-Wide (a New York corporation) (P). Claiming that no evidence showed it had any connection with Oklahoma whatsoever, World-Wide (P) sought a writ of prohibition to keep district court Judge Woodson (D) from exercising in personam jurisdiction. World-Wide (P) argued that a lack of sufficient contacts with the forum state made assertion of such jurisdiction improper under the Due Process Clause. The supreme court of Oklahoma denied the writ, noting that World-Wide (P) could foresee that the automobiles it sold would be taken into other states, including Oklahoma. The U.S. Supreme Court granted certiorari.

ISSUE: Must a defendant have "minimum contacts" with the forum state before it can exercise in personam jurisdiction over him?

HOLDING AND DECISION: (White, J.) Yes. Under the Due Process Clause, the exercise of in personam jurisdiction over a defendant is not constitutional unless he has sufficient "minimum contacts" with the forum state so that maintenance of the suit does not offend "traditional notions of fair play and substantial justice." Here, World-Wide (P) had no "contacts, ties, or relations" with Oklahoma, so personal jurisdiction could not be exercised.

As for the notion that it was foreseeable that cars sold in New York would wind up in Oklahoma, the foreseeability that is critical to due process analysis is not the mere likelihood that a product will find its way into the forum state. Rather, it is that the defendant's conduct and connection with the forum state are such that he should reasonably anticipate being hauled into court there. Such conduct and connection are simply missing in this case. Reversed.

DISSENT: (Brennan, J.) The automobile is designed specifically to facilitate travel from place to place, and the sale of one purposefully injects it into the stream of interstate commerce. Thus, this case is not unlike those where in personam jurisdiction is properly exercised over one who purposefully places his product into the stream of interstate commerce with the expectation it will be purchased by consumers in other states. Furthermore, a large part of the value of automobiles is the extensive, nationwide network of highways. State maintenance of such roads contributes to the value of World-Wide's (P) business. World-Wide (P) also participates in a network of related dealerships with nationwide service facilities. Having such facilities in Oklahoma also adds to the value of World-Wide's (P) business. Thus, it has the required minimum contacts with Oklahoma to render this exercise of personal jurisdiction constitutional.

▎ANALYSIS

Over the years, modern transportation and communication have made foreign-state suits much less of a burden to defendants. This resulted in a relaxing of the due process limits placed on state jurisdiction down to the "minimum contacts" concept. However, even if there were no inconvenience to the defendant, a state could not exercise personal jurisdiction over him if he had no "contacts, ties, or relations." This is true even if that state had a strong interest in applying its law to the controversy, and it was the most convenient location for litigation, etc. The reason is that the Due Process Clause serves two distinct functions: the first is as a guarantor against inconvenient litigation but the second is as a guardian of interstate federalism. It is in this second capacity that the Due Process Clause would prevent assumption of jurisdiction in the aforementioned instance by recognizing the "territorial limitations on the power of the respective states."

■▬▬■

Continued on next page.

Quicknotes

DUE PROCESS CLAUSE Clauses, found in the Fifth and Fourteenth Amendments to the United States Constitution, providing that no person shall be deprived of "life, liberty, or property, without due process of law."

IN PERSONAM JURISDICTION The jurisdiction of a court over a person as opposed to his interest in property.

MINIMUM CONTACTS The minimum degree of contact necessary in order to sustain a cause of action within a particular forum, consistent with the requirements of due process.

■═■

Burger King Corp. v. Rudzewicz

Fast-food corporation (P) v. Franchisee (D)

471 U.S. 462 (1985).

NATURE OF CASE: Appeal from reversal of award of damages and injunctive relief for breach of contract.

FACT SUMMARY: Burger King Corp. (P) brought an action against Rudzewicz (D), a defaulting franchisee, in Burger King's (P) home forum.

🏛 RULE OF LAW
Direct and continuous contacts by a franchisee with the franchisor may lead to the franchisee being subject to the jurisdiction of the franchisor's home forum.

FACTS: Rudzewicz (D) contracted for a Burger King franchise in Michigan with Burger King Corp. (P), a Florida corporation. A franchise was granted. The terms of the contract called for substantial supervision of the franchise's operations by Burger King (P), and also for the laws of Florida to apply. Despite the fact that Rudzewicz (D) was a sophisticated businessman, the business failed, and Burger King (P) brought suit for unpaid rent. The Florida district court granted damages and injunctive relief, but the Eleventh Circuit reversed, holding that Rudzewicz (D) was not amenable to Florida jurisdiction. Burger King (P) appealed.

ISSUE: May direct and continuous contacts by a franchisee with the franchisor lead to the franchisee being subject to the jurisdiction of the franchisor's home forum?

HOLDING AND DECISION: (Brennan, J.) Yes. Direct and continuous contacts by a franchisee with the franchisor may lead to the franchisee being subject to the jurisdiction of the franchisor's home forum. The main test for personal jurisdiction is whether a defendant's actions were such that he should have been put on notice of the possibility of becoming subject to the subject forum's jurisdiction. The yardstick here is the nature of that defendant's contacts with that forum. Here, Rudzewicz (D) contracted with a Florida franchisor and entered into a contract providing for a continuous relationship with that franchisor and constant monitoring by that franchisor. Further, the contract stated that it was to be construed a Florida contract. Considering the nature of Rudzewicz's (D) contacts with Florida, an ample basis for jurisdiction existed. Reversed and remanded.

DISSENT: (Stevens, J.) The typical franchise is a large operation connected with the franchisor's home office only in name. Since the business is purely local, only local jurisdiction should apply.

▶ ANALYSIS

Part of the rationale for the Court's opinion was the clause making the contract a Florida one. Most contracts involving parties in different states have such clauses. Exactly how much weight was given this was not spelled out by the Court, but the opinion did say that such a clause is not determinative.

■■■

Quicknotes

INJUNCTIVE RELIEF A count order issued as a remedy, requiring a person to do, or prohibiting that person from doing, a specific act.

MINIMUM CONTACTS The minimum degree of contact necessary in order to sustain a cause of action within a particular forum, consistent with the requirements of due process.

PERSONAL JURISDICTION The court's authority over a person or parties to a lawsuit.

■■■

Pavlovich v. Superior Court

Web-site creator (P) v. Superior Court (D)

Cal. Sup. Ct., 29 Cal. 4th 262, 58 P.3d 2 (2002).

NATURE OF CASE: Appeal of finding of personal jurisdiction over defendant.

FACT SUMMARY: When the trial court found specific personal jurisdiction over Pavlovich (P) based solely on his passive Internet Web site, Pavlovich (P) argued that personal jurisdiction may not be acquired over a defendant simply based on a posting on a passive Internet Web site.

RULE OF LAW

Personal jurisdiction may not necessarily be acquired over a defendant based on a posting on a passive Internet Web site.

FACTS: Matthew Pavlovich (P), a computer systems and network administrator, was a Texas resident who did not reside or work in California and never had a place of business, telephone listing, or bank account in California, and never owned property in California. Neither Pavlovich (P) nor his company (LiVid) ever solicited any business in California nor had any business contacts in California. Pavlovich (P) opened and operated a single-page passive Web site that only provided information, but did not solicit or transact any business and permitted no interactive exchange of information between its operators and visitors. The site sought to defeat certain DVD technology and enable the decryption and copying of DVDs containing motion pictures. LiVid posted the source code of a program named DeCSS on its Web site to allow users to circumvent the DVD technology and copy motion pictures. Real party in interest, DVD Copy Control Association, brought suit against Pavlovich (P) for posting this proprietary information, and the California superior court exercised specific personal jurisdiction over Pavlovich (P) based on his web site. The California Court of Appeals affirmed the finding of jurisdiction, and Pavlovich (P) appealed.

ISSUE: May personal jurisdiction necessarily be acquired over a defendant based on a posting on a passive Internet Web site?

HOLDING AND DECISION: (Brown, J.) No. Personal jurisdiction may not necessarily be acquired over a defendant based on a posting on a passive Internet Web site. A court may exercise specific jurisdiction over a nonresident defendant only if (1) the defendant has purposefully availed himself of forum benefits, (2) the controversy arises out of the defendant's contacts with the forum, and (3) the assertion of personal jurisdiction would comport with fair play and substantial justice. Here, Pavlovich's (P) sole contact with California was LiVid's posting of a DVD source code containing proprietary information on an Internet Web site accessible to any person with Internet access. A passive Web site, as here, that does little more than make information available to those who are interested in it is not grounds for the exercise of personal jurisdiction. In such case, the exercise of jurisdiction is determined by examining the level of interactivity and commercial nature of the exchange of information that occurs on the Web site. Here, LiVid's Web site merely posts information and has no interactive features. There is no evidence suggesting that the site targeted California. Indeed, there is no evidence that any California resident ever visited, much less downloaded the DeCSS source code from, the LiVid Web site. Pavlovich's (P) mere knowledge that his tortious conduct may harm industries centered in California, while relevant to the determination of personal jurisdiction, alone is insufficient to establish express aiming at the forum state as required to establish personal jurisdiction in the forum state. Hence, Pavlovich's (P) conduct was not, by itself, sufficient to subject him to California jurisdiction. Reversed and remanded.

DISSENT: (Baxter, J) The intended targets of Pavlovich (P) were entire businesses. He knew at least two of the targets: the movie industry and the computer industry, and both industries were centered in California. Thus, for purposes of specific personal jurisdiction, Pavlovich's (P) intentional act, even if committed outside California, was "expressly aimed" at California. In these particular circumstances, it cannot matter that Pavlovich (P) may not have known or cared about the exact identities or precise locations of each individual target, or that he happened to employ a so-called passive Internet Web site, or whether any California resident visited the site.

ANALYSIS

In *Pavlovich*, the court made clear that creating a Web site, like placing a product into the stream of commerce, may be felt nationwide, or even worldwide, but, without more, is not an act purposely directed toward the forum state. Otherwise, personal jurisdiction in Internet-related cases would almost always be found in any forum in the country. Such a result would violate long-held and inviolate principles of personal jurisdiction.

■■■

Continued on next page.

Quicknotes

FORUM A court or other location in which a legal remedy may be sought.

PERSONAL JURISDICTION The court's authority over a person or parties to a lawsuit.

■═■

J. McIntyre Machinery, Ltd. v. Nicastro

Product manufacturer (D) v. Injured worker (P)

_____ U.S. _____ 131 S. Ct. 2780 (2011).

NATURE OF CASE: Appeal of judgment by state supreme court.

FACT SUMMARY: A person who was injured when he used a piece of heavy machinery sued the foreign manufacturer in New Jersey state court. The company disputed the state's jurisdiction.

🏛 RULE OF LAW
In products liability cases, the "stream-of-commerce" doctrine cannot displace the general rule that the exercise of judicial power is not lawful unless the defendant purposefully avails itself of the privilege of conducting activities within the forum state, thus invoking the benefits and protections of its laws.

FACTS: Robert Nicastro (P) injured his hand while using a metal-shearing machine that was manufactured by J. McIntyre Machinery, Ltd. (J. McIntyre) (D). The machine was manufactured in England, where J. McIntyre (D) is incorporated and operates, and the injury occurred in New Jersey. Nicastro (P) filed suit in New Jersey. The New Jersey Supreme Court found that it had jurisdiction over J. McIntyre (D) because J. McIntyre (D) machines were sold in the United States, the company attended annual conventions for the scrap recycling industry to advertise, four machines were identified in New Jersey, and J. McIntyre (D) guided advertising and sales efforts for the U.S. distributor. J. McIntyre (D) appealed.

ISSUE: In products liability cases, can the "stream-of-commerce" doctrine displace the general rule that the exercise of judicial power is not lawful unless the defendant purposefully avails itself of the privilege of conducting activities within the forum state, thus invoking the benefits and protections of its laws?

HOLDING AND DECISION: (Kennedy, J.) No. In products liability cases, the "stream-of-commerce" doctrine cannot displace the general rule that the exercise of judicial power is not lawful unless the defendant purposefully avails itself of the privilege of conducting activities within the forum state, thus invoking the benefits and protections of its laws. The Supreme Court of New Jersey held that New Jersey's courts can exercise jurisdiction over a foreign manufacturer of a product as long as the manufacturer knows or reasonably should know that its products are distributed through a nationwide distribution system that might lead to those products being sold in any of the 50 states. That rule is from _Asahi Metal Industry Co. v. Superior Court of Cal, Solano County_, 480 U.S. 102 (1987). Based on that test, the court concluded that the British manufacturer of scrap metal machines was subject to New Jersey jurisdiction, even though the company had at no time advertised in, sent goods to, or in any way targeted the state. Those who live or operate primarily outside a state have a due process right not to be subjected to judgment in its courts, as a general rule. Where the individual or corporation explicitly consents to jurisdiction, is present in a state at the time a suit starts, is a citizen or has a domicile within the state, or is incorporated in the state, jurisdiction is proper, because all of those situations indicate an intent to submit to the laws of the state. The stream-of-commerce exception to the general rule refers to the movement of goods from manufacturers through distributors to consumers, and advocates of the exception argue that the placement of goods into the stream of commerce with the expectation that they will be purchased by consumers indicates purposeful availment. But the exception only holds where the activities manifest an intention to submit to the power of the sovereign. In this case, J. McIntyre (D) directed marketing and sales efforts at the United States, but not directly to New Jersey, and because of that, a federal court might have jurisdiction, but a New Jersey state court does not. It is J. McIntyre's (D) purposeful contacts with New Jersey, not with the United States, that are relevant. Because J. McIntyre has not engaged in conduct purposefully directed at New Jersey, New Jersey state courts did not have jurisdiction to hear the case. Reversed.

CONCURRENCE: (Breyer, J.) The judgment is correct, but it is determined by precedent. There is no reason to construct new general rules that limit jurisdiction, since on the basis of existing precedent, the case can be decided. No precedent finds that a single isolated sale, even if accompanied by the sales here, is sufficient. Nicastro (P) failed to meet his burden of showing that it was constitutionally proper to exercise jurisdiction over petitioner J. McIntyre (D).

DISSENT: (Ginsburg, J.) J. McIntyre (D) wanted to establish a market for its product in the United States and took steps to do so. Where in the United States buyers of the product live or operate is irrelevant to the manufacturer. The company simply wants to sell its product in the United States. Under _International Shoe_

Continued on next page.

Co. v. Washington, 326 U.S. 310 (1945), personal jurisdiction is established.

▶ *ANALYSIS*

The absence of a majority opinion makes it difficult to identify a reliable rule. Three justices voted to reverse on the basis of a new rule that limits jurisdiction more severely than precedent; three others voted to reverse on the basis of precedent, with making a new rule; and three others voted to affirm on the basis of precedent.

■══■

Quicknotes

FORUM STATE The state in which a court, or other location in which a legal remedy may be sought, is located.

PURPOSEFUL AVAILMENT An element in determining whether a defendant had the required minimum contacts in a forum necessary in order for a court to exercise jurisdiction over the party, whereby the court determines whether the defendant intentionally conducted activities in the forum and thus knows, or could reasonably expect, that such conduct could give rise to litigation in that forum.

■══■

Goodyear Dunlop Tires Operations, S.A. v. Brown

Foreign subsidiaries of U.S. corporation (D) v. Decedents' parents (P)

_____ U.S. _____, 131 S. Ct. 2846 (2011).

NATURE OF CASE: Appeal of state court's assertion of jurisdiction.

FACTS SUMMARY: The parents of two American boys killed in a bus accident in France brought suit in North Carolina, where the boys lived, against the tire company.

🏛 RULE OF LAW

A state may not exercise general personal jurisdiction over a foreign subsidiary of a U.S. corporation where the subsidiary lacks continuous and systematic business contacts with the state.

FACTS: The parents (P) of two American boys who were killed in a bus accident in France brought suit in North Carolina state court against Goodyear Tire and Rubber Company (D) and three Goodyear subsidiaries (D) operating in Turkey, France, and Luxembourg. The parents (P) claimed that the accident resulted from a defective tire manufactured at the Turkish subsidiary's plant. Although Goodyear USA (D) operates in North Carolina, the three foreign subsidiaries (D) have no place of business, employees, or bank accounts in the state and neither solicit nor do business in the state. A small percentage of the subsidiaries' (D) tires were distributed in North Carolina by other Goodyear USA (D) affiliates, however. The subsidiaries (D) moved to dismiss the claims against them for lack of personal jurisdiction. The trial court denied the motion, and the North Carolina Court of Appeals affirmed, holding that the court had general jurisdiction over the subsidiaries (D) because their tires had reached the state through "the stream of commerce."

ISSUE: May a state exercise general personal jurisdiction over a foreign subsidiary of a U.S. corporation where the subsidiary lacks continuous and systematic business contacts with the state?

HOLDING AND DECISION: (Ginsburg, J.) No. A state may not exercise general personal jurisdiction over a foreign subsidiary of a U.S. corporation where the subsidiary lacks continuous and systematic business contacts with the state. As stated in _International Shoe Co._ v. _Washington_, 326 U. S. 310, 316 (1945), and its progeny, a distinction exists between general and specific personal jurisdiction. General personal jurisdiction arises from a defendant's "continuous and systematic" affiliation with a state and permits a state to exercise personal jurisdiction over the defendant for any claim,

regardless of whether the claim itself has any connection to the defendant's activities in the state. Specific personal jurisdiction arises from a connection between the state and the underlying claim, and permits a state to exercise jurisdiction only with respect to that claim. In this case, the North Carolina courts conflated the two types of jurisdiction, improperly using the isolated presence of the subsidiaries' products in the state as a result of others' actions to justify jurisdiction over the subsidiaries for claims having nothing to do with those products. Reversed.

▶ ANALYSIS

Key to this case is the distinction between two types of personal jurisdiction: general and specific. General jurisdiction is all-purpose, in the sense that it allows any claim to be brought against a defendant as long as the defendant has "systematic and continuous" contacts with that forum. Specific jurisdiction exists where there is a connection between a forum and a particular controversy, and it is limited to that controversy. In this case, only general jurisdiction was in issue: The site of the accident and the factory where the tires were made were both outside of North Carolina, so there was no connection between the state and the controversy, and specific jurisdiction was therefore not properly at issue. As to whether general jurisdiction existed, the Court focused on "stream-of-commerce," and reached the conclusion that jurisdiction did not exist.

■=■

Quicknotes

GENERAL JURISDICTION Refers to the authority of a court to hear and determine all cases of a particular type.

PERSONAL JURISDICTION The court's authority over a person or parties to a lawsuit.

■=■

Burnham v. Superior Court

Husband and father (P) v. Court (D)

495 U.S. 604 (1990).

NATURE OF CASE: Appeal from denial of motion to quash service of process in dissolution action on the grounds that the court lacked personal jurisdiction.

FACT SUMMARY: Dennis Burnham (P) and his wife were living in New Jersey when they decided to separate. Mrs. Burnham moved with the children to California, filed for divorce in that state and served Mr. Burnham (P) while he was visiting.

RULE OF LAW
State courts have jurisdiction over nonresidents who are physically present in the state.

FACTS: Dennis Burnham (P) and his wife were living in New Jersey when they decided to separate. Mrs. Burnham moved with the children to California and filed for divorce in that state. Mr. Burnham (P) visited his children in January of 1988, at which time he was served with a California court summons and a copy of his wife's divorce petition. He made a special appearance in the California Superior Court (D) moving to quash the service of process on the ground that the Court (D) lacked personal jurisdiction over him because his only contacts with California were a few short visits to the state for the purpose of conducting business and visiting his children. The Superior Court (D) denied the motion, and the California Court of Appeals denied mandamus relief. The court held it to be a valid jurisdictional predicate for in personam jurisdiction that Mr. Burnham (P) was present in the forum state and personally served with process. The U.S. Supreme Court granted certiorari.

ISSUE: Do state courts have jurisdiction over nonresidents who are physically present in the state?

HOLDING AND DECISION: (Scalia, J.) Yes. State courts have jurisdiction over nonresidents who are physically present in the state. Jurisdiction based on physical presence alone constitutes due process because it is one of the continuing traditions of our legal system that define the due process standard of traditional notions of fair play and substantial justice. That standard was developed by analogy to physical presence, and it would be perverse to say it could now be turned against that touchstone of jurisdiction. Affirmed.

CONCURRENCE: (Brennan, J.) History is an important factor in establishing whether a jurisdictional rule satisfies due process requirements, but it is not the only factor such that all traditional rules of jurisdiction are, ipso facto, forever constitutional.

CONCURRENCE: (Stevens, J.) It is sufficient to note that the historical evidence and consensus identified by Justice Scalia, the considerations of fairness identified by Justice Brennan, and the common sense displayed by Justice White, all combine to demonstrate that this is, indeed, a very easy case.

▶ ANALYSIS

In a footnote to the above case, Justice Scalia explained that in *Helicopteros Nacionales de Columbia v. Hall*, 466 U.S. at 414 (1984), the Supreme Court held that due process is not offended by a state's subjecting a corporation to its jurisdiction when there are sufficient contacts between the state and the foreign corporation. However, the only holding supporting that statement involved regular service of summons upon a corporate president while in the forum state acting in that capacity. See *Perkins v. Benguet Consolidated Mining Co.*, 342 U.S. 437 (1952). It may be that whatever special rule exists permitting continuous and systematic contacts to support jurisdiction with respect to matters unrelated to activity in the forum applied only to corporations, which have never fitted comfortably within a jurisdictional regime based primarily upon de facto power over the defendant's person.

■■■

Quicknotes

PERSONAL JURISDICTION The court's authority over a person or parties to a lawsuit.

SERVICE OF PROCESS The communication of reasonable notice of a court proceeding to a defendant in order to provide him with an opportunity to be heard.

■■■

Carnival Cruise Lines, Inc. v. Shute

Cruise company (D) v. Customers (P)

499 U.S. 585 (1991).

NATURE OF CASE: Review of denial of defense motion for summary judgment in personal injury action.

FACT SUMMARY: Shute (P), an injured cruise ship passenger, filed suit in her home state despite a stipulation in her passenger ticket requiring all suits to be filed in Florida.

🏛 RULE OF LAW
Reasonable forum selection clauses contained in passenger tickets are presumptively valid.

FACTS: The Shutes (P), residents of Washington State, purchased passage for a seven-day cruise on a ship owned by Carnival Cruise Lines, Inc. (Carnival Cruise) (D). The cruise tickets they received contained a forum-selection clause setting the State of Florida as the forum where any disputes arising from the cruise would be litigated. Carnival Cruise (D) had its principal place of business in Florida, and many of its cruises departed from there. During the cruise, Mrs. Shute (P) was injured in a slip-and-fall accident. The Shutes (P) filed a negligence action in Washington. Carnival Cruise (D) moved for summary judgment, contending that the forum clause in the Shutes's (P) ticket required them to bring their suit in a Florida court. The Ninth Circuit denied its motion on the ground that the clause was not a product of negotiation, and the U.S. Supreme Court granted certiorari.

ISSUE: Are reasonable forum selection clauses contained in passenger tickets presumptively valid?

HOLDING AND DECISION: (Blackmun, J.) Yes. Reasonable forum selection clauses contained in passenger tickets are presumptively valid. They are permissible because a cruise line has a special interest in limiting the fora in which it potentially could be subject to suit. Such a clause also dispels any confusion about where a suit must be brought, thereby sparing litigants and courts the time and expense of litigating the issue. Finally, the passengers themselves benefit from forum clauses because fares are reduced commensurate with the money saved by the cruise line in limiting the fora where it may be sued. Since in this case there is no bad-faith motive apparent in Carnival Cruise's (D) forum provision, and the Shutes (P) have conceded that they had notice of the provision, the Ninth Circuit erred in refusing to enforce the clause. Reversed.

DISSENT: (Stevens, J.) The prevailing rule is that forum selection clauses are not enforceable if they were not freely bargained for, create additional expense for one party, or deny one party a remedy.

▶ ANALYSIS

Besides forum selection clauses, a contract may contain a choice of law clause, stipulating which jurisdiction's substantive law will govern, or an arbitration clause, requiring parties to use arbitration as their exclusive forum. The most extreme example of a contract provision limiting a defendant's right to appeal or to even raise a defense to an action is the "cognovit." A cognovit note is written authority of a debtor for entry of a judgment against him if the obligation set forth in the note is not paid when due. Such agreements are prohibited in many states.

■=■

Quicknotes

COGNOVIT NOTE A note signed by a debtor authorizing an attorney to enter judgment against him if payment is not made thereon.

FORUM SELECTION CLAUSE Provision contained in a contract setting forth the particular forum in which the parties would resolve a matter if a dispute were to arise.

■=■

Mullane v. Central Hanover Bank & Trust Co.

Guardian of trust beneficiaries (P) v. Bank (D)

339 U.S. 306 (1950).

NATURE OF CASE: Constitutional challenge of the sufficiency of the notice provision of the New York Banking Law relating to beneficiaries of common-trust funds.

FACT SUMMARY: Central Hanover Bank & Trust Co. (D) pooled a number of small trust funds, and beneficiaries (some of whom lived out of state) were notified by publication in a local newspaper.

RULE OF LAW
In order to satisfy due process challenges, notice must be by means calculated to inform the desired parties, and, where they reside outside of the state and their names and addresses are available, notice by publication is insufficient.

FACTS: A New York statute allowed corporate trustees to pool the assets of numerous small trusts administered by them. This allowed more efficient and economical administration of the funds. Each participating trust shared ratably in the common fund, but the trustees held complete control of all assets. A periodic accounting of profits, losses, and assets were to be submitted to the courts for approval. Beneficiaries were to be notified of the accounting so that they might object to any irregularities in the administration of the common fund. Once approved by the court, their claims would be barred. A guardian would be appointed to protect the interests of principal and income beneficiaries. Central Hanover Bank & Trust Co. (D) established a common fund by consolidating the corpus of 113 separate trusts under their control. Notice of the common fund was sent to all interested parties along with the relevant portions of the statute. Notice of accountings was by publication in a local New York newspaper. Mullane (P) was the appointed guardian for all parties known and unknown who had an interest in the trust's income. He objected to the sufficiency of the statutory notice provisions claiming that they violated the Due Process Clause of the Fourteenth Amendment. Notice by publication was not a reasonable method of informing interested parties that their rights were being affected, especially with regard to out-of-state beneficiaries. Mullane's (P) objections were overruled in state courts and the present federal appeal was brought by him.

ISSUE: Is notice by publication sufficient to satisfy due process challenges where the parties to be informed reside out of state and an alternative means, better calculated to give actual notice, is available?

HOLDING AND DECISION: (Jackson, J.) No. The purpose of a notice requirement is to inform parties that their rights are being affected. Therefore, the method chosen should, if at all possible, be reasonably designed to accomplish this end. Notice in a New York legal paper is not reasonably calculated to provide out-of-state residents with the desired information. While the state has a right to discharge trustees of their liabilities through the acceptance of their accounting, it must also provide beneficiaries with adequate notice so that their rights to contest the accounting are not lost. In cases where the identity or whereabouts of beneficiaries or future interest holders is unknown, then publication is the most viable alternate means available for giving notice. Publication is only a supplemental method of giving notice. However, the Court will approve its use where alternative methods are not reasonably possible or practical. Where alternative methods, better calculated to give actual notice, are available, publication is an impermissible means of providing notice. Notice to known beneficiaries via publication is inadequate, not because it in fact fails to inform everyone, but, because under the circumstances, it is not readily calculated to reach those who could easily be informed by other means at hand. Since publication to known beneficiaries is ineffective, the statutory requirement violates the Due Process Clause of the Fourteenth Amendment. These parties have, at least potentially, been deprived of property without due process of law. With respect to remote future interest holders and unknown parties, publication is permissible. Reversed and remanded.

ANALYSIS

Ineffective notice provisions violate procedural due process rights. As in all due process challenges, there must be a legitimate state interest and the means selected must be reasonably adapted to accomplish the state's purpose. While in *Mullane* the state's ends were permissible, the method of giving notice was unreasonable as it pertained to known parties. As has been previously stated, publication is only a supplementary method for giving notice. It is normally used in conjunction with other means when personal service by hand is unavailable or impractical. *Mullane* has been applied to condemnation cases where a known owner of property was never personally served. *Schroeder v. City of New York*, 371 U.S. 208 (1962). Factors considered by the Court involve the nature of the action,

Continued on next page.

whether the party's whereabouts or identity are known or unknown, whether he is a resident and whether or not he has attempted to avoid personal service. If an attempt to avoid service is made, then constructive service by publication in conjunction with substitute service by mail is permitted. Finally, foreign corporations are generally required to appoint resident agents authorized to accept service of process.

■■■

Quicknotes

DUE PROCESS The constitutional mandate requiring the courts to protect and enforce individuals' rights and liberties consistent with prevailing principles of fairness and justice and prohibiting the federal and state governments from such activities that deprive its citizens of life, liberty, or property interest.

NOTICE Communication of information to a person by one authorized or by an otherwise proper source.

■■■

Gibbons v. Brown

Automobile passenger (D) v. Fellow passenger (P)

Fla. Dist. Ct. App., 716 So. 2d 868 (1998).

NATURE OF CASE: Appeal from dismissal of a personal-injury action.

FACT SUMMARY: Mrs. Brown (P) filed a suit against Gibbons (D), a Texas resident, in Florida two years after Gibbons (D) had sued Mr. Brown in a Florida case involving the same auto accident.

🏛 RULE OF LAW
A prior decision to file a lawsuit in a state does not qualify as sufficient activity in the state to confer personal jurisdiction.

FACTS: Mr. Brown was driving a car in Canada, in which Mrs. Brown (P) and Gibbons (D) were passengers. After a collision, Gibbons (D), a Texas resident, sued Mr. Brown in Florida. Two years later, Mrs. Brown (P) filed suit against Gibbons (D) in Florida for allegedly causing the accident by giving faulty directions. The trial court dismissed the action based on a lack of personal jurisdiction over Gibbons (D). Mrs. Brown (P) appealed.

ISSUE: Does a prior decision to file a lawsuit in a state qualify as sufficient activity in the state to confer personal jurisdiction?

HOLDING AND DECISION: (Per curiam) No. A prior decision to file a lawsuit in a state does not qualify as sufficient activity in the state to confer personal jurisdiction. Obtaining personal jurisdiction over a nonresident defendant requires a two-pronged showing. First, there must be sufficient jurisdictional facts to bring the defendant within the long-arm statute. Then, there must be sufficient minimum contacts between the defendant and forum state that jurisdiction would not violate due process. Florida requires that nonresident defendants engage in substantial and not isolated activity within the state in order to be subject to personal jurisdiction. There is no doubt that when an out-of-state plaintiff brings an action in Florida, she is subject to jurisdiction in subsequent actions regarding the same subject matter. However, in the present case, there were two years separating Gibbons's (D) suit against Mr. Brown and Mrs. Brown's (P) current action. Additionally, Mrs. Brown (P) was not a party to the first suit. Given these facts, and the lack of any other contact between Gibbons (D) and Florida, the grounds for personal jurisdiction do not meet the state's requirements. Complaint dismissal ordered.

▶ ANALYSIS

The court acknowledged that Florida does not allow jurisdiction to the full range allowed by the U.S. Constitution. Thus, in the present case, it is possible that another state would have allowed the case against Gibbons (D) to proceed. However, the court never reached the issue of whether the minimum contacts required by due process had been met.

■━■

Quicknotes

LONG-ARM STATUTE A state statute conferring personal jurisdiction to state courts over a defendant not residing in the state, when the cause of action arises as a result of activities conducted within the state or affecting state residents.

PERSONAL JURISDICTION The court's authority over a person or parties to a lawsuit.

PROCEDURAL DUE PROCESS The constitutional mandate that if the state or federal government acts so as to deny a citizen of a life, liberty or property interest the individual is first entitled to notice and the right to be heard.

■━■

Dee-K Enterprises, Inc. v. Heveafil Sdn. Bhd.

Domestic purchaser (P) v. Foreign seller (D)

982 F. Supp. 1138 (E.D. Va. 1997).

NATURE OF CASE: Motion to dismiss antitrust action.

FACT SUMMARY: Heveafil Sdn. Bhd. (D), a Malaysian corporation, challenged jurisdiction and venue of Dee-K Enterprise Inc.'s antitrust action in U.S. federal court.

🏛 RULE OF LAW

The general venue statute, providing that aliens may be sued in any district, overrides special venue laws that place venue more specifically.

FACTS: Dee-K Enterprise Inc. (Dee-K) (P), a Virginia corporation, bought rubber thread from Heveafil Sdn. Bhd. (Heveafil) (D), a Malaysian company, and other companies for making bungee cords. Dee-K (P) alleged that Heveafil (D) and other corporations, both foreign and domestic, were involved in a conspiracy to fix prices. Dee-K (P) brought an antitrust action in the Eastern District federal court. Heveafil (D) argued that there was no basis for jurisdiction and venue and moved to dismiss the suit.

ISSUE: Does the general venue statute, providing that aliens may be sued in any district, override special venue laws that place venue more specifically?

HOLDING AND DECISION: (Ellis, J.) Yes. The general venue statute, providing that aliens may be sued in any district, overrides special venue laws that place venue more specifically. Section 12 of the Clayton Act provides for worldwide service of process when the antitrust defendant is a corporation. Thus, jurisdiction is proper if does not offend the requirements of due process. Since Heveafil (D) appointed an exclusive sales agent for the United States and customized its product for the U.S. market, personal jurisdiction does not offend notions of fair play and substantial justice. Section 12 also lays venue in any district where the defendant is found or where it transacts business. Heveafil (D) does not meet these requirements. However, 28 U.S.C § 1391 provides that aliens may be sued in any district. This overrides the special venue statute of the Clayton Act and eliminates the venue impediment. Thus, venue is proper for Heveafil (D) in Virginia district court. However, with regard to the American defendants, venue is proper only in a district where the events occurred or where the defendant resides. The allegations of the complaint are not specific enough to make this determination at this time.

▶ ANALYSIS

The court noted that there were indications that venue might have been proper in the western district of Virginia. The plaintiffs only had to show that one of the American defendants had enough connection to the eastern district in order to keep the case there. If they were unable to, the case could be transferred.

■=■

Quicknotes

28 U.S.C. § 1391 Permits venue to be placed where a substantial part of the events giving rise to the claim occurred.

VENUE The specific geographic location over which a court has jurisdiction to hear a suit.

■=■

Piper Aircraft v. Reyno

Aircraft company (D) v. Crash victims' representative (P)

454 U.S. 235 (1981).

NATURE OF CASE: Appeal from dismissal on the basis of forum non conveniens.

FACT SUMMARY: Reyno (P), the representative of five victims of an air crash, brought suit in California even though the location of the crash and the homes of the victims were in Scotland.

RULE OF LAW
A plaintiff may not defeat a motion to dismiss for forum non conveniens merely by showing that the substantive law that would be applied in the alternative forum is less favorable to him than that of the present forum.

FACTS: Reyno (P) was the representative of five air crash victims' estates and brought suit for wrongful death in United States district court in California, even though the accident occurred and all the victims resided in Scotland. Piper Aircraft (D) moved to dismiss for forum non conveniens, contending that Scotland was the proper forum. Reyno (P) opposed the motion on the basis that the Scottish laws were less advantageous to her than American laws. The district court granted the motion, while the court of appeals reversed. The U.S. Supreme Court granted certiorari.

ISSUE: May a plaintiff defeat a motion to dismiss for forum non conveniens merely on the basis that the laws of the alternative forum are less advantageous?

HOLDING AND DECISION: (Marshall, J.) No. A plaintiff may not defeat a motion to dismiss for forum non conveniens merely by showing that the substantive law of the alternative forum is less advantageous than that of the present forum. In this case, all the evidence, witnesses, and interests were in Scotland. Thus, the most convenient forum was there. As a result, the motion was properly granted. Reversed.

▶ ANALYSIS

The Court in this case specifically noted that under some circumstances, the fact that the chosen state's laws are less attractive to the defendant could be used to defeat a motion to dismiss for forum non conveniens. If the state chosen by the plaintiff has the only adequate remedy for the wrong alleged, then the motion may be denied.

Quicknotes

FORUM NON CONVENIENS An equitable doctrine permitting a court to refrain from hearing and determining a case when the matter may be more properly and fairly heard in another forum.

MOTION TO DISMISS Motion to terminate a trial based on the adequacy of the pleadings.

Subject Matter Jurisdiction of the Federal Courts

Quick Reference Rules of Law

Louisville & Nashville Railroad v. Mottley

Railroad company (D) v. Injured passengers (P)

211 U.S. 149 (1908).

NATURE OF CASE: Appeal of a decision overruling a demurrer in an action for specific performance of a contract.

FACT SUMMARY: Mottley (P) was injured on a train owned by Louisville & Nashville Railroad (D), which granted Mottley (P) a lifetime free pass, which he sought to enforce.

🏛 RULE OF LAW
Alleging an anticipated constitutional defense in the complaint does not give a federal court jurisdiction if there is no diversity of citizenship between the litigants.

FACTS: In 1871, Mottley (P) and his wife were injured while riding on the Louisville & Nashville Railroad (D). The Mottleys (P) released their claims for damages against the Louisville & Nashville Railroad (D) upon receiving a contract granting free transportation during the remainder of their lives. In 1907, the Louisville & Nashville Railroad (D) refused to renew the Mottleys' (P) passes, relying upon an act of Congress that forbade the giving of free passes or free transportation. The Mottleys (P) filed an action in a Circuit Court of the United States for the Western District of Kentucky. The Mottleys (P) and the Louisville & Nashville Railroad (D) were both citizens of Kentucky. Therefore, the Mottleys (P) attempted to establish federal jurisdiction by claiming that the Louisville & Nashville Railroad (D) would raise a constitutional defense in their answer, thus raising a federal question. The Louisville & Nashville Railroad (D) filed a demurrer to the complaint for failing to state a cause of action. The demurrer was denied. On appeal, the Supreme Court did not look at the issue raised by the litigants, but on their own motion raised the issue of whether the federal courts had jurisdiction to hear the case.

ISSUE: Does an allegation in the complaint that a constitutional defense will be raised in the answer raise a federal question that would give a federal court jurisdiction if no diversity of citizenship is alleged?

HOLDING AND DECISION: (Moody, J.) No. The Supreme Court reversed the lower court's ruling and remitted the case to that court with instructions to dismiss the suit for want of jurisdiction. Neither party to the litigation alleged that the federal court had jurisdiction in this case, and neither party challenged the jurisdiction of the federal court to hear the case. Because the jurisdiction of the circuit court is defined and limited by statute, the Supreme Court stated that it is their duty to see that such jurisdiction is not exceeded. Both parties to the litigation were citizens of Kentucky and so there was no diversity of citizenship. The only way that the federal court could have jurisdiction in this case would be if there was a federal question involved. Mottley (P) did allege in his complaint that the Louisville & Nashville Railroad (D) based their refusal to renew the free pass on a federal statute. Mottley (P) then attempted to allege information that would defeat the defense of the Louisville & Nashville Railroad (D). This is not sufficient. The plaintiff's complaint must be based upon the federal laws of the Constitution to confer jurisdiction on the federal courts. Mottley's (P) cause of action was not based on any federal laws or constitutional privileges; it was based on a contract. Even though it is evident that a federal question will be brought up at the trial, plaintiff's cause of action must be based on a federal statute or the constitution in order to have a federal question that would grant jurisdiction to the federal courts. Reversed and remanded.

▶ ANALYSIS

If Mottley (P) could have alleged that he was basing his action on a federal right, it would have been enough to have given the federal court jurisdiction. The federal court would have had to exercise jurisdiction at least long enough to determine whether there actually was such a right. If the federal court ultimately concludes that the claimed federal right does not exist, the complaint would be dismissed for failure to state a claim upon which relief can be granted rather than for lack of jurisdiction. The court has the power to determine the issue of subject matter jurisdiction on its own motion as it did in this case. Subject matter jurisdiction can be challenged at any stage of the proceeding.

◼◼◼

Quicknotes

DIVERSITY OF CITIZENSHIP The authority of a federal court to hear and determine cases involving $10,000 or more and in which the parties are citizens of different states, or in which one party is an alien.

FEDERAL QUESTION The authority of the federal courts to hear and determine in the first instance matters

Continued on next page.

pertaining to the federal Constitution, federal law, or treaties of the United States.

SUBJECT MATTER JURISDICTION The authority of the court to hear and decide actions involving a particular type of issue or subject.

■━━■

Redner v. Sanders

[Parties not identified.]

2000 WL 1161080 (S.D.N.Y. 2000).

NATURE OF CASE: Motion to dismiss for lack of diversity jurisdiction.

FACT SUMMARY: When plaintiff claimed he was a "resident" of France, defendants argued that only plaintiff's "citizenship" in France would satisfy federal diversity jurisdictional requirements.

🏛 RULE OF LAW
For purposes of diversity jurisdiction under 28 U.S.C. § 1332(a)(2), the controversy must be between citizens of a state and citizens or subjects of a foreign state, not merely "residents."

FACTS: Plaintiff filed a complaint in federal court, alleging that he was at all times mentioned "a citizen of the United States residing in France," and that defendants are residents of the State of New York. Defendants moved to dismiss for lack of subject matter jurisdiction, arguing that mere residency in a foreign country does not equate with citizenship of a foreign country as required by 28 U.S.C. § 1332(a)(2).

ISSUE: For purposes of diversity jurisdiction under 28 U.S.C. § 1332(a)(2), must the controversy be between citizens of a state and citizens or subjects of a foreign state, not merely "residents?"

HOLDING AND DECISION: (Griesa, J.) Yes. For purposes of diversity jurisdiction under 28 U.S.C. § 1332(a)(2), the controversy must be between citizens of a state and citizens or subjects of a foreign state, not merely "residents." Here, plaintiff's complaint speaks of his "residing" in France, whereas the statute speaks of citizenship. The two are not synonymous. It appears in fact that defendants are citizens of the State of New York. However, for jurisdiction to exist under (a)(2), plaintiff would need to be a citizen of a foreign state, not merely a resident, and the complaint itself actually alleges that plaintiff is a citizen of the United States. Thus, the case does not involve an action between citizens of the United States and a citizen of a foreign state. Accordingly, there is no jurisdiction under § 1332(a)(2). Motion granted and suit dismissed.

▶ ANALYSIS

In *Redner*, the court noted that plaintiff's affidavit was entirely lacking in details about what his living in France involved. Plaintiff provided no information about exactly where he lived, what kind of a residence he had, whether he had any family in France, or what professional activities he carried out in France.

■━■

Hertz Corp. v. Friend

Rental car company (D) v. Employees (P)

130 S. Ct. 1181 (2010).

NATURE OF CASE: Appeal from state supreme court.

FACT SUMMARY: [Hertz Corp. (D) tried to remove a class action against it to federal court on the basis of diversity jurisdiction. The employees (P) objected, arguing that because Hertz (D) derived more revenue from California than any other, and because the plurality of its business activities occurred there, California was its principal place of business.]

🏛 RULE OF LAW
The phrase "principal place of business" in the federal diversity jurisdiction statute refers to the place where the corporation's high level officers direct, control, and coordinate the corporation's activities.

FACTS: [California-based employees (P) of Hertz Corp. (D) claimed in a class action that Hertz (D) violated California's wage and hours laws. Hertz (D) tried to remove to federal court on the basis of diversity jurisdiction. The federal diversity jurisdiction statute provides that "a corporation shall be deemed to be a citizen of any state by which it has been incorporated and of the state where it has its principal place of business." The employees (P) objected, arguing that because Hertz (D) derived more revenue from California than any other, and because the plurality of its business activities occurred there, California was its principal place of business.]

ISSUE: Does the phrase "principal place of business" in the federal diversity jurisdiction statute refer to the place where the corporation's high level officers direct, control, and coordinate the corporation's activities?

HOLDING AND DECISION: (Breyer, J.) Yes. The phrase "principal place of business" in the federal diversity jurisdiction statute refers to the place where the corporation's high level officers direct, control, and coordinate the corporation's activities. Some courts refer to this test as the "nerve center" test. Normally, this would be where the corporation maintains its headquarters, provided headquarters is not simply an office where the corporation holds its board meetings. This interpretation is supported by the statute's language. The statute uses the word "place" in the singular form of the word, not the plural. It is also supported by its advancement of administrative simplicity, which demands that courts be provided straightforward rules under which they can readily assure themselves of their power to hear a case.

And it is supported by the statute's legislative history, which suggests that the words "principal place of business" should be interpreted to be no more complex than the initial test put forth by the Judicial Conference, the "half of gross income" test, a test the Conference rejected as too impractical to apply. A "nerve center" test offers greater simplicity. There may be no perfect test that satisfies all administrative and purposive criteria, but some complication must be accepted in view of the necessity of having a clearer rule.

▶ *ANALYSIS*

Remember that the nerve center is a single place within a state and not a measure of corporate activity statewide. In the Court's view, this aspect of the nerve center test makes it relatively easy to apply, will promote greater predictability, and is consistent with legislative history suggesting that determining corporate citizenship should not be a complex and impractical task. *Hertz* should promote predictability and uniformity in determining corporate citizenship, particularly in circuits that previously applied multifactor tests or compared corporate activity within multiple states to determine a company's principal place of business.

■=■

Quicknotes

DIVERSITY JURISDICTION The authority of a federal court to hear and determine cases involving a statutory sum and in which the parties are citizens of different states, or in which one party is an alien.

■=■

In re Ameriquest Mortgage Co. Mortgage Lending Practices Litigation

Real estate appraiser (D) v. Mortgager (P)

2007 U.S. Dist. LEXIS 70805 (N.D. Ill. 2007).

NATURE OF CASE: Motion to dismiss state law claims that were based on the court's supplemental jurisdiction.

FACT SUMMARY: Barbara Skanes (P) claimed that house appraiser Douglas Trevino (D) inflated the value of Skanes's (P) property to increase the loan amount for which she could qualify, and increase Ameriquest's (D) potential profit.

🏛 RULE OF LAW
Supplemental jurisdiction is proper where there is a sufficient nexus between state and federal claims, and statutory discretionary factors do not weigh in favor of a decision to decline to exercise supplemental jurisdiction.

FACTS: Barbara Skanes (P) claimed that house appraiser Douglas Trevino (D) inflated the value of Skanes's (P) property to increase the loan amount for which she could qualify, and increase Ameriquest's (D) potential profit. She filed a federal claim under the Truth in Lending Act, seeking rescission of the mortgage and statutory damages. She also claimed that at the time of her closing Ameriquest (D) gave her improper and misleading disclosures of her right to cancel her mortgage. In the second and third counts of her claim, she alleged state law fraud claims against Ameriquest (D) and Trevino (D). Trevino (D) moved to dismiss the state law claims.

ISSUE: Is supplemental jurisdiction proper where there is a sufficient nexus between state and federal claims, and statutory discretionary factors do not weigh in favor of a decision to decline to exercise supplemental jurisdiction?

HOLDING AND DECISION: (Aspen, J.) Yes. Supplemental jurisdiction is proper where there is a sufficient nexus between state and federal claims, and statutory discretionary factors do not weigh in favor of a decision to decline to exercise supplemental jurisdiction. Where a court already has jurisdiction over some federal claim, it also has supplemental jurisdiction over state claims that are factually connected to the federal claim. The factual connection is sufficient as long as the facts are common and operative. To determine whether the federal and state law claims are connected by common and operative facts, the facts necessary to prove the federal claim are compared with those necessary to the success of the state claim. In this case, Skanes (P) explicitly connected her federal and state claims. She did not fully know of her right to cancel her mortgage, she paid too much during the life of the loan because the mortgage was overstated, and she has not been able to refinance the mortgage due to the over-statement. The connection is operative, in that if the court were to dismiss the state law claims, it may not be able to grant the rescission of the mortgage under the federal Truth in Lending Act (TILA). Because the court cannot conclude that the resolution of one of her state claims will have no effect on the resolution on her federal claims, supplemental jurisdiction is proper. In addition, there is no reason to choose not to exercise that jurisdiction under discretionary powers.

▶ ANALYSIS

In this case, the court says that the factual bases for the federal and state claims are essentially the same, and the resolution of one claim impacts the other. But the connection between the facts need not be as tight as they are in this case to support a finding that supplemental jurisdiction is proper.

▬▬▬

Quicknotes

SUPPLEMENTAL JURISDICTION A doctrine granting authority to a federal court to hear a claim that does not invoke diversity jurisdiction if it arises from the same transaction or occurrence as the primary action.

▬▬▬

Szendrey-Ramos v. First Bancorp

Employee (P) v. Employer (D)

2007 U.S. Dist. LEXIS 74896 (D.P.R. 2007).

NATURE OF CASE: Motion to dismiss employment discrimination claim.

FACT SUMMARY: A bank's general counsel was fired after finding that some bank officials violated the bank's code of ethics. She sued under Title VII of the 1964 Civil Rights Act for discrimination and retaliation, and under Puerto Rican law for wrongful discharge, defamation, tortious interference with contract, and violations of the Puerto Rican constitution.

🏛 RULE OF LAW
A court may decline to exercise supplemental jurisdiction where (1) the state law claims raise complex or novel issues, or (2) the state law claims substantially predominate over the federal claim.

FACTS: Carmen Szendrey-Ramos (P) was general counsel for First Bancorp (D) in Puerto Rico. When an outside law firm sent Szendrey (P) a report alleging possible ethical and legal violations by bank officials, Szendrey (D) conducted an investigation. Szendrey (D) found that there were some violations of the bank's (D) code of ethics. The bank (D) fired Szendrey (P), blaming her for some of the events she had investigated. She sued under the federal Title VII of the 1964 Civil Rights Act for discrimination and retaliation, and under Puerto Rican law for wrongful discharge, defamation, tortious interference with contract, and violations of the Puerto Rican constitution.

ISSUE: May a court decline to exercise supplemental jurisdiction where (1) the state law claims raise complex or novel issues, or (2) the state law claims substantially predominate over the federal claim?

HOLDING AND DECISION: (Casellas, J.) Yes. A court may decline to exercise supplemental jurisdiction where (1) the state law claims raise complex or novel issues, or (2) the state law claims substantially predominate over the federal claim. Here, the state law claims exceed the federal claims in number and scope. Some of the state claims mimic the federal claims, but most—including wrongful discharge, tortious interference with contracts, and defamation—are distinct and have their own elements of proof, which is not necessary to establish the Title VII claims. The predominance of the state claims over the federal claims is enough to decline to exercise supplemental jurisdiction. But Puerto Rican law claims require a more probing analysis of Szendrey's (P) performance as general counsel, and any shortcomings she may have had, and this leads to another reason for declining to exercise supplemental jurisdiction, which is the presence of complex or novel issues of state law. The interpretation of the relevant Puerto Rico laws is usually the province of the Puerto Rico Supreme Court. The laws at issue in this case are silent on the issue of a lawyer's claim against her former client, and the possibility of divulging confidential information in order to pursue such a claim, and Puerto Rican courts have not yet addressed the issue. Therefore, the Puerto Rico law claims will be dismissed without prejudice, so they may be refiled in Puerto Rican courts.

▌ANALYSIS

Note that the court could have declined to exercise supplemental jurisdiction on the basis of the predominance of the Puerto Rican claims alone. But the court considered it significant that neither Puerto Rican statutes nor Puerto Rican courts had addressed the issues underlying the non-federal claims. Given that the Puerto Rican claims presented issues of first impression, the federal court declined to exercise jurisdiction on that point as well.

■■■

Quicknotes

SUPPLEMENTAL JURISDICTION A doctrine granting authority to a federal court to hear a claim that does not invoke diversity jurisdiction if it arises from the same transaction or occurrence as the primary action.

■■■

Caterpillar, Inc. v. Lewis

Manufacturer (D) v. Injured person (P)

519 U.S. 61 (1996).

NATURE OF CASE: Appeal of judgment vacating verdict for the defense in personal-injury case.

FACT SUMMARY: A federal district court denied a motion to remand a case to state court even though the case lacked complete diversity and later entered judgment after the nondiverse defendant had settled out of the case.

🏛 RULE OF LAW
A district court's error in failing to remand a case improperly removed does not prevent adjudication if the jurisdictional requirements are satisfied at the time of judgment.

FACTS: Lewis (P) filed a personal-injury claim in state court. The case was removed to federal district court at Caterpillar Inc.'s (D) request although there was not complete diversity of citizenship among the parties. After the removal, Lewis (P) moved to remand the case to state court for lack of federal jurisdiction. The district court denied the motion. Subsequently, the nondiverse defendant settled out of the case. At trial, Caterpillar (D) prevailed. Lewis (P) appealed, claiming that the district court did not have jurisdiction at the time of removal. The court of appeals agreed and vacated the judgment. Caterpillar (D) appealed.

ISSUE: Does a district court's error in failing to remand a case improperly removed prevent adjudication if the jurisdictional requirements are satisfied at the time of judgment?

HOLDING AND DECISION: (Ginsburg, J.) No. A district court's error in failing to remand a case improperly removed does not prevent adjudication if the jurisdictional requirements are satisfied at the time of judgment. The lack of subject matter jurisdiction at the time of removal is not fatal to later adjudication of the case. The only issue is whether the jurisdictional requirements are met at the time the judgment is entered. In the present case, allowing removal when there was not complete diversity was a mistake by the district court. However, when judgment was entered, complete diversity did exist. Thus, there was sufficient subject matter jurisdiction to adjudicate the case. Reversed and remanded.

▶ ANALYSIS

In the present case, the nondiverse defendant settled out of the litigation prior to judgment. It would present a more difficult question if the nondiverse defendant had not been dismissed from the case by the district court. In such circumstances, the federal court would be acting without any subject matter jurisdiction.

■■■

Quicknotes

DIVERSITY OF CITIZENSHIP The authority of a federal court to hear and determine cases involving $10,000 or more and in which the parties are citizens of different states, or in which one party is an alien.

SUBJECT MATTER JURISDICTION A court's ability to adjudicate a specific category of cases based on the subject matter of the dispute.

■■■

CHAPTER 4

State Law in Federal Courts: Erie and its Entailments

Quick Reference Rules of Law

Erie Railroad v. Tompkins

Railroad company (D) v. Pedestrian (P)

304 U.S. 64 (1938).

NATURE OF CASE: Action to recover damages for personal injury allegedly caused by negligent conduct.

FACT SUMMARY: In a personal-injury suit, a federal district court trial judge refused to apply applicable state law because such law was "general" (judge-made) and not embodied in any statute.

🏛 RULE OF LAW
Although the 1789 Rules of Decision Act left federal courts unfettered to apply their own rules of procedure in common-law actions brought in federal court, state law governs substantive issues. State law includes not only statutory law, but case law as well.

FACTS: Tompkins (P) was walking in a right of way parallel to some railroad tracks when an Erie Railroad (Erie) (D) train came by. Tompkins (P) was struck and injured by what he would, at trial, claim to be an open door extending from one of the rail cars. Under Pennsylvania case law (the applicable law since the accident occurred there), state courts would have treated Tompkins (P) as a trespasser in denying him recovery for other than wanton or willful misconduct on Erie's (D) part. Under "general" law, recognized in federal courts, Tompkins (P) would have been regarded as a licensee and would only have been obligated to show ordinary negligence. Because Erie (D) was a New York corporation, Tompkins (P) brought suit in a federal district court in New York, where he won a judgment for $30,000. Upon appeal to a federal circuit court, the decision was affirmed.

ISSUE: Was the trial court in error in refusing to recognize state case law as the proper rule of decision in deciding the substantive issue of liability?

HOLDING AND DECISION: (Brandeis, J.) Yes. The Court's opinion is in four parts: (1) *Swift v. Tyson*, 41 U.S. (16 Pet.) 1 (1842), which held that federal courts exercising jurisdiction on the ground of diversity of citizenship need not, in matters of general jurisprudence, apply the unwritten law of the state as declared by its highest court, is overruled. Section 34 of the Federal Judiciary Act of 1789, c. 20, 28 U.S. § 725 requires that federal courts in all matters, except those where some federal law is controlling, apply as their rules of decision the law of the state, unwritten as well as written. Up to this time, federal courts had assumed the power to make "general law" decisions even though Congress was powerless to enact "general law" statutes. (2) *Swift* had numerous political and social defects. The hoped-for

uniformity among state courts had not occurred; there was no satisfactory way to distinguish between local and general law. On the other hand, *Swift* introduced grave discrimination by noncitizens against citizens. The privilege of selecting the court for resolving disputes rested with the noncitizen who could pick the more favorable forum. The resulting far-reaching discrimination was due to the broad province accorded "general law" in which many matters of seemingly local concern were included. Furthermore, local citizens could move out of the state and bring suit in a federal court if they were disposed to do so; corporations, similarly, could simply reincorporate in another state. More than statutory relief is involved here; the unconstitutionality of *Swift* is clear. (3) Except in matters governed by the federal Constitution or by acts of Congress, the law to be applied in any case is the law of the state. There is no federal common law. The federal courts have no power derived from the Constitution or by Congress to declare substantive rules of common law applicable in a state whether they are "local" or "general" in nature. (4) The federal district court was bound to follow the Pennsylvania case law, which would have denied recovery to Tompkins (P). Reversed.

CONCURRENCE: (Reed, J.) It is unnecessary to go beyond interpreting the meaning of "laws" in the Rules of Decision Act. Article III and the Necessary and Proper Clause of Article I of the Constitution, might provide Congress with the power to declare rules of substantive law for federal courts to follow.

▶ ANALYSIS

Erie can fairly be characterized as the most significant and sweeping decision on civil procedure ever handed down by the Supreme Court. As interpreted in subsequent decisions, *Erie* held that while federal courts may apply their own rules of procedure, issues of substantive law must be decided in accord with the applicable state law: usually the state in which the federal court sits. Note, however, how later Supreme Court decisions have made inroads into the broad doctrine enunciated here.

■■■

Quicknotes

DIVERSITY OF CITIZENSHIP The authority of a federal court to hear and determine cases involving $10,000 or more

Continued on next page.

and in which the parties are citizens of different states, or in which one party is an alien.

FEDERAL JURISDICTION The authority of federal courts to hear and determine cases of a particular nature derived from the United States Constitution and rules promulgated by Congress pursuant thereto.

SUBJECT MATTER JURISDICTION The authority of the court to hear and decide actions involving a particular type of issue or subject.

■══■

Guaranty Trust Co. v. York

Trustee (D) v. Note holder (P)

326 U.S. 99 (1945).

NATURE OF CASE: Class action alleging fraud and misrepresentation.

FACT SUMMARY: York (P), barred from filing suit in state court because of the state statute of limitations, brought an equity action in federal court based upon diversity of citizenship jurisdiction.

🏛 RULE OF LAW
Where a state statute that would completely bar recovery in state court has significant effect on the outcome-determination of the action, even though the suit is brought in equity, the federal court is bound by the state law.

FACTS: York (P) sued Guaranty Trust Co. (D) in a federal diversity action. New York substantive law governed. Guaranty Trust (D) asserted the defense of the statute of limitations. York (P) argued that the statute of limitations did not bar the suit because it was on the "equity side" of federal court. The federal court of appeals ruled the suit was not barred, and Guaranty Trust (D) appealed.

ISSUE: Does a state statute of limitations, which would bar a suit in state court, also act as a bar to the same action if the suit is brought in equity in federal court and jurisdiction being based on diversity of citizenship?

HOLDING AND DECISION: (Frankfurter, J.) Yes. A state statute of limitations, which would bar a suit in state court, may also act as a bar to the same action if the suit is brought in equity in federal court and jurisdiction is based on diversity of citizenship. *Erie Railroad Co. v. Tompkins*, 304 U.S. 64 (1938), overruled a particular way of looking at law after its inadequacies had been laid bare. The question is not whether a statute of limitations is deemed a matter of "procedure" in some sense. The question is whether such a statute concerns merely the manner and the means by which a right to recover, as recognized by the state, is enforced, or whether such statutory limitation is a matter of substance in the aspect that alone is relevant to the problem, namely, whether it significantly affects the result of a litigation for a federal court to disregard a law of a state that would be controlling in an action upon the same claim by the same parties in a state court. In essence, the intent of *Erie* was to insure that, in all cases where a federal court is exercising jurisdiction solely because of the diversity of citizenship of the parties, the outcome of the litigation in the federal court should be substantially the same, so far as legal rules determine the outcome of a litigation, as it would be if tried in a state court. Reversed and remanded.

▶ ANALYSIS

While clarifying *Erie*, the legal foundation supporting *Guaranty Trust* may be undergoing a process of slow erosion by contemporary courts. *Hanna v. Plumer*, 380 U.S. 460 (1965), held that where state law conflicts with the Federal Rules of Civil Procedure, the latter prevails regardless of the effect on the outcome of the litigation. And in *Byrd v. Blue Ridge Elec. Cooperative*, 356 U.S. 525 (1958), the Court suggested that some constitutional doctrines (there, the right to a jury trial in federal court) are so important as to be controlling over state law, regardless of whether application of such constitutional doctrines would result in an outcome different than that which would result under the law of the state in which the federal court sits.

■=■

Quicknotes

COMITY A rule pursuant to which courts in one state give deference to the statutes and judicial decisions of another.

DIVERSITY OF CITIZENSHIP Parties are citizens of different states, or one party is an alien; a factor, along with a statutorily set dollar value of the matter in controversy, that allows a federal district court to exercise its authority to hear a lawsuit based on diversity jurisdiction.

ERIE DOCTRINE Federal courts must apply state substantive law and federal procedural law.

■=■

Byrd v. Blue Ridge Rural Electric Cooperative

Injured employee (P) v. Electric utility (D)

356 U.S. 525 (1958).

NATURE OF CASE: Negligence action for damages.

FACT SUMMARY: Byrd (P) was injured while connecting power lines for a subcontractor of Blue Ridge Electric Cooperative, Inc. (D).

> ## 🏛 RULE OF LAW
> The *Erie* doctrine requires that federal courts in diversity cases must respect the definitions of rights and obligations created by state courts, but state laws cannot alter the essential characteristics and functions of the federal courts, and the jury function is such an essential function (provided for in the Seventh Amendment).

FACTS: Byrd (P) was injured while on a construction job for Blue Ridge Electric Cooperative, Inc. (Blue Ridge) (D) and sued Blue Ridge (D) in tort. Although Byrd (P) was employed by an independent contractor, Blue Ridge (D) argued that Byrd (P) was performing the same work as Blue Ridge's (D) regular employees and was therefore a "statutory" employee whose exclusive remedy was under the South Carolina workers' compensation legislation. Blue Ridge (D) contended that despite the *Erie* doctrine, South Carolina law could not be allowed to preclude his right to a jury.

ISSUE: Do *Erie* doctrine considerations require that all state determinations of rights be upheld regardless of their intrusions into federal determinations?

HOLDING AND DECISION: (Brennan, J.) No. The *Erie* doctrine requires that federal courts in diversity cases must respect the definitions of rights and obligations created by state courts, but state laws cannot alter the essential characteristics and functions of the federal courts, and the jury function is such an essential function (provided for in the Seventh Amendment). The South Carolina determination here that immunity is a question of law to be tried by a judge is merely a determination of the form and mode of enforcing immunity. It does not involve any essential relationship or determination of right created by the state. Of course, the *Erie* doctrine will reach even such form and mode determinations where no affirmative countervailing considerations can be found. Here, however, the Seventh Amendment makes the jury function an essential factor in the federal process protected by the Constitution. Reversed and remanded.

▶ ANALYSIS

This case points up a major retreat by the Court in its interpretation of the *Erie* doctrine. The *Guaranty Trust* case, 326 U.S. 99 (1945), had stated that the *Erie* doctrine required that federal courts not tamper with state remedies for violations of state-created rights. In *Byrd*, the Court retreats, stating that questions of mere "form and mode" of remedy (i.e., trial by jury or judge) is not necessarily the province of the states where essential federal rights (i.e., Seventh Amendment) are involved. Note that the Court does not abandon the *Guaranty Trust* rationale, however (that the outcome of a case should not be affected by the choice of court in which it is filed). The Court expresses doubt that the permitting of trial by jury here will make any difference in the final determination of the case. Note the inconsistency of argument here since the Court first states that trial by jury is an essential right, and then states that it is really insignificant after all.

■═■

Quicknotes

ERIE DOCTRINE Federal courts must apply state substantive law and federal procedural law.

■═■

Hanna v. Plumer

Injured claimant (P) v. Executor of defendant (D)

380 U.S. 460 (1965).

NATURE OF CASE: Appeal of dismissal in federal diversity tort action.

FACT SUMMARY: Hanna (P) filed tort action in federal court in Massachusetts, where Plumer (D) resided, for an auto accident that occurred in South Carolina.

🏛 RULE OF LAW
The *Erie* doctrine mandates that federal courts are to apply state substantive law and federal procedural law, but, where matters fall roughly between the two and are rationally capable of classification as either, the Constitution grants the federal court system the power to regulate their practice and pleading (procedure).

FACTS: In this diversity suit for personal injuries, Plumer (D) represented the estate of one of the drivers involved. Massachusetts law provided that suits required personal service of process on the estate's executor. Process was instead served under Fed. R. Civ. P. 4[(e)(2)(B)], which allowed for the summons and complaint to be left with a competent adult at the defendant's residence. The federal circuit court agreed with the federal district court that the claim should be dismissed because of Hanna's (P) failure to comply with the state's method of serving process within the applicable limitations period. Hanna (P) appealed.

ISSUE: Does the *Erie* doctrine classification of "substantive law questions" extend to embrace questions involving both substantive and procedural considerations merely because such a question might have an effect on the determination of the substantive outcome of the case?

HOLDING AND DECISION: (Warren, C.J.) No. The *Erie* doctrine mandates that federal courts are to apply state substantive law and federal procedural law, and, where matters fall roughly between the two and are rationally capable of classification as either, the Constitution grants the federal court system the power to regulate their practice and pleading (procedure). It is well settled that the Enabling Act for the Federal Rules of Civil Procedure requires that a procedural effect of any rule on the outcome of a case be shown to actually "abridge, enlarge, or modify" the substantive law in a case for the *Erie* doctrine to come into play. Where, as here, the question only goes to procedural requirements (i.e., service of summons, a dismissal for improper service here would not alter the substantive right of Hanna

[P] to serve Plumer [D] personally and refile or effect the substantive law of negligence in the case), Article III and the Necessary and Proper Clause provide that the Congress has a right to provide rules for the federal court system such as Fed. R. Civ. P. 4[(e)(2)(B)]. "Outcome determination analysis was never intended to serve as a talisman" for the *Erie* doctrine. The judgment of the appellate court must be reversed.

CONCURRENCE: (Harlan, J.) I agree with the result of the Court and its rejection of the outcome-determination test. However, the Court was wrong in stating that anything arguably procedural is constitutionally placed within the province of the federal government to regulate. The test for "substantive" would be whether "the choice of rule would substantially affect those primary decisions respecting human conduct which our constitutional system leaves to state regulation."

▶ ANALYSIS

This case points a return to the basic rationales of *Erie R. Co. v. Tompkins*, 304 U.S. 64 (1938). First, the Court asserts that one important consideration in determining how a particular question should be classified (substantive or procedural) is the avoidance of "forum shopping" (the practice of choosing one forum such as federal, to file in, in order to gain the advantages of one), which permits jurisdictions to infringe on the substantive law-defining powers of each other. Second, the Court seeks to avoid inequitable administration of the laws that would result from allowing jurisdictional considerations to determine substantive rights. Justice Warren here, in rejecting the "outcome determination" test, asserts that any rule must be measured ultimately against the Federal Rules Enabling Act and the Constitution.

■■■

Quicknotes

PROCEDURAL LAW Law relating to the process of carrying out a lawsuit and not to the substantive rights asserted by the parties.

SUBSTANTIVE LAW Law that pertains to the rights and interests of the parties and upon which a cause of action may be based.

■■■

Semtek Intl. Inc. v. Lockheed Martin Corp.

Injured party (P) v. Alleged wrongdoer (D)

531 U.S. 497 (2001).

NATURE OF CASE: Appeal from affirmance of dismissal of state action on res judicata grounds, giving effect to dismissal by federal court sitting in diversity jurisdiction.

FACT SUMMARY: When Semtek International, Inc.'s (Semtek's) (P) breach of contract and tort claims against Lockheed Martin Corp. (D) were barred by California's two-year statute of limitations, Semtek (P) filed the same claims in state court in Maryland, which had a three-year statute of limitations.

🏛 RULE OF LAW
As a matter of federal common law, a state rule of claim preclusion applies to dismissals ordered by either state or federal courts, except where state law is incompatible with federal interests.

FACTS: Semtek International, Inc. (Semtek) (P) sued Lockheed Martin Corp. (Lockheed) (D) for breach of contract and tort claims. After removal to federal court in California, the action was dismissed because it was barred by California's two-year statute of limitations. Semtek (P) filed the same claims in state court in Maryland, which had a three-year statute of limitations. The Maryland court dismissed the case on the ground of res judicata. In affirming, the Maryland Court of Special Appeals held that, regardless of whether California state law would have accorded claim preclusive effect to a statute-of-limitations dismissal by one of its own courts, the California federal court's dismissal barred the Maryland complaint because the res judicata effect of federal diversity judgments is prescribed by federal law, under which the earlier dismissal was on the merits and claim preclusive.

ISSUE: As a matter of federal common law, does a state rule of claim preclusion apply to dismissals ordered by either state or federal courts, except where state law is incompatible with federal interests?

HOLDING AND DECISION: (Scalia, J.) Yes. As a matter of federal common law, a state rule of claim preclusion applies to dismissals ordered by either state or federal courts, except where state law is incompatible with federal interests. Semtek (P) asserts that *Dupasseur v. Rochereau*, 21 Wall. 130 (1875), which held that the res judicata effect of a federal diversity judgment "is such as would belong to judgments of the State courts rendered under similar circumstances," governs here. That case is not dispositive, however, because it was decided under the Conformity Act of 1872, which required federal courts to apply the procedural law of the forum state in nonequity cases. However, claim-preclusive effect is not, as Lockheed (D) asserts, required by Fed. R. Civ. P. § 41(b), which provides that, unless the court "otherwise specifies," an involuntary dismissal, other than a dismissal for lack of jurisdiction, improper venue, or failure to join a party under Rule 19, "operates as an adjudication upon the merits." Although the original connotation of a judgment "on the merits" was one that passes directly on the substance of a claim (which would be claim-preclusive), the meaning of the term has changed, and does not necessarily designate a judgment effecting claim preclusion. There are a number of reasons that support this conclusion. First, it would be peculiar to announce a federally prescribed rule on claim preclusion in a default rule for determining a dismissal's import, or to find a rule governing the effect to be accorded federal judgments by other courts ensconced in rules governing the internal procedures of the rendering court itself. Moreover, if the rule were interpreted as Lockheed (D) suggests, it would in many cases violate the federalism principle of *Erie R. Co. v. Tompkins*, 304 U.S. 64 (1938), by engendering substantial variations in outcomes between state and federal litigation which would likely influence forum choice. Finally, the Court itself has never relied upon Rule 41(b) when recognizing the claim-preclusive effect of federal judgments in federal-question cases. Rule 41(a) makes clear that "an adjudication upon the merits" in Rule 41(b) is the opposite of a dismissal without prejudice, which means that it prevents refiling of the claim in the same court. That is undoubtedly a necessary condition, but not a sufficient one, for claim-preclusive effect in other courts. Given that neither Semtek's (P) approach, nor Lockheed's (D) approach is satisfactory, what does govern the claim-preclusive effect of the California federal diversity judgment in Maryland state court? The answer is that federal common law governs the claim-preclusive effect of a dismissal by a federal court sitting in diversity, and that it is up to this Court to determine the appropriate federal rule. Since in diversity cases state, rather than federal, substantive law is at issue, there is no need for a uniform federal rule; and nationwide uniformity is better served by having the same claim-preclusive rule (the state rule) apply whether the dismissal has been ordered by a state or a federal court. Any other rule would produce the sort of forum shopping and inequitable administration of the

Continued on next page.

laws that *Erie* seeks to avoid. While the federal reference to state law will not be workable in situations in which the state law is incompatible with federal interests, no such conflict exists here. Reversed and remanded.

▶ *ANALYSIS*

An example of where federal reference to state law will not work is where state law has not given claim-preclusive effect to dismissals for willful violation of discovery orders. In such a case, the federal courts' interest in the integrity of their own processes might justify a federal rule of claim preclusion that does not reflect state law. Of course, that kind of exceptional case was not before the court.

■■■■

Quicknotes

CLAIM PRECLUSION A procedural rule or order prohibiting the support or opposition to certain claims or defenses.

***ERIE* DOCTRINE** Federal courts must apply state substantive law and federal procedural law.

RES JUDICATA The rule of law that a final judgment by a court precludes subsequent litigation between the parties regarding the same cause of action.

■■■■

CHAPTER 5

Incentives to Litigate

Quick Reference Rules of Law

State Farm Mutual Automobile Insurance Co. v. Campbell

Insurance company (D) v. Insured motorist (P)

538 U.S. 408 (2003).

NATURE OF CASE: Appeal from a punitive damages award.

FACT SUMMARY: When Campbell (P) received a jury award of $1 million in compensatory damages and $145 million in punitive damages, State Farm Mutual Automobile Insurance Co. (D) appealed, arguing that such a disproportionate award of punitive damages violated due process.

RULE OF LAW

Punitive damages may be awarded only when they are reasonable and proportionate to the wrong committed.

FACTS: Campbell (P), driving on the wrong side of a two-lane highway, caused an oncoming vehicle to swerve and crash, killing its driver and permanently disabling another driver. In the ensuing wrongful death suit and tort action against him, Campbell (P) insisted he was not at fault. Campbell's insurer, State Farm Mutual Automobile Insurance Co. (State Farm) (D), against the advice of its own investigators, contested Campbell's (P) liability and refused to settle with the families of the deceased and injured. Instead, State Farm (D) took the case to trial where a jury determined that Campbell (P) was 100 percent at fault and returned a judgment of $185,849 against Campbell (P), far more than the amount offered in settlement. After State Farm (D) refused to cover Campbell's (P) excess liability, the injured parties and Campbell (P) reached an agreement by which the estate would not seek satisfaction of their claim against Campbell (P) in exchange for which Campbell (P) would pursue a bad faith action against State Farm (D) and would give most of the recovery, if any, to the injured parties. Campbell filed the suit and went to trial, resulting in a jury award of $2.6 million (later reduced to $1 million) in compensatory damages and $145 million in punitive damages. State Farm (D) appealed.

ISSUE: May punitive damages be awarded only when they are reasonable and proportionate to the wrong committed?

HOLDING AND DECISION: (Kennedy, J.) Yes. Punitive damages may be awarded only when they are reasonable and proportionate to the wrong committed. This case is neither close nor difficult. It was error to reinstate the jury's $145 million punitive damages award. While State Farm's (D) handling of Campbell's (P) claim merits no praise, a more moderate punishment for its reprehensible conduct could have satisfied the state's legitimate objectives, and the state courts should have gone no further. This case, instead, was wrongfully used as a platform to expose, and punish, the perceived deficiencies of State Farm's (D) operations throughout the country. Furthermore, the Utah courts erred in relying upon evidence of State Farm's (D) practices in other states and conduct that bore no relation to Campbell's (P) harm. Due process does not permit courts, in the calculation of punitive damages, to adjudicate the merits of other parties' hypothetical claims against a defendant under the guise of the reprehensibility analysis. Single-digit multipliers are more likely to comport with due process, while still achieving the state's goals of deterrence and retribution, than awards with ratios of 500 to 1 or, as here, 145 to 1. Finally, the wealth of a defendant cannot justify an otherwise unconstitutional punitive damages award. Reversed and remanded.

DISSENT: (Ginsburg, J.) Rules that are essentially legislative must not be laid down by the Court using the Constitution. The Supreme Court has no warrant to reform state law governing awards of punitive damages.

▌ ANALYSIS

In *State Farm*, the Court noted that although punitive damages awards serve the same purposes as criminal penalties, defendants subjected to punitive damages in civil cases have not been accorded the protections applicable in a criminal proceeding. This fact, said the Court, increases the Court's concern over the imprecise manner in which punitive damages systems are administered.

■=■

Quicknotes

PUNITIVE DAMAGES Damages exceeding the actual injury suffered for the purposes of punishment, deterrence and comfort to plaintiff.

■=■

Sigma Chemical Co. v. Harris

Chemical company employer (P) v. Purchasing agent (D)

605 F. Supp. 1253 (E.D. Mo. 1985).

NATURE OF CASE: Action for permanent injunction and determination of the validity of a restrictive covenant.

FACT SUMMARY: In its action against Harris (D) for breach of a restrictive covenant, Sigma Chemical Co. (P) contended that a permanent injunction should be entered against Harris (D) for violating the terms of the employment contract because he was aware of the restrictions imposed upon him by the contract and he took a voluntary risk by deciding to violate the contract.

> ### RULE OF LAW
> The main prerequisite to obtaining injunctive relief is a finding that plaintiff is being threatened by some injury for which he has no adequate legal remedy.

FACTS: Sigma Chemical Co. (Sigma) (P) employed Harris (D) as a purchasing agent whose job consisted of matching the right chemical supplier with a chemical product sold by Sigma (P). When he went to work for Sigma (P), Harris (D) signed an agreement stating that he would not work for a competitor for two years after leaving Sigma (P), and even after that period would not disclose any confidential information acquired from Sigma (P). Harris (D) became dissatisfied with Sigma (P), began looking for another job and, after finding one with a competitor of Sigma's (P), quit his Sigma (P) job. At the new job, Harris (D) used information acquired during his employment at Sigma (P) that helped his new employer find new sources of various chemicals. Sigma (P) then sued Harris (D) for breach of his employment contract, contending that a permanent injunction should be entered against Harris (D) for violating the terms of the contract because Harris (D) was aware of the restrictions imposed upon him by that contract and he took a voluntary risk by deciding to violate the contract.

ISSUE: Is the main prerequisite to obtaining injunctive relief a finding that plaintiff is being threatened by some injury for which he has no adequate legal remedy?

HOLDING AND DECISION: (Nangle, C.J.) Yes. The main prerequisite to obtaining injunctive relief is a finding that plaintiff is being threatened by some injury for which he has no adequate legal remedy. Also, a determination whether to issue an injunction involves a balancing of the interests of the parties who might be affected by the court's decision—the hardship on plaintiff if relief is denied as opposed to the hardship to defendant if it is granted. Here, it is clear that Harris (D) is violating the restrictive covenant by working for Sigma's (P) competitor. Under these circumstances, there is a strong threat of irreparable injury to Sigma (P). The harm that would occur to Harris (D) if the injunction should be granted is not insubstantial, but the threat of harm to Sigma (P) greatly outweighs the threat of harm to Harris (D). Permanent injunctive relief granted to Sigma (P).

▶ ANALYSIS

Courts consider two factors in discussing the propriety of issuing an injunction: the inadequacy of legal remedy and the balance of hardships to the two parties. Injunctions are by far the most prevalent form of equitable relief, and with an injunction, courts will order parties to do things or to refrain from doing them.

Quicknotes

EQUITABLE RELIEF A remedy that is based upon principles of fairness as opposed to rules of law.

INJUNCTION A remedy imposed by the court ordering a party to cease the conduct of a specific activity.

RESTRICTIVE COVENANT A promise contained in a deed to limit the uses to which the property will be made.

Evans v. Jeff D.

Mentally disabled children (P) v. State (D)

475 U.S. 717 (1986).

NATURE OF CASE: Review of settlement approved by court in class action for injunctive relief.

FACT SUMMARY: The legal aid attorney representing a class of handicapped children (P) accepted settlement offer that denied attorney fees.

🏛 RULE OF LAW
A court may in its discretion accept a settlement that denies statutorily authorized fees.

FACTS: Johnson, an Idaho Legal Aid Society attorney, represented a class of emotionally and mentally disturbed children (P) seeking injunctive relief from the State of Idaho (D) to improve their treatment. Johnson accepted a settlement offer that granted the plaintiff class generous injunctive relief, but denied Johnson his statutorily authorized fees. Legal Aid contended that the court abused its discretion in accepting a settlement conditioned on the denial of attorney fees and sought appellate review. Legal Aid argued that Johnson was forced to accept the settlement to obtain the most favorable relief for his clients because of his ethical obligation to his clients, and, therefore, the court had a duty to reject the settlement. The appellate court found an abuse of discretion. The State (D) appealed.

ISSUE: May a court in its discretion accept a settlement that denies statutorily authorized fees?

HOLDING AND DECISION: (Stevens, J.) Yes. A court may in its discretion accept a settlement that denies statutorily authorized fees. The Fees Act and its legislative history do not indicate that Congress intended to ban fee waivers conditioned on favorable settlement terms. Courts may appraise the reasonableness of settlement offers that deny fees on a case-by-case basis until Congress commands that fees be paid. Reversed.

▶ ANALYSIS

Ethical issues abound in the area of attorney fees. It is good practice to discuss the issue of fees with clients early on in representation. Many states have statutes that require the attorney fee agreement to be in writing if the fees are likely to exceed a set amount. If Johnson had a written fee-agreement with his clients, this might have provided him with some leverage. If Johnson had disclosed the fact that he had a written fee-agreement and the State (D) had continued to push for a settlement without fees, this might be construed as tortious interference with contract.

Quicknotes

INJUNCTIVE RELIEF A court order issued as a remedy, requiring a person to do, or prohibiting that person from doing, a specific act.

SETTLEMENT OFFER An offer made by one party to a lawsuit to the other agreeing upon the determination of rights and issues between them, thus disposing of the need for judicial determination.

Buckhannon Board and Care Home, Inc. v. West Virginia Department of Health and Human Resources

Declaratory-relief complainant (P) v. State (D)

532 U.S. 598 (2001).

NATURE OF CASE: Appeal of denial of attorney's fees award.

FACT SUMMARY: Buckhannon Board and Care Home, Inc. (Buckhannon) (P) brought suit to declare provisions of a state statute invalid as violating a federal statute. When the state statute was amended to delete the attacked provisions, Buckhannon (P) sought attorney's fees under the federal statute even though its federal court suit was dismissed as moot.

RULE OF LAW
An award of attorney's fees and costs to a "prevailing party" under federal statutes may be awarded only to a party who has secured a judgment on the merits or a court-ordered consent decree.

FACTS: Buckhannon Board and Care Home, Inc. (Buckhannon) (P), which operated care homes and assisted living facilities, ran afoul of a state regulation that required residents to be sufficiently ambulatory to get out of a burning building. After receiving a cease and desist order from the West Virginia Department of Health and Human Resources (D) requiring closure of its residential-care facilities, Buckhannon (P) brought suit against the latter, seeking declaratory and injunctive relief that the self-preservation requirement violated the Fair Housing Amendments Act of 1990. The West Virginia Legislature subsequently enacted legislation eliminating the self-preservation requirement, and the federal district court dismissed Buckhannon's (P) suit as moot. Buckhannon (P) thereupon requested attorney's fees as the "prevailing party" under the Fair Housing Amendments Act. The court denied the motion, the court of appeals affirmed, and Buckhannon (P) appealed.

ISSUE: May an award of attorney's fees and costs to a "prevailing party" under federal statutes be awarded only to a party who has secured a judgment on the merits or a court-ordered consent decree?

HOLDING AND DECISION: (Rehnquist, C.J.) Yes. An award of attorney's fees and costs to a "prevailing party" under federal statutes may be awarded only to a party who has secured a judgment on the merits or a court-ordered consent decree. In designating those parties eligible for an award of litigation costs, Congress employed the term "prevailing party," a legal term of art that indicates one who has been awarded some relief

by the court. Enforceable judgments on the merits and court-ordered consent decrees create the "material alteration of the legal relationship of the parties" necessary to permit an award of attorney's fees. However, the "catalyst theory," which would allow an award where there is no judicially sanctioned change in the relationship of the parties, should not give rise to an attorney fees award. A defendant's voluntary change in conduct, although perhaps accomplishing what the plaintiff sought to achieve by the lawsuit, lacks the necessary judicial imprimatur on the change. The legislative history on the issue is at best ambiguous as to the availability of the "catalyst" theory for awarding attorney's fees. Particularly in view of the "American Rule" that attorney's fees will not be awarded absent explicit statutory authority, such legislative history is clearly insufficient to alter the accepted meaning of the statutory term. Affirmed.

DISSENT: (Ginsburg, J.) To "prevail" so as to receive attorney's fees, it should not be a requirement that the court enter a judgment on the merits. Nor should there necessarily be any finding of wrongdoing. A court-approved settlement will do. The catalyst rule, as applied by the clear majority of federal circuits, is a key component of the fee-shifting statutes Congress adopted to advance enforcement of civil rights.

▶ ANALYSIS

In *Buckhannon*, the Supreme Court noted that, in addition to judgments on the merits, settlement agreements enforced through a consent decree may serve as the basis for an award of attorney's fees.

■══■

Quicknotes

AMERICAN RULE The rule that attorneys' fees are not recoverable, unless expressly provided by law or pursuant to a contract.

CONSENT DECREE A decree issued by a court of equity ratifying an agreement between the parties to a lawsuit; an agreement by a defendant to cease illegal activity.

JUDGMENT ON THE MERITS A determination of the rights of the parties to litigation based on the presentation evidence, barring the party from initiating the same suit again.

■══■

Winter v. Natural Resources Defense Council, Inc.

U.S. Navy (D) v. Environmental defense organization (P)

555 U.S. 7 (2008).

NATURE OF CASE: Challenge to a preliminary injunction.

FACT SUMMARY: The Natural Resources Defense Council (P) filed suit against the U.S. Navy (the Navy) (D) to stop the Navy (D) from using sonar in its training programs due to the effect sonar may have on marine mammals. A federal district court granted a preliminary injunction against the Navy (D), and the U.S. Court of Appeals for the Ninth Circuit upheld it.

RULE OF LAW

A plaintiff who seeks a preliminary injunction must establish that he is likely to succeed on the merits, that he is likely to suffer irreparable harm in the absence of preliminary relief, that the balance of equities tips in his favor, and that an injunction is in the public interest.

FACTS: The U.S. Navy (the Navy) (D) prepares for war through training exercises at sea. The exercises include training in the use of modern sonar to detect and track enemy submarines, and sonar has been part of the training for 40 years. Active sonar, which involves emitting pulses of sound underwater and then receiving the acoustic waves that echo off the target, is the most effective technology for identifying submerged submarines in torpedo range. But the Natural Resources Defense Council (the Council) (P) believes that active sonar harms marine mammals that share the waters with the Navy. Such harm can include permanent hearing loss, decompression sickness, and major behavioral disruptions. A federal law—the Marine Mammal Protection Act of 1972—prohibits harassing marine mammals, but the Secretary of Defense may exempt any action or category of actions from the law if such actions are necessary for national defense. The Navy (D) had been granted an exemption for the training that occurred in this case. Another federal law—the National Environmental Policy Act of 1969—requires federal agencies "to the fullest extent possible" to prepare an environmental impact statement for every major federal action significantly affecting the quality of the human environment, unless the agency determines that the proposed action will not have a significant impact on the environment, and bases that conclusion on a shorter environmental assessment (EA). The Navy (D) had concluded that the training exercises would not have a significant impact on the environment, and issued an EA to that effect in 2007. The Council (P) then filed suit against the Navy

(D) to stop the Navy (D) from using sonar in its training programs. A federal district court granted a preliminary injunction against the Navy (D), and the U.S. Court of Appeals for the Ninth Circuit upheld it.

ISSUE: Must a plaintiff who seeks a preliminary injunction establish that he is likely to succeed on the merits, that he is likely to suffer irreparable harm in the absence of preliminary relief, that the balance of equities tips in his favor, and that an injunction is in the public interest?

HOLDING AND DECISION: (Roberts, C.J.) Yes. A plaintiff who seeks a preliminary injunction must establish that he is likely to succeed on the merits, that he is likely to suffer irreparable harm in the absence of preliminary relief, that the balance of equities tips in his favor, and that an injunction is in the public interest. First, the district court and the Ninth Circuit held that when a plaintiff demonstrates a strong likelihood of prevailing on the merits, a preliminary injunction may be entered based only on a "possibility" of irreparable harm. This "possibility" standard is too lenient. Irreparable injury must be likely, not merely possible, for an injunction to be justified. It is an extraordinary remedy that can only be awarded on a clear showing that the plaintiff is entitled to such relief. But even though the courts both stated the incorrect standard, it appears from the record that they found that the Council (P) had in fact established a "near certainty" of irreparable harm, so the statement of the incorrect standard did not cause harm. Second, even if the Council (P) had shown irreparable injury from the Navy's (D) training exercises, any injury is outweighed by the public interest and the Navy's (D) interest in effective, realistic training of its sailors. Consideration of these factors requires denial of the preliminary injunction. The threat posed by enemy submarines and the need for extensive sonar training to counter the threat is absolutely necessary. The seriousness of the possible harm to the ecological, scientific, and recreational interests advanced by the Council (P) is substantial, but the balance of equities and consideration of the overall public interest tip strongly in favor of the Navy (D). The most serious possible injury caused by the sonar would be to harm an unknown number of the marine mammals that the Council (P) studies and observes, but forcing the Navy (D) to deploy an inadequately trained antisubmarine force jeopardizes the safety of the fleet. This is not a judgment on the underlying merits of the

Continued on next page.

claims, but this judgment does make clear that it would be an abuse of discretion to enter a permanent injunction, after final decision on the merits, along the same lines as the preliminary injunction. Reversed, and the preliminary injunction is vacated.

DISSENT: (Ginsburg, J.) Equity jurisdiction allows for flexibility and courts must evaluate claims for equitable relief on a sliding scale, awarding relief based on a lower likelihood of harm when the likelihood of success is very high.

▶ ANALYSIS

It is unusual for the Supreme Court to hear a challenge to a preliminary injunction. Typically, it hears the merits of a petitioner's claims. But the court made very clear that its belief in the overriding national security interest associated with the Navy's training program should lead the lower court to reject a permanent injunction after a decision on the merits as well, thus influencing a final judgment by the district court even if the district court finds that the Navy violated an environmental statute. This case also illustrates the Court's rejection of the Ninth Circuit's "mere possibility" test, which the United States government had been seeking for some time.

■═■

Quicknotes

IRREPARABLE HARM Such harm that because it is either too great, too small or of a continuing character that it cannot be properly compensated in damages, and the remedy for which is typically injunctive relief.

PRELIMINARY INJUNCTION A judicial mandate issued to require or restrain a party from certain conduct; used to preserve a trial's subject matter or to prevent threatened injury.

■═■

Fuentes v. Shevin

Owner of chattels (P) v. Court (D)

407 U.S. 67 (1972).

NATURE OF CASE: Constitutional challenge to Florida's prejudgment replevin procedure on due process grounds.

FACT SUMMARY: Margarita Fuentes (P) had her stove and stereo picked up by the sheriff prior to the adjudication of a suit filed by Firestone Tire and Rubber Co. for nonpayment of the installment sales contract.

🏛 RULE OF LAW
Procedural due process requires that parties whose rights are to be affected are entitled to be heard at a meaningful time; and in order that they may enjoy that right they must be notified.

FACTS: Margarita Fuentes (Fuentes) (P) purchased a gas stove and service policy, and later a stereo, from Firestone Tire and Rubber Co. (Firestone). After a year, there arose a dispute between Fuentes (P) and Firestone over the servicing of the stove. Firestone filed an action for replevin of both the stove and the stereo, claiming Fuentes (P) had defaulted on her installment payments. Before she was served with the complaint, Firestone obtained a writ of replevin and the sheriff seized the stove and stereo. The prejudgment replevin statutes did not require a convincing showing that the goods were wrongfully detained before seizure. A person could merely file a complaint, post a bond, and request a writ. To obtain a hearing, the person whose property was seized had to initiate a suit for a hearing. Fuentes (P) attacked the prejudgment replevin statute as violative of due process. The state court upheld the legislation, and Fuentes (P) appealed.

ISSUE: Are these state statutes constitutionally defective in that they fail to provide for a hearing at a meaningful time?

HOLDING AND DECISION: (Stewart, J.) Yes. Procedural due process requires that a party whose rights are being affected be given a meaningful opportunity to be heard; and in order that they may enjoy that right they must be notified. The constitutional right to be heard is a basic aspect of the duty of government to follow a fair process of decision-making when it acts to deprive a person of his possessions. This right to be heard minimizes substantively unfair or mistaken deprivations of property, a danger that is especially great when the state seizes goods simply upon the application of and for the benefit of a private party. Without due process of law, there would be no safeguards to protect a

person's property from governmental interference. The right to speak out in one's own defense before an impartial arbitrator is a fundamental right that must be protected. If the right to notice and a hearing is to serve its full purpose, then it is clear that it must be granted at a time when the deprivation can still be prevented. While return of possession and damages can be granted at a later hearing, nothing can undo the fact that a person's property was arbitrarily taken from him without procedural due process of law. That the hearing required by due process is subject to waiver, and is not fixed in form, does not affect its root requirement that an individual be given an opportunity for a hearing before he is deprived of any significant property interest, except for extraordinary situations where some valid governmental interest is at stake that justifies postponing the hearing until after the event. The statute's requirements of requesting a writ, posting bond, and stating in a conclusory fashion that the property is wrongfully held merely test the applicant's own belief in his rights. Since his private gain is at stake, the danger is all too great that his confidence in his cause will be misplaced. While possession may be reinstated by the posting of a counter-bond, it is well settled that a temporary, nonfinal deprivation of property is nonetheless violative of the Due Process Clause of the Fourteenth Amendment. Moreover, the Due Process Clause encompasses both the possessory rights to property and situations where the title is in dispute. Situations requiring a postponement of notice and hearing are truly unusual. They require an important governmental purpose, a special need for prompt action, and are initiated by and for the benefit of the government as opposed to a private individual (e.g., war effort, economic disaster, etc.). The contention that the parties waived their constitutional rights is also without merit, since waiver requires clear and explicit language indicating exactly the rights to be waived. For the above-mentioned reasons, both Florida's and Pennsylvania's prejudgment replevin statutes violate the Due Process Clause of the Fourteenth Amendment. Vacated and remanded.

▶ ANALYSIS

In California, Michigan, and a large number of other states, the writ of replevin is now referred to as claim and delivery. In California, this action is contained in § 511.010, et seq. of the Code of Civil Procedure. A hearing is required for the granting of a writ of possession (comparable to the prior writ of replevin) under the

Continued on next page.

guidelines set out in § 512.010. Exceptions are made for property feloniously taken, credit cards and property acquired in the normal course of trade or business for commercial use. It must be alleged that the property is not necessary for the support of the defendant or his family and that there is a danger that the property will become unavailable to levy, its value will be substantially impaired, and it is necessary to protect the property (§ 512.020). At the hearing, the court will make its determination based on affidavits, pleadings, and other evidence on record. Upon showing of good cause, the court may admit additional evidence or continue the hearing until the new evidence can be obtained (§ 512.050). Finally, with regard to waiver of a hearing requirement, it appears that it is permissible if the parties are acting at arm's length and have equal bargaining power, *D.H. Overmeyer Co. v. Frick Co.*, 405 U.S. 174 (1972); however, if the consumer has no option but to buy on credit, the parties are not equal in bargaining power and the clause is unconscionable, *Kosches v. Nichols*, 327 N.Y.S. 2d 968 (1971). This is but another example of consumer protection. The businessman can waive his constitutional rights, but the consumer cannot.

■≡■

Quicknotes

GARNISHMENT Satisfaction of a debt by deducting payments directly from the debtor's wages before they are paid to him by his employer; due process requires that the debtor be first given notice and an opportunity to be heard.

PROCEDURAL DUE PROCESS The constitutional mandate that if the state or federal government acts so as to deny a citizen of a life, liberty or property interest the individual is first entitled to notice and the right to be heard.

REPLEVIN An action to recover personal property wrongfully taken.

■≡■

Quick Reference Rules of Law

Haddle v. Garrison (S.D. Ga. 1996)

Employee (P) v. Employer (D)

Unpublished Opinion. Docket No. 96-00029-CV-1 (S.D. Ga. 1996).

NATURE OF CASE: Motion to dismiss for failure to state a claim.

FACT SUMMARY: Haddle (P) sued his employer for allegedly conspiring to fire him to deter from testifying at a federal criminal trial.

🏛 RULE OF LAW
A Civil Rights Act § 1985(2) claim requires that the plaintiff suffer actual injury, and discharge from at-will employment does not constitute actual injury.

FACTS: Haddle (P), an employee at Healthmaster (D), alleged that he was terminated in an attempt to deter his participation as a witness at a federal criminal trial. Haddle (P) filed suit in district court for violation of § 1985(2) of the Civil Rights Act. Healthmaster (D) and their officers (D) moved to dismiss for failure to state a claim upon which relief can be granted. They argued that because Haddle (P) was an at-will employee, there was no actual injury as required by § 1985(2).

ISSUE: Does discharge from at-will employment constitute actual injury for purposes of Civil Rights Act § 1985(2)?

HOLDING AND DECISION: (Alaimo, J.) No. A Civil Rights Act § 1985(2) claim requires that the plaintiff suffer actual injury, and discharge from at-will employment does not constitute actual injury. Section 1985(2) provides that one or more persons may not engage in a conspiracy to deter, intimidate, or threaten another from attending and testifying at a federal court proceeding and cause an injury. Fed. R. Civ. P. 12(b)(6) permits a defendant to move to dismiss a complaint where the plaintiff has failed to state a claim upon which relief can be granted. This motion attacks the legal sufficiency of the complaint. Consequently, a court must assume that all of the factual allegations of the complaint are true in deciding the motion. In the present case, the Eleventh Circuit has already ruled that at-will employees have no constitutionally protected property interest in continued employment and thus suffer no actual injury under § 1985(2) when discharged. Accordingly, Haddle (P) has failed to state a federal claim, even if his allegations about the conspiracy to deter him from testifying are true. The motion to dismiss is granted.

▶ ANALYSIS

On appeal, the Eleventh Circuit affirmed this decision in per curiam decision, holding that precedent forecloses Michael A. Haddle's (P) arguments on appeal (unpublished opinion, Docket No. 96-8856 (11th Cir. 1997)). However, the Supreme Court eventually took up the case because it conflicted with the decisions in two other circuits. In the end, Haddle's (P) appeal was upheld and the dismissal reversed.

■=■

Quicknotes

FED. R. CIV. P. 12 Allows for successive motions to dismiss for failure to state a claim.

■=■

Haddle v. Garrison (1998)

Employee (P) v. Employer (D)

525 U.S. 121 (1998).

NATURE OF CASE: Appeal from dismissal of Civil Rights Act action.

FACT SUMMARY: Haddle (P) sued his employer for allegedly conspiring to fire him to deter him from testifying at a federal criminal trial.

🏛 RULE OF LAW
A Civil Rights Act claim under § 1985(2) does not require an injury to a constitutionally protected property interest.

FACTS: Healthmaster (D) and officers Garrison (D) and Kelly (D) were indicted by a federal grand jury in 1995. Haddle (P), an employee, had cooperated with the investigation and was expected to appear as a witness at the resulting criminal trial. Garrison (D) and Kelly (D) allegedly conspired with the other officers at Healthmaster (D) to terminate Haddle (P) in retaliation. Haddle (P) filed suit in district court for violation of § 1985 of the Civil Rights Act. Healthmaster (D) and the officers (D) moved to dismiss for failure to state a claim upon which relief can be granted. The district court ruled that because Haddle (P) was an at-will employee, there was no actual injury as required by § 1985. The dismissal motion was granted and the court of appeals affirmed. Since the Eleventh Circuit's decision conflicted with the holdings in two other circuits, the U.S. Supreme Court granted certiorari.

ISSUE: Does a Civil Rights Act claim under § 1985(2) require an injury to a constitutionally protected property interest?

HOLDING AND DECISION: (Rehnquist, C.J.) No. A Civil Rights Act claim under § 1985(2) does not require an injury to a constitutionally protected property interest. Section 1985(2) provides that one or more persons may not engage in a conspiracy to deter, intimidate, or threaten another from attending and testifying at a federal court proceeding. The Eleventh Circuit held that there was no injury to Haddle (P) because he had no property interest in at-will employment that could give rise to damages. However, nothing in the language of § 1985(2) or the remedial provisions establishes this requirement. The section is directed against intimidation or retaliation against witnesses, not the deprivation of property. The fact that employment at will is not property does not mean that the loss of this employment does not cause injury. Such harm has long been a compensable injury under tort law and is similar to intentional interference with contractual relations. Dismissal of Haddle's (P) complaint for failure to state a claim was in error. Reversed and remanded.

▶ ANALYSIS

The employment term for "at-will employees" is not definite, and when *Haddle* was decided, very few Supreme Court cases addressed the issue of at-will employment. In addition, amici in the case included the National Whistleblowers Association. The Court's reversal arguably could have caused a significant increase in the number of whistleblower cases filed in federal court.

Quicknotes

SUPPLEMENTAL JURISDICTION A doctrine granting authority to a federal court to hear a claim that does not invoke diversity jurisdiction if it arises from the same transaction or occurrence as the primary action.

Ashcroft v. Iqbal

Former U.S. Attorney General (D) v. Pakistani citizen (P)

556 U.S. 662 (2009).

NATURE OF CASE: Certiorari to determine complaint sufficiency in constitutional claim.

FACT SUMMARY: Javaid Iqbal (P), a Pakistani citizen, was arrested in the United States on criminal charges and detained by federal officials soon after the 9/11 terrorist attacks. He claimed his confinement conditions violated his constitutional rights. The federal official defendants moved to dismiss Iqbal's (P) complaint as facially insufficient.

RULE OF LAW
A well-pleaded complaint requires nonconclusory, plausible, factual pleadings.

FACTS: United States officials arrested Javaid Iqbal (P), a Pakistani citizen and Muslim, on criminal charges and detained him after the 9/11 terrorist attacks. Iqbal (P) filed a federal complaint alleging he was deprived of certain constitutional rights while confined. He alleged the deprivations occurred because of his race, religion, or national origin. He named former U.S. Attorney General John Ashcroft (D) and FBI Director Robert Mueller (D) in addition to several others. Ashcroft (D) and Mueller (D) moved to dismiss the complaint as facially insufficient and raised the defense of qualified immunity based on their official status at the time of the confinement. The district court denied the motion and Ashcroft (D) and Mueller (D) took an interlocutory appeal to the Second Circuit Court of Appeals. The Second Circuit affirmed, and the U.S. Supreme Court granted certiorari.

ISSUE: Does a well-pleaded complaint require nonconclusory, plausible, factual pleadings?

HOLDING AND DECISION: (Kennedy, J.) Yes. A well-pleaded complaint requires nonconclusory, plausible, factual pleadings. Iqbal's (P) complaint alleges the federal government had a policy of detaining Arab Muslims after the 9/11 attacks until the individuals were "cleared" by the FBI. Iqbal (P) claimed Ashcroft (D) was the "architect" of this policy and Mueller (D) was instrumental in its "adoption, promulgation, and implementation." This Court held in *Bell Atlantic Corp. v. Twombly*, 550 U.S. 544 (2007), that pleadings required factual content that allows the court to draw the reasonable inference that the defendant is liable for the alleged misconduct. The plausibility standard did not rise to a probability but requires more than conclusions of misconduct. *Twombly* supported the principles that a court accepts factual allegations as true but need not accept conclusory allegations as true. Fed. R. Civ. P. 8 may now permit more flexibility but it does not permit mere conclusions. Further, only a complaint that states a plausible claim survives a motion to dismiss. The courts may begin their analysis with determining which pleadings include factual allegations that will be entitled to a presumption of truth. Here, Iqbal (P) states only conclusory allegations that Ashcroft (D) was the principal architect and Mueller (D) was the principal implementer of the policies. These conclusory allegations are not entitled to a presumption of truth. Iqbal (P) fails to include factual allegations supporting his conclusions that Ashcroft (D) and Mueller (D) knew of the federal officials' behavior regarding his confinement. The consideration then becomes whether the complaint suggests an entitlement to relief. It does not. Iqbal (P) was plausibly held for reasons other than race, religion, or national origin. Detaining such suspects until cleared does not violate constitutional protections. Iqbal (P) argues *Twombly* should be limited to antitrust pleadings, but nothing supports this theory. *Twombly* is the pleading standard for all civil actions. Iqbal (P) finally argues Fed. R. Civ. P. 9(b) permits him "general" rather than "specific" pleading for an alleged constitutional violation. Rule 9(b) does not override the factual pleading requirements of Rule 8 but merely requires even greater specificity for the enumerated claims. Reversed and remanded.

DISSENT: (Souter, J.) Consistent with *Twombly*, nonconclusory allegations should be taken as true unless they are "sufficiently fantastic to defy reality." The key allegations here are not conclusory and the complaint was facially sufficient.

DISSENT: (Breyer, J.) The lower court expressly rejected minimally intrusive discovery in favor of dismissal. That would have been appropriate because the discovery could have been in anticipation of a summary judgment motion.

ANALYSIS

Pleading requirements have become stricter so general notice is no longer sufficient. The defendant is not merely put on notice of the plaintiff's claim but is entitled to factual allegations informing it of the support for the claim. Some analysts were concerned about the future of litigation because of a fear that pleadings would have to be so specific that most plaintiffs would not be able to proceed. Most courts, however, have

Continued on next page.

required factual pleading for a long time and did not become more stringent after *Iqbal*. The rule stated in *Iqbal* is "plausibility" not "probability" so the allegations do not have to be proven on the face of the complaint but the facts alleged must be plausible and permit a reasonable inference of defendant's misconduct.

■━■

Quicknotes

INTERLOCUTORY APPEAL The appeal of an issue that does not resolve the disposition of the case, but is essential to a determination of the parties' legal rights.

■━■

Stradford v. Zurich Insurance Co.

Insured (P) v. Insurer (D)

2002 WL 31027517 (S.D.N.Y. 2002).

NATURE OF CASE: Motion to dismiss counterclaim.

FACT SUMMARY: When Dr. Stradford (P) sued his insurer, Zurich Insurance Company (Northern) (D), for property damage, Northern (P) counterclaimed for fraud, contending that Stradford (P) was fully aware the damage had occurred during a period in which the policy had lapsed for nonpayment of premiums. Stradford (P) moved to dismiss the fraud claim.

🏛 **RULE OF LAW**
Under Fed. R. Civ. P. 9(b), the time, place, and nature of alleged misrepresentations must be disclosed to a party accused of fraud.

FACTS: Dr. Stradford (P), a dentist, brought suit against his insurer, Zurich Insurance Company (Northern) (D), for water damage allegedly occurring to his property during a period that Northern (D) claimed was an interim period when the insurance had lapsed because of Stradford's (P) failure to make premium payments. Northern (D), accordingly, counterclaimed against Stradford (P), contending that Stradford (P), by making the claim and filing the suit, knowingly had devised a scheme and artifice to defraud the insurer and obtain money by false pretenses and representations. Stradford (P) moved to dismiss the counterclaim that was based in fraud for failure to state the fraud claim with sufficient particularity.

ISSUE: Under Fed. R. Civ. P. 9(b), must the time, place, and nature of alleged misrepresentations be disclosed to a party accused of fraud?

HOLDING AND DECISION: (Buchwald, J.) Yes. Under Fed. R. Civ. P. 9(b), the time, place, and nature of alleged misrepresentations must be disclosed to a party accused of fraud. Here, Northern's (D) counterclaims simply failed to identify the statement made by Stradford (P) that they claimed to be false. Thus, it is unclear from the face of the counterclaims whether Northern (D) was asserting that Stradford's (P) claimed losses were improperly inflated, that Stradford's (P) office never even flooded, or that the offices flooded, but not during the term of the insurance policy. In essence, Northern (D) claimed that Stradford (P) lied, but failed to identify the lie. The primary purpose of Rule 9(b) is to afford a litigant accused of fraud fair notice of the claim and the factual ground upon which it is based. Here, Northern's (D) counterclaims failed to provide Stradford (P) with fair notice of precisely which statement, or which aspect of his claim, Northern (D) alleged to be false. The counterclaims were therefore insufficient under Rule 9(b) and must be dismissed. However, in accordance with the practice of the Second Circuit, Northern (D) is permitted to file an amended pleading, which it has done, which cures the defects found in the counterclaims by making it clear that it was alleging that Stradford's (P) office was flooded at a time when he had permitted the insurance policy to lapse, yet that he misrepresented the date of the loss to try to bring the loss within the coverage period. Defendant's request for permission to move for summary judgment is granted.

▶ **ANALYSIS**

Fed. R. Civ. P. 9(b) provides that in all averments of fraud or mistake, the circumstances constituting fraud or mistake shall be stated with particularity. Malice, intent, knowledge, and other condition of mind of a person may be averred generally.

■═■

Quicknotes

FED. R. CIV. P. 9(B) Sets forth the requirements for pleading fraud or mistake and requires the circumstances constituting fraud or mistake to be plead with particularity; malice, intent, knowledge and other conditions of the mind of a person may be plead generally.

■═■

Jones v. Bock

Prisoner (P) v. State (D)

549 U.S. 199 (2007).

NATURE OF CASE: Appeal to Supreme Court on issue of pleading requirements.

FACT SUMMARY: Lorenzo Jones (P) was a prisoner in Michigan. He sued the State (D) after he suffered injuries in custody when the staff refused to reassign him to work he could perform in light of his injuries.

🏛 RULE OF LAW
A plaintiff need not plead and demonstrate exhaustion of administrative remedies in the complaint.

FACTS: Lorenzo Jones (P) was a prisoner in Michigan. He sued the state after he suffered injuries in custody when the staff refused to reassign him to work he could perform in light of his injuries.

ISSUE: Must a plaintiff plead and demonstrate exhaustion of administrative remedies in the complaint?

HOLDING AND DECISION: (Roberts, C.J.) No. A plaintiff need not plead and demonstrate exhaustion of administrative remedies in the complaint. The Federal Rules of Civil Procedure do not require that exhaustion be pleaded, and Rule 8(c) identifies a non-exhaustive list of affirmative defenses that must be pleaded in response, leaving room for exhaustion as an affirmative defense. In addition, the Prison Litigation Reform Act, which deals extensively with the subject of exhaustion, is silent on the issue whether exhaustion must be pleaded by the plaintiff or as an affirmative defense by the defendant. This supports the fact that the usual practice should be followed, and the usual practice under the Federal Rules is to regard exhaustion as an affirmative defense. The reasons behind the decisions of some lower courts to impose a pleading requirement on plaintiffs in this context, which are to separate, when it comes to prisoner suits, those claims that have merit and those that have none and will merely clog the process, are understandable. But the way to establishing higher pleading requirements is to amend the rules, not on a case-by-case basis in courts.

▶ ANALYSIS

The outcome of this case is in keeping with the Roberts Court's general idea that policy considerations and courts should not expand the requirements of the Federal Rules of Civil Procedure. The general belief is that expansion of the Rules should be made through the Rules amendment process.

Quicknotes

AFFIRMATIVE DEFENSE A manner of defending oneself against a claim not by denying the truth of the charge, but by the introduction of some evidence challenging the plaintiff's right to bring the claim.

EXHAUSTION REMEDIES Requirement that a party exhaust all administrative remedies available before a court will intervene in the controversy.

Walker v. Norwest Corp.

Minor (P) v. Fiduciary (D)

108 F.3d 158 (8th Cir. 1996).

NATURE OF CASE: Appeal of an award of Rule 11 sanctions.

FACT SUMMARY: Jimmy Lee Walker, III (P), his guardian, Cynthia Walker (P), and their attorney, Massey, appealed Fed. R. Civ. P. 11 sanctions imposed against Massey when Massey failed to amend or dismiss a clearly defective complaint he had filed.

RULE OF LAW
Fed. R. Civ. P. 11 sanctions may be appropriate for an attorney's filing of a clearly defective complaint and taking no steps to amend or dismiss it.

FACTS: Jimmy Walker (P), a minor, through his attorney, Massey, filed a complaint in federal court against Norwest (D), in which the attorney failed to plead complete diversity of citizenship, and indeed, pleaded facts that tended to show there was not complete diversity. Upon receiving the complaint, Norwest (D) wrote to Massey informing him that the complaint showed on its face that there was no diversity jurisdiction. The letter asked Massey to dismiss the complaint and warned that if he did not, Norwest (D) would seek sanctions, including attorney's fees. Massey acknowledged Norwest's (D) correspondence, but made no substantive response to the deficiency that Norwest's (D) counsel had pointed out. The federal district court granted Norwest's (D) motion to dismiss and for Fed. R. Civ. P. 11 sanctions against Walker (P) and Massey, and Walker (P) and Massey appealed.

ISSUE: May Fed. R. Civ. P. 11 sanctions be appropriate for an attorney's filing of a clearly defective complaint and taking no steps to amend or dismiss it?

HOLDING AND DECISION: (Gibson, J.) Yes. Fed. R. Civ. P. 11 sanctions may be appropriate for an attorney's filing of a clearly defective complaint and taking no steps to amend or dismiss it. Even though it was the Walkers' (P) burden to plead, and if necessary, prove diversity, they did not allege that all of the defendants were domiciled in a state other than South Dakota. Instead, they argued that finding out the defendants' (D) citizenship would be more trouble than they should be expected to take. However, this is a burden that plaintiffs desiring to invoke diversity jurisdiction have assumed since the days of Chief Justice Marshall. As to Massey's contention that the court should have inquired into his financial circumstances before imposing the monetary sanction, not only did Massey fail to argue this point to

the district court, but there was no evidence in the record to support such an argument. Finally, Massey never did allege citizenship for many of the defendants and never identified which defendants should be dismissed to create diversity jurisdiction. Affirmed.

ANALYSIS

In *Walker*, the court made clear that a district court is not obliged to do a party's research for them.

Quicknotes

DIVERSITY JURISDICTION The authority of a federal court to hear and determine cases involving $10,000 or more and in which the parties are citizens of different states, or in which one party is an alien.

DIVERSITY OF CITIZENSHIP The authority of a federal court to hear and determine cases involving $10,000 or more and in which the parties are citizens of different states, or in which one party is an alien.

FED. R. CIV. P. 11 Sets forth: the requirement that every pleading or written paper be signed by at least one attorney of record; the representations made by the attorney to the court upon the signing of such document; and the sanctions for violation of the provision.

Christian v. Mattel, Inc.

Alleged infringed toymaker (P) v. Alleged infringing toymaker (D)

286 F.3d 1118 (9th Cir. 2003).

NATURE OF CASE: Appeal of an award of Fed. R. Civ. P. 11 sanctions.

FACT SUMMARY: When the court awarded Fed. R. Civ. P. 11 sanctions against Claudene Christian (P) and her attorney, Hicks, for a combination of frivolous pleading and improper discovery tactics, Christian (P) and Hicks argued that Rule 11 sanctions must be limited to papers signed in violation of the rule, not to other conduct.

> ## RULE OF LAW
> Fed. R. Civ. P. 11 sanctions are limited to papers signed in violation of the rule, not to other conduct.

FACTS: Claudene Christian (P), who created and marketed a cheerleader doll, filed a complaint alleging that the toymaker Mattel, Inc. (D) infringed the copyright on her doll. Mattel (D) proferred evidence that its copyright predated Christian's (P) doll. However, Christian (P), through her attorney Hicks, refused voluntarily to dismiss the suit. The federal district court granted Mattel's (D) motion for summary judgment and for Fed. R. Civ. P. 11 sanctions, finding that Christian's (P) attorney, Hicks, had filed a meritless claim and that Hicks had demonstrated that his conduct fell far below the proper standards of attorneys, including, among other things, unprofessional behavior during discovery proceedings and misrepresentations to the court during oral arguments. The court awarded Mattel (D) $501,565 in attorneys' fees. Christian (P) and Hicks appealed.

ISSUE: Are Fed. R. Civ. P. 11 sanctions limited to papers signed in violation of the rule, not to other conduct?

HOLDING AND DECISION: (McKeown, J.) Yes. Fed. R. Civ. P. 11 sanctions are limited to papers signed in violation of the rule, not to other conduct. While the laundry list of Hicks's outlandish conduct is a long one and raises questions as to his respect for the judicial process, nonetheless Rule 11 sanctions are limited to papers signed. Conduct in depositions, discovery meetings of counsel, oral representations at hearings and behavior in prior proceedings do not fall within the ambit of Rule 11. Here, the orders clearly demonstrate that the district court decided, at least in part, to sanction Hicks because he signed and filed a factually and legally meritless complaint and also strongly suggest that the court considered "extra-pleadings conduct" as

a basis for the Rule 11 sanctions. Because it cannot from the record be determined for certain whether the district court granted Mattel's (P) Rule 11 motion as a result of an impermissible intertwining of its conclusion about the complaint's frivolity and Hicks's extrinsic misconduct, the district court Rule 11 order is vacated and the matter remanded to delineate the factual and legal basis for its sanctions orders.

▌ ANALYSIS

In *Christian*, the court emphasized that Fed. R. Civ. P. 11 does not authorize sanctions for "extra-pleadings conduct" such as, for example, discovery abuses or misstatements made to the court during an oral presentation.

■■■■

Quicknotes

FED. R. CIV. P. 11 Sets forth: the requirement that every pleading or written paper be signed by at least one attorney of record; the representations made by the attorney to the court upon the signing of such document; and the sanctions for violation of the provision.

■■■■

Zielinski v. Philadelphia Piers, Inc.

Injured forklift operator (P) v. Rival forklift company (D)

139 F. Supp. 408 (E.D. Pa. 1956).

NATURE OF CASE: Action in torts to recover damages for personal injuries.

FACT SUMMARY: Philadelphia Piers (D) was estopped to deny ownership of a forklift and the agency of the operator.

🏛 RULE OF LAW
In the federal courts, a defendant who knowingly makes inaccurate statements may be estopped from denying those inaccurate statements at the trial.

FACTS: Zielinski (P) was injured on February 9, 1953, while operating a forklift on Pier 96 for J.A. McCarthy. Zielinski (P) alleged in his complaint that Sandy Johnson was operating a forklift owned by Philadelphia Piers (D) and was their agent as well. Because of the negligent manner in which Sandy Johnson operated the forklift, Zielinski (P) was injured. A complaint was served on Philadelphia Piers (D). Actually, Sandy Johnson worked for Carload Contractors, Inc., who had leased the forklift from Philadelphia Piers, Inc. (D). Sandy Johnson had worked for Philadelphia Piers (D) for the previous 15 years and wasn't aware that he was now working for Carload Contractors, Inc. Sandy Johnson testified at a deposition taken August 18, 1953, that he had worked for Philadelphia Piers, Inc. (D). As soon as Carload Contractors, Inc. found out about the accident, they made a report to their insurance company. When Philadelphia Piers (D) received the complaint, they forwarded it on to their insurance company, which was the same insurance company of Carload Contractors, Inc., telling them of the mistake and asking them to take care of it. Philadelphia Piers (D) was at the deposition when Sandy Johnson testified that he worked for Philadelphia Piers (D), and by receiving the complaint and the letter they sent to their insurance company, it was clear that they knew of Zielinski's (P) mistake. Zielinski (P) didn't find out that he was suing the wrong party until the pretrial conference held on September 27, 1955. Zielinski (P) requested a ruling that for the purposes of this case the forklift operated by Sandy Johnson was owned by Philadelphia Piers (D), and that Sandy Johnson was its agent acting in the course of his employment. In other words, Philadelphia Piers (D) would be estopped to deny the facts they allowed Zielinski (P) to believe.

ISSUE: If a defendant makes an ineffective denial of part of the complaint and knowingly allows the plaintiff to continue to rely on the facts as stated in the complaint, may the defendant be estopped to deny the facts as they are contained in the complaint?

HOLDING AND DECISION: (Van Dusen, J.) Yes. Philadelphia Piers (D) made a general denial of the paragraph in the complaint that alleged that Sandy Johnson was an agent of Philadelphia Piers (D) and was driving their forklift. It was clear from interrogatories that they were aware of the accident and the facts involved because they made an investigation and forwarded their report to their insurance company. Philadelphia Piers (D) should have made a specific denial of parts of the complaint they believed and knew to be false and admitted the parts that were true. This would have warned Zielinski (P) that he was suing the wrong party. This case was being tried in the district court sitting in Pennsylvania and there were no federal court decisions on this point, so the Pennsylvania law was used. The Pennsylvania rule is that where an improper and ineffective answer has been filed, an allegation of agency in the complaint requires a statement to the jury that agency is admitted if the time allowed to amend an answer has already passed. Philadelphia Piers (D) was under no duty to advise Zielinski (P) of his error other than by appropriate pleadings, but neither did they have a right, knowing of the mistake, to foster it by its acts of omission. Therefore, Philadelphia Piers (D) will be estopped to deny Sandy Johnson's agency and their ownership of the forklift and the jury will be instructed as Zielinski (P) requested. Philadelphia Piers (D) will not be prejudiced by having to defend this action, because it will be its insurance company who will have to do it and they are the insurance company for the proper defendants. A pre-trial order may be modified at trial if justice so requires.

▶ ANALYSIS

Fed. R. Civ. P. 8(b) requires that denials fairly meet the substance of the averments denied. This requirement, together with the basic requirement of good faith in pleading contained in Fed. R. Civ. P. 11, probably would provide adequate grounds for the decision in this case. Rule 8(b) also requires that the party shall state in short and plain terms his defenses to each claim asserted against him. If Philadelphia Piers (D) had stated that their defense to the complaint was that they were not the employers or owners of the personnel or machinery involved, Zielinski (P) would have been able to

Continued on next page.

bring this action against the proper party. Philadelphia Piers (D) seemed to lack the good faith that the federal rules require because they waited until the time of trial to raise their defense that Zielinski had sued the wrong party.

■■■■

Quicknotes

COMPLAINT The initial pleading commencing litigation which sets forth a claim for relief.

FED. R. CIV. P. 8 Sets forth the general rules of pleading a claim for relief.

GENERAL DENIAL Type of pleading contradicting all the assertions of a former pleading.

■■■■

Beeck v. Aquaslide 'N' Dive Corp.

Injured slide user (P) v. Slide manufacturer (D)

562 F.2d 537 (8th Cir. 1977).

NATURE OF CASE: Appeal from grant of leave to amend.

FACT SUMMARY: Beeck (P) was injured on a pool slide alleged to have been manufactured by Aquaslide 'N' Dive Corp. (Aquaslide) (D), and after Aquaslide (D) admitted manufacture in its answer, the district court granted it leave to amend to deny manufacture over Beeck's (P) objection.

🏛 RULE OF LAW
The opponent of a motion for leave to amend must show he will be prejudiced by the grant of leave under Fed. R. Civ. P. 15(a)[2].

FACTS: Beeck (P) was injured while using the slide at a social gathering at Kimberly Village, Davenport, Iowa. Beeck (P) then brought this action in district court under diversity jurisdiction alleging that Aquaslide 'N' Dive Corp. (Aquaslide) (D) was liable under theories of negligence, strict liability, and breach of implied warranty. Aquaslide (D) answered the complaint, admitting that it manufactured the slide in question in reliance upon the opinions of insurance investigators. The district court then granted Aquaslide (D) leave to amend the answer to deny this fact and permitted a separate trial on the question of manufacture over the objection of Beeck (P). The jury found for Aquaslide (D) and the court entered summary judgment against Beeck (P). By the time of the amendment, the statute of limitations for Beeck's (P) cause of action had run, and Beeck (P) appealed.

ISSUE: Must an opponent of a motion for leave to amend show he will be prejudiced by the grant of leave under Fed. R. Civ. P. 15(a)[2]?

HOLDING AND DECISION: (Benson, J.) Yes. Fed. R. Civ. P. 15(a)[2] provides that "leave shall be freely given when justice so requires." The grant or denial of such leave to amend is within the sound discretion of the trial judge. The party opposing the motion for leave must show he will be prejudiced by the grant of leave under Fed. R. Civ. P. 15(a)[2]. In this case, Aquaslide (D) relied upon the conclusions of three separate insurance companies and their investigators and were thus not negligent in determining the facts in question, and it was not an abuse of discretion to give Aquaslide (D) a chance to correct a fact disputed. Beeck (P) alleged that he was prejudiced because his action was foreclosed by the running of the statute of limitations. This argument required the trial judge to assume that Aquaslide (D)

would prevail on the manufacturing issue, and the judge properly refused to so presume. Neither was the grant of separate trials improper. A substantial issue of material fact was raised that would exonerate Aquaslide (D) if resolved in its favor. There was thus no abuse of discretion. Affirmed.

▶ ANALYSIS

Because of the running of the statute of limitations, it would be unlikely, if not impossible, that Beeck (P) would be able to move against any other party. The court had to counterbalance this injustice against that of precluding Aquaslide (D) from proving that it did not manufacture the slide that caused the injury. Since the amendment and the separate trial gave Beeck (P) a chance to disprove Aquaslide's (D) argument, and since the Federal Rules of Civil Procedure technically permitted the amendment and severance, the balance was struck in Aquaslide's (D) favor.

■■■

Quicknotes

AMENDMENT TO PLEADING The modification of a pleading either as a matter of course upon motion to the court or by consent of both parties; a party is entitled to change its pleading once as a matter of course before a responsive pleading has been served.

ISSUE OF MATERIAL FACT A fact that is disputed between two or more parties to litigation that is essential to proving an element of the cause of action or a defense asserted or would otherwise affect the outcome of the proceeding.

■■■

Moore v. Baker

Patient (P) v. Physician (D)

989 F.2d 1129 (11th Cir. 1993).

NATURE OF CASE: Appeal of denial of motion to amend pleading in nonconsent action.

FACT SUMMARY: Moore (P) initially alleged that Dr. Baker (D) violated the informed-consent law, but then sought to include a claim for medical malpractice.

⚖ RULE OF LAW
A claim that does not arise out of the same conduct, transaction, or occurrence as the original claim does not relate back to the original pleading.

FACTS: Moore (P) consulted Dr. Baker (D) to correct a blockage of her carotid artery. Baker (D) recommended surgery and warned Moore (P) of the risks. The operation left Moore (P) permanently disabled. Moore's (P) initial complaint alleged only a violation of Georgia's informed-consent law. The trial court granted Baker's (D) motion for summary judgment. The statute of limitations ran the day after Moore (P) filed the original complaint. Moore (P) then sought to amend the complaint to include a claim for negligence, asserting that the new claim should relate back to the date of the original complaint. The trial court denied Moore's (P) motion, and Moore (P) appealed.

ISSUE: May a claim that does not arise out of the same conduct, transaction, or occurrence as the original claim relate back to the original pleading?

HOLDING AND DECISION: (Morgan, J.) No. A claim that does not arise out of the same conduct, transaction, or occurrence as the original claim may not relate back to the original pleading. In this case, the new claim arises out of alleged actions that are distinct in time and involve separate and distinct conduct. The failure-to-warn claim focused on actions prior to surgery, while the negligence claim focuses on actions during and post-surgery. Affirmed.

▶ ANALYSIS

Whether the conduct, transaction, or occurrence in the amended complaint relates back to the original complaint to avoid the bar of a statute of limitations is a subjective test open to argument and interpretation. The role of the appellate court is to decide whether the trial court abused its discretion in applying this test to the facts of the case.

Quicknotes

AMENDMENT TO PLEADING The modification of a pleading either as a matter of course upon motion to the court or by consent of both parties; a party is entitled to change its pleading once as a matter of course before a responsive pleading has been served.

RELATION BACK DOCTRINE Doctrine that holds that a party may not amend its pleading to set forth a new or different claim or defense unless it involves the subject matter of the original pleading; under Fed. R. Civ. P. 15(c), if a party amends its pleading as a matter of course before a responsive pleading is served, such amendment is said to relate back to the original pleading if it involves the subject matter of the original pleading.

■■■

Bonerb v. Richard J. Caron Foundation

Injured basketball player (P) v. Foundation (D)

159 F.R.D. 16 (W.D.N.Y. 1994).

NATURE OF CASE: Motion to amend complaint in personal-injury action.

FACT SUMMARY: After Bonerb (P) filed suit for injuries received on a basketball court while he was being treated at the Richard J. Caron Foundation (Foundation) (D), he sought to amend his complaint to add a cause of action for "counseling malpractice."

🏛 RULE OF LAW
When allegations in an amended complaint and the original complaint derive from the same nucleus of operative facts, the amended complaint relates back to the date of the original complaint.

FACTS: Bonerb (P) slipped and fell while playing basketball at the Richard J. Caron Foundation (Foundation) (D) while participating in the Foundation's (D) mandatory exercise program. Bonerb's (P) original complaint alleged the Foundation's (D) basketball court was negligently maintained. Bonerb (P) sought to amend the complaint to include a new claim for counseling malpractice. Bonerb (P) sought to relate back the malpractice claim to the date of the original complaint since the statute of limitations had expired for asserting a malpractice claim.

ISSUE: May allegations in an amended complaint relate back to the date of the original complaint when the new claim derives from the same nucleus of operative facts as the original complaint?

HOLDING AND DECISION: (Heckman, J.) Yes. Allegations in an amended complaint may relate back to the date of the original complaint when the new claim derives from the same nucleus of operative facts as the original complaint. The determining factor is whether the facts stated in the original complaint put the defendant on notice of the claim which plaintiff later seeks to add. Here, Bonerb (P) is using the same factual allegations in the amended complaint as in the original complaint. Bonerb (P) has merely changed the legal theory upon which the claim is based. Motion to amend is granted.

▶ ANALYSIS

Amendment to a pleading may occur in an answer as well as a complaint. Fed. R. Civ. P. 15(a) allows relation back for claims and defenses asserted in the original pleading or attempted to be set forth in the original pleading which arose from the conduct, transaction, or occurrence of the original pleading.

■═■

Quicknotes

NUCLEUS OF OPERATIVE FACTS An underlying fact situation common to those pleadings asserting it.

RELATION BACK DOCTRINE Doctrine that holds that a party may not amend its pleading to set forth a new or different claim or defense unless it involves the subject matter of the original pleading; under Fed. R. Civ. P. 15(c), if a party amends its pleading as a matter of course before a responsive pleading is served, such amendment is said to relate back to the original pleading if it involves the subject matter of the original pleading.

■═■

Discovery

Quick Reference Rules of Law

Davis v. Precoat Metals

Employee (P) v. Employer (D)

2002 WL 1759828 (N.D. Ill. 2002).

NATURE OF CASE: Motion to compel discovery.

FACT SUMMARY: When Davis (P), a minority employee of Precoat Metals (Precoat) (D), and others sued Precoat for discrimination under federal civil rights legislation and requested discovery regarding similar complaints of other employees, Precoat (D) argued that such information was not a proper subject for a discovery request.

RULE OF LAW
Discovery requests that are narrowly tailored to the specific claims of the case are proper.

FACTS: Davis (P) and other African-American and Latino employees working at Precoat Metal's (Precoat) (D) Chicago plant brought suit against their employer, Precoat (D), alleging race and national origin discrimination and retaliation in violation of Title VII of the Civil Rights Act of 1964. They alleged a hostile working environment, including being subjected to racially insulting and derogatory comments by management-level employees of Precoat (D). Davis (P) sought discovery regarding other employees' complaints made against Precoat (D) by nonclerical/non-administrative employees who worked at the same plant as Davis (P), namely, the Chicago plant. Precoat (D) argued that such information was nondiscoverable.

ISSUE: Are discovery requests that are narrowly tailored to the specific claims of the case proper?

HOLDING AND DECISION: (Nolan, J.) Yes. Discovery requests that are narrowly tailored to the specific claims of the case are proper. In their discovery motion, plaintiffs have limited their request to: (1) the time period of the alleged discrimination; (2) complaints by employees who worked at the same Chicago plant where the plaintiffs worked; and (3) complaints of race and national original discrimination, the same types of discrimination alleged in plaintiffs' complaint. Here, such request for information is properly discoverable and is narrowly tailored to this specific lawsuit. Davis (P) is correct in his argument that other employees' complaints of discrimination may be relevant to establish pretext since an employer's general policy and practice with respect to minority employment may certainly be relevant to a discrimination issue. Here, Davis (P) does not seek discovery related to all alleged unequal employment practices by Precoat Metals (D), nor does Davis (P) seek complaints by employees who did not work at the Chicago plant. Rather, plaintiffs have limited their discovery requests to complaints alleging race and national origin discrimination filed by other employees who worked at the same plant as the plaintiffs. The motion of Davis (P) to compel discovery is granted.

ANALYSIS

Fed. R. Civ. P. 26(b)(1) permits discovery into any matter, not privileged, that is relevant to the claim or defense of any party. Discoverable information is not limited to that which would be admissible at trial. Information is relevant for purposes of Rule 26 if the discovery appears reasonably calculated to lead to the discovery of admissible evidence.

Quicknotes

DISCOVERY Pretrial procedure during which one party makes certain information available to the other.

TITLE VII OF THE CIVIL RIGHTS ACT OF 1964 Law prohibiting discrimination in employment on the basis of race, color, religion, sex, and national origin.

Steffan v. Cheney

Homosexual naval candidate (P) v. Secretary of Defense (D)

920 F.2d 74 (D.C. Cir. 1990).

NATURE OF CASE: Appeal from dismissal of action for wrongful discharge from U.S. Naval Academy.

FACT SUMMARY: Steffan (P), who was discharged from the U.S. Naval Academy after he truthfully responded in the affirmative to a superior's inquiry as to whether he was homosexual, argued that his wrongful-discharge action should not have been dismissed because the district court erroneously allowed irrelevant questions as to whether he had engaged in homosexual activities during or after his tenure as a midshipman.

RULE OF LAW
Only evidence that is relevant to the issue being litigated may be discovered.

FACTS: Steffan (P), while he was a midshipman at the U.S. Naval Academy, responded truthfully to a superior who asked him if he was a homosexual. Steffan (P) resigned from the Academy after an administrative board, shortly before he was to graduate at the head of his class, recommended that Steffan (P) be discharged, based solely on his statement. Steffan (P) brought suit against Secretary of Defense Cheney (D), alleging that he was constructively discharged from the service and challenging the constitutionality of the regulation that provided for discharge of homosexuals. During discovery, Steffan (P), invoking his Fifth Amendment privilege against self-incrimination, refused to answer questions as to whether he had ever engaged in homosexual activities during the time he was a midshipman or after his discharge. Additionally, he objected that the questions were not relevant to the legality of his separation. After giving a warning, the district court dismissed Steffan's (P) action for failure to comply with discovery orders, but the court acknowledged that Steffan (P) was discharged for his statement, not for acts. The court held, however, that the questions were relevant because the Navy could "refuse reinstatement on the grounds an individual has engaged in homosexual acts." Steffan (P) appealed.

ISSUE: May evidence that is irrelevant to the issue being litigated be discovered?

HOLDING AND DECISION: (Per curiam) No. Only evidence that is relevant to the issue being litigated may be discovered. The law is quite clear on this issue. Further, judicial review must be confined to the grounds upon which the action was based. Here, the action was brought for invalid separation from the Naval Academy. If the basis for separation from the Academy was

homosexual conduct, then the questions may have been relevant and the information discoverable. However, in the instant case, the basis for separation was a statement made by Steffan (P) in response to an inquiry by Academy supervisors. This does not put into question whether he engaged in the potentially disqualifying activity. Therefore, this area was not discoverable, unless the court could find another ground to assert relevance. Reversed and remanded.

⬤ ANALYSIS

Discovery is allowed on issues that are admissible or will lead to admissible evidence. However, discovery may be denied even when the issue is relevant if it invades the right of privacy of the individual. In these instances, the court must weigh the judicial concept of fair play requiring disclosure of evidence relevant to a claim against the constitutional rights of the individual. Clearly, if the right being invaded is a fundamental right, then discovery will be denied, unless the government can demonstrate a compelling need.

Quicknotes

DISCOVERY Pretrial procedure during which one party makes certain information available to the other.

FUNDAMENTAL RIGHT A liberty that is either expressly or impliedly provided for in the United States Constitution, the deprivation or burdening of which is subject to a heightened standard of review.

RELEVANT EVIDENCE Evidence having any tendency to prove or disprove a disputed fact.

Silvestri v. General Motors Corp.

Injured motorist (P) v. Car company (D)

271 F.3d 583 (4th Cir. 2001).

NATURE OF CASE: Appeal of dismissal for spoliation of evidence.

FACT SUMMARY: Mark Silvestri (P) sued General Motors Corp. (D) after the airbag in the Monte Carlo he was driving failed to deploy when he hit a utility pole. Silvestri (P) failed to give General Motors notice of his claim before the vehicle was repaired. The district court dismissed the case for the spoliation of evidence.

RULE OF LAW

A party's duty to preserve material evidence extends to the period before litigation, when a party reasonably should know that the evidence may be relevant to anticipated litigation, and therefore the object of discovery.

FACTS: Mark Silvestri (P) sued General Motors Corp. (D) after the airbag in the Monte Carlo he was driving failed to deploy when he hit a utility pole, causing him injuries. While he was in the hospital, his parents retained an attorney, who retained two accident reconstructionists to examine the vehicle. They concluded that the airbag was defective, and told Silvestri's (P) attorney that he should let General Motors (D) see the vehicle. Neither Silvestri (P) nor his lawyer took steps to preserve the vehicle or to notify General Motors of the existence of the vehicle, until almost three years later when Silvestri (P) began this action. The district court dismissed the case for the spoliation of evidence.

ISSUE: Does a party's duty to preserve material evidence extend to the period before litigation, when a party reasonably should know that the evidence may be relevant to anticipated litigation, and therefore the object of discovery?

HOLDING AND DECISION: (Niemeyer, J.) Yes. A party's duty to preserve material evidence extends to the period before litigation, when a party reasonably should know that the evidence may be relevant to anticipated litigation, and therefore the object of discovery. Silvestri (P) had access to the vehicle, and the vehicle was preserved in its post-accident condition for two to three months, or more, during which time Silvestri (P) or his lawyer and his experts recognized not only that they would be suing General Motors (D) but also that General Motors (D) should be given the opportunity to inspect the vehicle. Silvestri (P) therefore breached his duty not to spoliate evidence. And while dismissal is severe and constitutes the ultimate sanction for spoliation, it is necessary here because the prejudice to General Motors (D) is extraordinary, denying it the ability to adequately defend its case. Affirmed.

ANALYSIS

Note that it was the particular facts of the case that supported the "ultimate sanction" for spoliation in this case. The court determined that General Motors could not adequately defend its case without being given the opportunity to examine the car, the object of the litigation in this products liability case.

Quicknotes

DISCOVERY Pretrial procedure during which one party makes certain information available to the other.

EVIDENCE Any type of proof offered at a trial in order to prove or disprove a disputed fact or issue.

Hickman v. Taylor

Representative of deceased (P) v. Tug owner (D)

329 U.S. 495 (1947).

NATURE OF CASE: Action for damages for wrongful death.

FACT SUMMARY: Five crew members drowned when a tug sank. In anticipation of litigation, the attorney for Taylor (D), the tug owner, interviewed the survivors. Hickman (P), as representative of one of the deceased, brought this action and tried by means of discovery to obtain copies of the statements Taylor's (D) attorney obtained from the survivors.

🏛 RULE OF LAW
Material obtained by counsel in preparation for litigation is the work product of the lawyer, and while such material is not protected by the attorney-client privilege, it is not discoverable on mere demand without a showing of necessity or justification.

FACTS: Five of nine crew members drowned when a tug sank. A public hearing was held at which the four survivors were examined. Their testimony was recorded and was made available to all interested parties. A short time later, the attorney for Taylor (D), the tug owner, interviewed the survivors, in preparation for possible litigation. He also interviewed other persons believed to have information on the accident. Ultimately, claims were brought by representatives of all five of the deceased. Four were settled. Hickman (P), the fifth claimant, brought this action. He filed interrogatories asking for any statements taken from crew members as well as any oral or written statements, records, reports, or other memoranda made concerning any matter relative to the towing operation, the tug's sinking, the salvaging and repair of the tug, and the death of the deceased. Taylor (D) refused to summarize or set forth the material on the ground that it was protected by the attorney-client privilege.

ISSUE: Does a party seeking to discover material obtained by an adverse party's counsel in preparation for possible litigation have a burden to show a justification for such production?

HOLDING AND DECISION: (Murphy, J.) Yes. The deposition-discovery rules are to be accorded a broad and liberal treatment, since mutual knowledge of all the relevant facts gathered by both parties is essential to proper litigation. But discovery does have ultimate and necessary boundaries. Limitations arise upon a showing of bad faith or harassment or when the inquiry seeks material that is irrelevant or privileged. In this case, the material sought by Hickman (P) is not protected by the attorney-client privilege. However, such material as that sought here does constitute the work product of the lawyer. The general policy against invading the privacy of an attorney in performing his various duties is so well recognized and so essential to the orderly working of our legal system that the party seeking work-product material has a burden to show reasons to justify such production. Interviews, statements, memoranda, correspondence, briefs, mental impressions, etc., obtained in the course of preparation for possible or anticipated litigation fall within the work product. Such material is not free from discovery in all cases. Where relevant and nonprivileged facts remain hidden in an attorney's file and where production of those facts is essential to the preparation of one's case, discovery may be had. But there must be a showing of necessity and justification. In this case, Hickman (P) seeks discovery of oral and written statements of witnesses whose identity is well known and whose availability to Hickman (P) appears unimpaired. Here no attempt was made to show why it was necessary that Taylor's (D) attorney produce the material. No reasons were given to justify this invasion of the attorney's privacy. Hickman's (P) counsel admitted that he wanted the statements only to help him prepare for trial. That is insufficient to warrant an exception to the policy of protecting the privacy of an attorney's professional activities.

CONCURRENCE: (Jackson, J.) A common law trial is and always should be an adversary proceeding. Discovery was hardly intended to enable a learned profession to perform its functions either without wits or on wits borrowed from the adversary. I can conceive of no practice more demoralizing to the bar than to require a lawyer to write out and deliver to the adversary an account of what witnesses have told him.

▶ ANALYSIS

The *Hickman* decision left open a number of questions as to the scope of the work product doctrine and the showing needed to discover work product material. In 1970, Fed. R. Civ. P. 26(b)(3) was added to deal with the discovery of work product. It provides that documents and tangible things that were prepared in anticipation of litigation or for trial are discoverable only upon a showing that the party seeking such materials has substantial need of them and that he is unable without

Continued on next page.

undue hardship to obtain the substantial equivalent of the materials by other means. The rule states that mental impressions, conclusions, opinions, or legal theories of an attorney or other representative of a party are to be protected against disclosure.

■≡■

Quicknotes

ATTORNEY-CLIENT PRIVILEGE A doctrine precluding the admission into evidence of confidential communications between an attorney and his client made in the course of obtaining professional assistance.

ATTORNEY WORK-PRODUCT DOCTRINE A doctrine excluding from discovery work performed by an attorney in preparation for litigation.

DEPOSITION A pretrial discovery procedure whereby oral or written questions are asked by one party of a witness of the opposing party under oath in preparation for litigation.

DISCOVERY Pretrial procedure during which one party makes certain information available to the other.

■≡■

Thompson v. The Haskell Co.

Sexually harassed employee (P) v. Employer (D)

65 F. Empl. Prac. Cas. (BNA) 1088 (M.D. Fla. 1994).

NATURE OF CASE: Motion for protective order in sexual-harassment suit.

FACT SUMMARY: Thompson (P) sought to protect her psychologist's report from discovery.

🏛 RULE OF LAW
Under exceptional circumstances, if it is impractical for the party seeking discovery to obtain facts or opinions on the same subject by other means, a party may, by interrogatories or by deposition, discover information by an expert who has been retained or specially employed by another party in anticipation of litigation and who is not to be called as a witness.

FACTS: Thompson (P) sued The Haskell Co. (D) and Zona (D), a supervisor of The Haskell Co. (D), alleging sexual harassment and that her employment with The Haskell Co. (D) was terminated when she refused to acquiesce to Zona's (D) advances. Thompson's (P) former counsel employed Dr. Lucas, a psychologist, to perform a diagnostic review and personality profile ten days after Thompson (P) was terminated. Thompson (P) sought an order to protect the psychological records possessed by Dr. Lucas.

ISSUE: May a party, under exceptional circumstances, obtain discovery of information by an opposing party's expert who has been retained or employed by a party in anticipation of litigation and who is not to be called as a witness?

HOLDING AND DECISION: (Snyder, J.) Yes. Under exceptional circumstances, a party may obtain discovery of information by an opposing party's expert who has been retained or employed by a party in anticipation of litigation and who is not to be called as a witness. Here, Dr. Lucas's report was made ten days after Thompson (P) was terminated and is the only evidence available which is probative of Thompson's (P) emotional state at that time. Motion denied.

▌ANALYSIS

Thompson (P) did not file her complaint until several months after she was terminated. Thus, opposing counsel had no opportunity to obtain psychological information from Thompson (P) shortly after her termination that would be probative of her emotional state during that time. This factor provided the exceptional circumstance in the present case.

Quicknotes

DEPOSITION A pretrial discovery procedure whereby oral or written questions are asked by one party of a witness of the opposing party under oath in preparation for litigation.

DISCOVERY Pretrial procedure during which one party makes certain information available to the other.

EXPERT WITNESS A witness providing testimony at trial who is specially qualified regarding the particular subject matter involved.

INTERROGATORY A method of pretrial discovery in which written questions are provided by one party to another who must respond in writing under oath.

■══■

Chiquita International Ltd. v. M/V Bolero Reefer

Shipper (P) v. Cargo carrier (D)

1994 U.S. Dist. LEXIS 5820 (S.D.N.Y. 1994).

NATURE OF CASE: Motion to compel discovery.

FACT SUMMARY: International Reefer Ltd. (D), a carrier, sought to compel discovery of a marine surveyor who had evaluated its loading cranes and side ports.

RULE OF LAW
A nontestifying expert is immune from discovery unless exceptional circumstances apply.

FACTS: Shipper Chiquita International Ltd. (Chiquita) (P) sued International Reefer Services, S.A. (D), a cargo carrier, for cargo loss and damage. Chiquita (P) alleged that loading cranes and side ports on International Reefer's (D) carrier failed to function properly, which prevented the carrier from shipping the full load of Chiquita (P) bananas to Germany and unloading them before spoilage in accord with their contract. International Reefer (D) requested an order compelling discovery from Winer, a marine surveyor Chiquita (P) had employed to inspect the carrier upon arrival in Germany. International Reefer (D) asserted that Winer was a fact witness rather than an expert and that even if Winer were a nontestifying expert, exceptional circumstances existed to compel discovery. Chiquita (P) objected.

ISSUE: May a nontestifying expert be subject to discovery?

HOLDING AND DECISION: (Francis, J.) No. A nontestifying expert may not be subject to discovery unless exceptional circumstances apply. A fact witness is a witness whose information was obtained in the normal course of business; however, a nontestifying expert is a person hired to make an evaluation in connection with expected litigation. Winer was hired by Chiquita (P) to make an observation in anticipation of litigation; thus, he is a nontestifying expert. Because International Reefer (D) could have employed its own expert to examine its carrier, and Chiquita (P) did not prevent another expert from being retained, no exceptional circumstances apply here. Application for Winer's deposition is denied.

▶ ANALYSIS

It is often not clear whether a person is a fact witness or nontestifying expert; thus, this is a favorite topic for law school examinations. Another favorite topic is determining if exceptional circumstances apply that would warrant compelling discovery from a nontestifying expert.

Quicknotes

DEPOSITION A pretrial discovery procedure whereby oral or written questions are asked by one party of a witness of the opposing party under oath in preparation for litigation.

DISCOVERY Pretrial procedure during which one party makes certain information available to the other.

EXPERT WITNESS A witness providing testimony at trial who is specially qualified regarding the particular subject matter involved.

■■■

Stalnaker v. Kmart Corp.

Employee (P) v. Employer (D)

71 Fair Empl. Prac. Cas. (BNA) 705 (D. Kan. 1996).

NATURE OF CASE: Motion for protective order in sexual-harassment action.

FACT SUMMARY: Stalnaker (P) sought to discover information about her coworkers' voluntary romantic conduct for use in her sexual-harassment suit.

🏛 RULE OF LAW
Protective orders are appropriate to preclude discovery of irrelevant and private information.

FACTS: Stalnaker (P) brought a sexual-harassment suit against her employer, Kmart (D) and another employee, Graves (D). Stalnaker (P) alleged that Graves (D) created a hostile working environment and inappropriately touched her. As part of discovery, Stalnaker (P) sought to discover information concerning the voluntary romantic conduct of four other employees who were not parties to the action. Kmart (D) moved for a protective order against this discovery.

ISSUE: Are protective orders appropriate to preclude discovery of irrelevant and private information?

HOLDING AND DECISION: (Rushfelt, J.) Yes. Protective orders are appropriate to preclude discovery of irrelevant and private information. Fed. R. Civ. P 26 provides for broad and liberal discovery, including information that may not be admissible at trial. However, courts have the discretion to enter a protective order against discovery in order to protect a person from annoyance, embarrassment, oppression or undue burden. The party seeking the protective order has the burden to show good cause. In the present case, Fed. R. Evid. 412 should also be considered. Rule 412(a) aims to safeguard victims from the invasion of privacy associated with the public disclosure of intimate sexual details. It is not controlling with respect to persons who are not the victims of alleged misconduct, so it does not directly apply to Kmart's (D) sought protective order. Thus, the best grounds for entering a protective order are that there is no relationship between voluntary romantic and sexual activities of nonparty witnesses and the allegations of Stalnaker (P). The only possibly relevant information is Graves's (D) relationship with the nonparty witnesses. This might show that he encouraged or solicited that type of conduct in the workplace. Accordingly, the protective order is granted except to the limited question of whether the nonparty witnesses had romantic contact with Graves (D).

▶ ANALYSIS

Stalnaker (P) had already conceded that the information she sought should not be disseminated outside the parties and their attorneys. The court allowed a small part of the discovery sought, but ordered that this could not be disclosed to anyone outside the case. In this sense, Fed. R. Evid. 412 played a small role in the decision.

■≡■

Quicknotes

PROTECTIVE ORDER Court order protecting a party against potential abusive treatment through use of the legal process.

■≡■

Zubulake v. UBS Warburg LLP

Former employee (P) v. Former employer (D)

220 F.R.D. 212 (S.D.N.Y. 2003).

NATURE OF CASE: Motion to compel discovery of electronic data at the producing party's expense.

FACT SUMMARY: In litigation for gender discrimination and illegal retaliation, Laura Zubulake (P) requested all internal e-mails about her from her former employer, UBS Warburg LLP (UBS) (D). UBS (D) produced some e-mails, but clearly failed to produce perhaps several hundred e-mails in response to Zubulake's (P) request. Zubulake (P) moved for an order compelling production, with UBS (D) to bear the cost of production.

🏛 **RULE OF LAW**
A company with potentially extensive relevant e-mail records should be ordered to produce those records at its own expense if they are relatively accessible and inexpensive to produce.

FACTS: Zubulake (P) filed suit against her former employer, UBS Warburg LLP (UBS) (D), for alleged gender discrimination and illegal retaliation under federal, state, and local law. Her case required access to UBS's (D) e-mail records, many of which existed only on archiving media that were not readily accessible; Zubulake's (P) production request sought all electronic documents about her. Early disputes over this request resulted in an agreement under which UBS (D) unconditionally agreed to produce all e-mails from the e-mail accounts of five UBS (D) employees identified by Zubulake (P). UBS (D) failed to produce any additional e-mails beyond the 100 pages of e-mails it had already produced before the agreement. In failing to produce more e-mails, though, UBS (D), citing excessive expense (estimated at $300,000 and eventually $175,000), did not search its electronic archives for more e-mails. Zubulake (P) objected to UBS's (D) failure to produce more e-mails because she had produced about 450 pages of her own e-mails from her time at UBS (D), and UBS (D) thus clearly had deleted, or tried to delete, several responsive e-mails involving Zubulake from its e-mail system. Given the company's heavy reliance on e-mail communications, UBS (D) regularly preserved its e-mails on backup tapes and optical disks. With the strong likelihood that many relevant electronic documents were actually available, Zubulake (P) filed a motion to compel production of UBS's e-mail records, with UBS (D) to bear the costs of producing its e-mail records.

ISSUE: Should a company with potentially extensive relevant e-mail records be ordered to produce those records at its own expense if they are relatively accessible and inexpensive to produce?

HOLDING AND DECISION: (Scheindlin, J.) Yes. A company with potentially extensive relevant e-mail records should be ordered to produce those records at its own expense if they are relatively accessible and inexpensive to produce. The Federal Rules create a rebuttable presumption that the producing party should bear the cost of production; if production requests place an undue burden or expense on the producing party, the Rules permit conditioning an order compelling production on the requesting party's payment of the costs of production. Under the influential analysis of *Rowe Entertainment, Inc. v. William Morris Agency, Inc.*, 205 F.R.D. 421, 429 (S.D.N.Y. 2002), deciding whether to shift discovery costs to the requesting party requires review of eight factors: (1) how specific the requests are, (2) the likelihood that the requests will succeed, (3) how available the requested information is from other sources, (4) why the producing party keeps the requested information, (5) how the requested information benefits each party, (6) how much the production costs, (7) each party's ability and incentive to control costs of disclosing the information, (8) and each party's resources. In this case, UBS (D) clearly must make additional disclosures of its internal e-mails to Zubulake (P). Two categories of the company's e-mail records are both readily accessible and inexpensive to access: the active e-mail files and the e-mails saved on optical disks. UBS (D) thus will bear the expense of disclosing such files, as the Federal Rules typically require. The third category of UBS's (D) e-mail records, however, those on backup tapes, are not readily accessible and will be expensive to produce. Therefore, at its own expense, UBS (D) shall produce all relevant e-mails from its optical disks and active e-mail files; and UBS (D) shall produce, also at its own expense, all relevant e-mails from any five backup tapes of Zubulake's (P) choice, with the issue of cost-shifting for production of the backup tapes reserved for decision until UBS (D) knows its specific costs for that production. Motions for instruction and reconsideration denied. Motion granting costs for additional depositions granted.

Continued on next page.

▶ *ANALYSIS*

As so often happens in litigation both sides "won," to some extent, in *Zubulake*. Zubulake (P) prevailed on the substantive issues supporting the order compelling production of UBS's (D) e-mail records. UBS (D) also won an important victory here, though, with the trial judge reserving the cost-shifting analysis until the judge can assess the actual reasonable costs that UBS (D) incurs for producing the electronic documents. Although Zubulake (P) has an excellent chance of gaining "damages [that] may be substantial" from her suit, any damages she recovers will now also likely cost her a substantial amount to review UBS's (D) e-mail records.

■══■

Quicknotes

DAMAGES Monetary compensation that may be awarded by the court to a party who has sustained injury or loss to his person, property or rights due to another party's unlawful act, omission or negligence.

DISCOVERY Pretrial procedure during which one party makes certain information available to the other.

■══■

Resolution Without Trial

Quick Reference Rules of Law

Peralta v. Heights Medical Center

Employer/guarantor (P) v. Hospital (D)

485 U.S. 80 (1988).

NATURE OF CASE: Review of summary judgment dismissing bill of review.

FACT SUMMARY: A trial court refused to set aside a default entered after improper service when Peralta (D) could not show a meritorious defense to the action.

> ## RULE OF LAW
> A meritorious defense is not required to set aside a default entered after improper service.

FACTS: Heights Medical Center, Inc. (Heights Medical) (D) sued Peralta (P) on a guarantee to pay medical expenses on an employee of Peralta (P). Peralta (P) was improperly served. Heights Medical (D) nonetheless entered a default on Peralta's (P) failure to respond and a judgment lien was placed on certain real estate belonging to Peralta (P). The property was sold at a marshal's sale at a large discount. Peralta (P), upon discovering the sale, filed an action to void the sale and have the default set aside, as the service was invalid. The trial court granted summary judgment, dismissing the action, holding that Peralta (P) had to show meritorious defense to the underlying action, which he could not do. The Texas Court of Appeals affirmed. The Supreme Court accepted review.

ISSUE: Is a meritorious defense required to set aside a default entered after improper service?

HOLDING AND DECISION: (White, J.) No. A meritorious defense is not required to set aside a default entered after improper service. It is basic to due process before a judgment can be entered against a person, he must be given legally sufficient notice of the action and be given an opportunity to defend. It is no defense to a due process claim that the defendant would have lost on the merits. There are avenues that can be employed by a litigant in a losing posture, such as settling or impleading other parties. For the defendant to do this, he must have notice of the suit. Here, Peralta (P) was not given such notice, and due process therefore demands that the default be set aside. Reversed.

▶ ANALYSIS

Various avenues exist to challenge a default. The most direct manner is to move for relief in the same action in which the default is entered. However, most states place time limitations on this, as did Texas in this instance. This forced Peralta (P) to file a bill of review, a collateral proceeding.

Quicknotes

DEFAULT JUDGMENT A judgment entered against a defendant due to his failure to appear in a court or defend himself against the allegations of the opposing party.

SERVICE OF PROCESS The communication of reasonable notice of a court proceeding to a defendant in order to provide him with an opportunity to be heard.

SHERIFF'S SALE A sale of property by a sheriff pursuant to a judgment.

Matsushita Elec. Industrial Co. v. Epstein

Merging companies (D) v. Class of stockholders (P)

516 U.S. 367 (1996).

NATURE OF CASE: Appeal from dismissal of a class action for breach of fiduciary duty.

FACT SUMMARY: A class-action suit against Matsushita Elec. Industrial Co. (Matsushita) (D) was settled in Delaware and purported to release pending federal claims against Matsushita (D) in a separate action.

RULE OF LAW
Settlement of class-action suits in state court may release exclusively federal claims pending in federal court.

FACTS: In 1990, Matsushita Elec. Industrial Co. (Matsushita) (D) made a tender offer for MCA (D), a Delaware corporation, and eventually acquired MCA (D). A class action was filed in Delaware state court against the directors of MCA (D) for failing to maximize shareholder value. While this action was pending, another suit was filed in federal court in California for violations of the Williams Act. The Securities Exchange Act of 1934 gives federal courts exclusive jurisdiction over these claims. The federal court failed to certify the class, and the decision was appealed. While the federal case was under appeal, the parties to the Delaware suit negotiated a settlement that included a global release of all claims arising out of the acquisition. The chancery court approved this settlement if the Delaware Supreme Court affirmed. Matsushita (D) invoked this settlement to the Ninth Circuit, which was considering the federal suit, but the Ninth Circuit held that the settlement could not preclude claims that were exclusively federal. The U.S. Supreme Court granted certiorari to clear up the issue.

ISSUE: May the settlement of class-action suits in state court release exclusively federal claims pending in federal court?

HOLDING AND DECISION: (Thomas, J.) Yes. Settlement of class-action suits in state court may release exclusively federal claims pending in federal court. The Full Faith and Credit Act mandates that the judicial proceedings of any state shall have the same full faith and credit in every United States court. Federal courts must accept the rules chosen by the state from which the judgment was taken in determining the effect of the state judgment. Judgments entered in class actions, like all other actions, are presumptively entitled to full faith and credit. Delaware courts have decided that a global release of claims precludes future federal court litigations of released claims. Thus, Delaware courts would give preclusive effect to a settlement, notwithstanding their lack of jurisdiction over federal claims. The only situation in which federal claims could not be released is if the state court did not have subject matter jurisdiction over the case. In the present case, the Delaware courts had proper jurisdiction over the action and understood that the global release approved in the settlement would release the federal claims. Therefore, the release must be given full effect. Reversed and remanded.

ANALYSIS

The majority noted that it is an extremely rare occasion when a federal statute expressly or impliedly repeals the Full Faith and Credit Act. For an implicit repeal, the two statutes must cause an irreconcilable conflict. This has happened in only a few instances in history.

■■■

Quicknotes

CLASS ACTION A suit commenced by a representative on behalf of an ascertainable group that is too large to appear in court, who shares a commonality of interests and who will benefit from a successful result.

FULL FAITH AND CREDIT ACT As provided in the U.S. Constitution, Article IV, any state judicial proceedings shall have such faith and credit given them in every court in the United States as they would in their own state.

■■■

Kalinauskas v. Wong

Former employee (P) v. Employer (D)

151 F.R.D. 363 (D. Nev. 1993).

NATURE OF CASE: Motion for protective order.

FACT SUMMARY: Caesars Palace Hotel & Casino (D) sought to enforce a confidential settlement agreement with a former employee.

RULE OF LAW
A protective order or confidentiality agreement can be modified to place private litigants in a position they would otherwise reach only after repetition of another's discovery if modification would not tangibly prejudice substantial rights of the party opposing modification.

FACTS: Kalinauskas (P) sued Desert Palace, Inc. (D), doing business as Caesars (D), for sexual discrimination. She sought to depose Thomas, a former Caesars (D) employee, who had sued Caesars (D) for sexual harassment the previous year. Thomas had settled her claim with Caesars (D) and agreed to a confidential settlement agreement that stated in part that Thomas "shall not discuss any aspect of plaintiff's employment at Caesars other than to state the dates of her employment and her job title." Caesars (D) sought a protective order to enforce the confidential settlement agreement and to bar Thomas's deposition. Kalinauskas (P) opposed the order.

ISSUE: May a protective order or confidentiality agreement be modified to place private litigants in a position they would otherwise reach only after repetition of another's discovery if modification would not tangibly prejudice substantial rights of the party opposing modification?

HOLDING AND DECISION: (Johnston, J.) Yes. A protective order or confidentiality agreement can be modified to place private litigants in a position they would otherwise reach only after repetition of another's discovery if modification would not tangibly prejudice substantial rights of the party opposing modification. Here, Kalinauskas's (P) claim duplicates Thomas's claim both factually and legally. Thus, to force Kalinauskas (P) to duplicate all of Thomas's work would be wasteful. The protective order is granted to the extent that during the deposition of Thomas no information regarding the settlement itself may be disclosed and is denied as to all other aspects. Protective order granted in part and denied in part.

▶ ANALYSIS

The party seeking to enforce a protective order against a party seeking discovery information has the burden of showing that allowing modification of the order would substantially prejudice that party's rights. As the case above indicates, this burden could be met by showing that an applicable privilege applies to the information sought to be disclosed or that the party would suffer potential injury or prejudice if the information were to be disclosed.

■■■

Quicknotes

DISCOVERY Pretrial procedure during which one party makes certain information available to the other.

PROTECTIVE ORDER Court order protecting a party against potential abusive treatment through use of the legal process.

■■■

Ferguson v. Countrywide Credit Industries, Inc.

Employee (P) v. Employer (D)

298 F.3d 778 (9th Cir. 2002).

NATURE OF CASE: Appeal of denial of motion to compel arbitration.

FACT SUMMARY: Misty Ferguson (P) sued Countrywide Credit Industries Inc. (Countrywide) (D) and her supervisor for sexual harassment, retaliation, and hostile work environment, and Countrywide (D) moved to compel the matter to arbitration. The district court denied Countrywide's (D) motion.

🏛 RULE OF LAW

An arbitration agreement is unconscionable, and therefore unenforceable, where it is a prerequisite to employment, job applicants are not permitted to modify the terms of the agreement, and the terms are one sided, favoring the employer.

FACTS: Misty Ferguson (P) sued Countrywide Credit Industries Inc. (Countrywide) and her supervisor for sexual harassment, retaliation, and hostile work environment. Countrywide (D) moved to compel the matter to arbitration pursuant to an employment contract, which required Ferguson (P) to arbitrate her claims. The district court refused to compel arbitration, holding that the arbitration agreement was unenforceable under the doctrine of unconscionability.

ISSUE: Is an arbitration agreement unconscionable, and therefore unenforceable, where it is a prerequisite to employment, job applicants are not permitted to modify the terms of the agreement, and the terms are one-sided, favoring the employer?

HOLDING AND DECISION: (Pregerson, J.) Yes. An arbitration agreement is unconscionable, and therefore unenforceable, where it is a prerequisite to employment, job applicants are not permitted to modify the terms of the agreement, and the terms are one sided, favoring the employer. A contract is unenforceable under the doctrine of unconscionability where there is both procedural and substantive unconscionability. Procedural unconscionability exists here, because the bargaining power of each party is unequal: Ferguson (P) had to sign the agreement, and accept all of its terms, or not get the job applied for. Substantive unconscionability also exists here, because the terms of the agreement are one sided: The agreement compels arbitration of Ferguson's (P) claims, but exempts from arbitration the claims of Countrywide (D). In addition, Countrywide's (D) agreement requires Ferguson (P) to pay filing fees for arbitration, which could exceed the costs of litigation.

Finally, the agreement includes limitations on the number of subjects Ferguson (P) could raise during discovery. While the discovery provision in the arbitration agreement is not so one sided it alone could be called unconscionable, in the context of an arbitration agreement that overall favors Countrywide (D), it too is unconscionable. Affirmed.

▶ ANALYSIS

The outcome of this case, decided in California, stands in direct contrast to *Carter v. Countrywide Credit Industries, Inc.*, 362 F.3d 294 (5th Cir. 2004), also set forth in your casebook. *Carter* was decided in Texas, which is generally much more lenient on arbitration agreements.

■══■

Quicknotes

SUBSTANTIVE UNCONSCIONABILITY Rule of law whereby a court may excuse performance of a contract, or of a particular contract term, if it determines that such terms are unduly oppressive or unfair to one party to the contract and violate the subordinate party's reasonable expectations.

■══■

AT&T Mobility LLC v. Concepción

Mobile phone company (D) v. Customers (P)

_____ U.S. _____, 131 S. Ct. 1740 (2011).

NATURE OF CASE: Grant of petition for certiorari.

FACT SUMMARY: Vincent and Liza Concepción (P) and members of a class (P) who had entered into an agreement for the sale and servicing of cellular telephones with AT&T Mobility LCC (AT&T) (D) filed suit against AT&T (D) for deceptive advertising. AT&T (D) moved to compel arbitration under the contract. The district court denied AT&T's (D) motion, and the U.S. Court of Appeals for the Ninth Circuit affirmed. AT&T (D) appealed to the U.S. Supreme Court.

> ## 🏛 RULE OF LAW
> The Federal Arbitration Act of 1925 preempts state law that prohibits contracts disallowing class action arbitration.

FACTS: Vincent and Liza Concepción (P) entered into an agreement for the sale and servicing of cellular telephones with AT&T Mobility LCC (AT&T) (D). They filed suit against AT&T (D) when they discovered they had to pay tax on the phones that were advertised by the company as being free, and the suit grew into a class action. The contract with AT&T (D) required all claims to be resolved through arbitration, and provided that the arbitration could not move forward as a class. AT&T (D) moved to compel arbitration under the contract, and the Concepcións (P) opposed the motion, arguing that the arbitration agreement was unconscionable and unlawfully exculpatory under California law because it disallowed class-wide procedures. The district court denied AT&T's (D) motion, approving of the arbitration agreement generally, but finding that the anti-class arbitration provision was unconscionable because AT&T (D) had not shown that bilateral arbitration adequately substituted for the deterrent effects of class actions. AT&T (D) appealed, arguing that the Federal Arbitration Act of 1925 (FAA) preempts the state law. The U.S. Court of Appeals for the Ninth Circuit affirmed, finding the provision unconscionable under California law under _Discover Bank v. Superior Court_, 36 Cal. 4th 148 (2005), and holding that _Discover Bank_ rule was not preempted by the FAA because that rule was simply a refinement of the unconscionability analysis applicable to contracts generally in California. AT&T (D) appealed to the U.S. Supreme Court.

ISSUE: Does the Federal Arbitration Act of 1925 preempt state law that prohibits contracts disallowing class action arbitration?

HOLDING AND DECISION: (Scalia, J.) No. The Federal Arbitration Act of 1925 preempts state law that prohibits contracts disallowing class action arbitration. The _Discover Bank_ rule interferes with a fundamental attribute of arbitration and creates a scheme inconsistent with the FAA by requiring the availability of class arbitration, despite the parties' agreement to the contrary. The argument that the _Discover Bank_ rule is limited to adhesion contracts is unpersuasive, because in fact, nearly all consumer contracts are adhesion contracts to some degree. The states are free to take steps to address concerns related to adhesion contracts, but such steps cannot conflict with the FAA or frustrate its purpose to ensure that arbitration agreements are enforced according to their terms. Class arbitration, to the extent it is manufactured by _Discover Bank_ rather than consensual, is inconsistent with the FAA. If class arbitration is imposed, the changes to the process are fundamental. Class arbitration takes away the primary advantage of arbitration—informality—and makes the process slower, more costly and, most likely, more procedurally formal. Class arbitration also greatly increases the risks to AT&T (D) because of the possibility of much greater losses in a class arbitration proceeding that does not have the same review and appeal procedures as court litigation. Thus, AT&T (D) will be pressured into settling questionable claims. The dissent's argument that class proceedings are necessary to prosecute small-dollar claims that might otherwise slip through the legal system is unpersuasive. States cannot require a procedure that is inconsistent with the FAA, even if it is desirable for unrelated reasons. Further, it is unlikely that the claim at issue will go unresolved if it cannot be brought as part of a class because the Concepcións (P) are better off under their arbitration agreement with AT&T than as participants in a class action. Reversed and remanded.

DISSENT: (Breyer, J.) California contemplates circumstances in which class action waivers in any contract are unenforceable. It is not a blanket policy against class action waivers in the consumer context, but a more general unconscionability principle. That law is consistent with the Federal Arbitration Act's language and objective. It applies equally to class action litigation waivers in contracts without arbitration agreements, and to class arbitration waivers. It falls within the scope of the Act's exception permitting courts to refuse to enforce arbitration agreements on grounds that exist for the revocation of any contract.

Continued on next page.

▶ *ANALYSIS*

The arbitration agreement in this decision was considered by all courts to be fair to all parties. The decision leaves open the possibility that a less consumer-friendly agreement may not be looked upon as favorably by the Court, and a one-sided arbitration agreement may be susceptible to an unconscionability argument on grounds separate and apart from whether it contains a class action waiver. Finally, the decision does not address the enforceability of class action waivers in agreements providing for resolution of disputes through litigation, as opposed to arbitration.

■══■

Quicknotes

ADHESION CONTRACT A contract that is not negotiated and is usually prepared by the dominant party on a "take it or leave it" basis.

ARBITRATION CLAUSE Provision contained in a contract pursuant to which both parties agree that any disputes arising thereunder will be resolved through arbitration.

CLASS ACTION A suit commenced by a representative on behalf of an ascertainable group that is too large to appear in court, who shares a commonality of interests and who will benefit from a successful result.

UNCONSCIONABILITY A situation in which a contract, or a particular contract term, is unenforceable if the court determines that such terms are unduly oppressive or unfair to one party to the contract.

■══■

Ferguson v. Writers Guild of America, West

Screenwriter (P) v. Professional organization (D)

Cal. Ct. App., 226 Cal. App. 3d 1382 (1991).

NATURE OF CASE: Appeal of dismissal of action to set aside arbitration decision.

FACT SUMMARY: After a Writers Guild (D) arbitration proceeding supported a Guild (D) determination that Ferguson (P) should get only a partial writing credit on a film, Ferguson (P) sued to set aside the arbitration proceeding.

RULE OF LAW
Judicial review of arbitration proceedings is limited to whether the parties agreed to arbitration, whether the arbitration procedures provide a fair opportunity to be heard, and whether the arbitrators exceeded their powers.

FACTS: A collective-bargaining agreement gave the Writers Guild (the Guild) (D) the power to make determinations on writing credits for films. The agreement also provided that disputes could not be taken to court. Instead, any dispute had to be submitted to arbitration by the Guild (D). Anonymous arbitrators were chosen through a specified procedure. Their decision could be appealed to the Guild's (D) policy review board only for deviation from Guild (D) policy or procedure, not for matters of substance. Board approval of a determination was final. The Guild (D) gave Ferguson (P) partial credit on a film. Ferguson (P) initiated arbitration proceedings to have himself declared the sole writer. Ferguson (P) lost his arbitration and appealed to the review board on the substance of the dispute. After the review board declared the determination of partial credit final, Ferguson (P) sued in state court, urging the court to make its own determination and award him sole writing credit. In the alternative, Ferguson (P) asked the court to vacate the arbitration decision based on certain procedural defects and to require the Guild (D) to make a new determination of the writing credits. The Guild (D) argued that the collective-bargaining agreement made disputes over writing credits nonjusticiable. The trial court dismissed Ferguson's (P) case, and he appealed.

ISSUE: Is judicial review of arbitration proceedings limited to whether the parties agreed to arbitration, whether the arbitration procedures provide a fair opportunity to be heard, and whether the arbitrators exceeded their powers?

HOLDING AND DECISION: (Klein, J.) Yes. Judicial review of arbitration proceedings is limited to whether the parties agreed to arbitration, whether the arbitration procedures provide a fair opportunity to be heard, and whether the arbitrators exceeded their powers. Courts accord considerable deference to the determination of arbitration review boards because of their expertise, which courts lack, in their specialized field. The Guild's (D) review board is such a body. Additionally, the principle of exhaustion of administrative remedies prevented Ferguson (P) from pursuing a judicial remedy for any alleged procedural defects in the Guild's (D) conduct of the arbitration and review, since he failed to raise them before the policy review board. Even if he had preserved the procedural defects issue, Ferguson's (P) claims were without merit. There was no material and prejudicial departure from the Guild's (D) procedures. Affirmed.

▶ ANALYSIS

The use of arbitration in place of judicial resolution has increased significantly in recent years. Parties often prefer arbitration because they can control the substantive and procedural rules that apply to their dispute, they can ensure having a fact finder with expertise in the area of the dispute, and they can save time and money as arbitration is often faster and cheaper. Moreover, while courts traditionally looked with disfavor on arbitration agreements, modern courts usually uphold arbitration agreements because they are a mechanism for reducing the increasingly heavy caseloads of civil courts.

■■■

Quicknotes

ADMINISTRATIVE REMEDIES Relief that is sought before an administrative body as opposed to a court.

ARBITRATION An agreement to have a dispute heard and decided by a neutral third party, rather than through legal proceedings.

■■■

Celotex Corp. v. Catrett

Asbestos product manufacturer (D) v. Wife of decedent (D)

477 U.S. 317 (1986).

NATURE OF CASE: Appeal from reversal of summary judgment denying damages for asbestos exposure.

FACT SUMMARY: In Catrett's (P) action against Celotex Corp. (D) for the death of her husband as a result of his exposure to asbestos manufactured by Celotex (D), Celotex (D) moved for summary judgment, contending that Catrett (P) had failed to identify, in answering interrogatories specifically requesting such information, any witnesses who could testify about the decedent's exposure to Celotex's (D) asbestos.

> ## 🏛 RULE OF LAW
> The plain language of Fed. R. Civ. P. 56(c) mandates the entry of summary judgment, after adequate time for discovery, against a party who fails to make a showing sufficient to establish the existence of an element essential to that party's case.

FACTS: Catrett (P) sued Celotex Corp. (D), alleging that the death of her husband resulted from his exposure to products containing asbestos manufactured by Celotex (D). At trial, Celotex (D) moved for summary judgment, contending that Catrett (P) had failed to identify, in answering interrogatories specifically requesting such information, any witnesses who could testify about the decedent's exposure to Celotex's (D) asbestos products. The district court granted Celotex's (D) motion because there was no showing that the decedent was exposed to Celotex's (D) product within the statutory period. Catrett (P) appealed.

ISSUE: Does the plain language of Fed. R. Civ. P. 56(c) mandate the entry of summary judgment, after adequate time for discovery, against a party who fails to make a showing sufficient to establish the existence of an element essential to that party's case?

HOLDING AND DECISION: (Rehnquist, J.) Yes. The plain language of Fed. R. Civ. P. 56(c) mandates the entry of summary judgment, after adequate time for discovery, against a party who fails to make a showing sufficient to establish the existence of an element essential to that party's case. In such a situation, there can be "no genuine issue as to any material fact," since a complete failure of proof concerning an essential element of the nonmoving party's case necessarily renders all other facts immaterial. Here, Catrett (P) failed to identify any witnesses who could testify about her husband's exposure to Celotex's (D) asbestos products. There was also no showing that the decedent was exposed to Celotex's

(D) product within the statutory period. Catrett's (P) failure to show sufficient evidence to establish essential elements of her case makes summary judgment proper. [Reversed and remanded.]

CONCURRENCE: (White, J.) If respondent Catrett (P) had named a witness to support her claim, summary judgment could not have been granted without Celotex (D) somehow showing that the named witness's testimony raised no genuine issue of material fact.

DISSENT: (Brennan, J.) The nonmoving party may defeat a motion for summary judgment that asserts that the nonmoving party has no evidence by calling the court's attention to the supporting evidence in the record that was overlooked by the moving party.

▶ ANALYSIS

Celotex is an important case in two ways. First, it integrates the burden of proof borne by the parties at trial with the corresponding burdens on a summary judgment motion. Second, it hints at a larger, more significant role for summary judgment in deciding cases.

■═▪

Quicknotes

MATERIAL FACT A fact without the existence of which a contract would not have been entered.

SUMMARY JUDGMENT Judgment rendered by a court in response to a motion by one of the parties, claiming that the lack of a question of material fact in respect to an issue warrants disposition of the issue without consideration by the jury.

■═▪

Bias v. Advantage International, Inc.

Estate of basketball player (P) v. Business affairs representative (D)

905 F.2d 1558 (D.C. Cir. 1990).

NATURE OF CASE: Appeal of the granting of a motion for summary judgment.

FACT SUMMARY: Basketball star Leonard Bias (P) died from a cocaine overdose. When his estate sued Bias's business manager, Advantage International, Inc. (D) for failure to procure insurance for Bias (P) as it had promised to do, Advantage International (D) argued that no insurer would have insured a cocaine user.

🏛 RULE OF LAW
Once a moving party has made a prima facie showing to support a motion for summary judgment, the motion will be granted unless the non-moving party establishes specific facts showing a genuine issue for trial.

FACTS: The estate of basketball star Leonard Bias (P) brought suit against Advantage International, Inc. (Advantage) (D) which was Bias's (P) management company, for failing to secure life insurance for Bias (P) as it had promised to do. Bias (P) died from a cocaine overdose without the $1-million dollar life insurance policy that Advantage (D) had represented it had obtained. Advantage (D) moved for a summary judgment on the grounds that Bias's estate (P) did not suffer any damage from the failure of Advantage (D) to try to obtain life insurance for Bias (P) because even if they had attempted to obtain such a policy, they would not have been able to do so because of Bias's (P) known cocaine use. The district court agreed and granted the motion. Bias's estate (P) appealed.

ISSUE: Once a moving party has made a prima facie showing to support a motion for summary judgment, will the motion be granted unless the nonmoving party establishes specific facts showing a genuine issue for trial?

HOLDING AND DECISION: (Sentelle, J.) Yes. Once a moving party has made a prima facie showing to support a motion for summary judgment, the motion will be granted unless the nonmoving party establishes specific facts showing a genuine issue for trial. Here, Advantage (D) offered testimony of witnesses that clearly tended to show that Bias (P) was a cocaine user who would therefore have been uninsurable. Bias's estate (P) could have deposed these witnesses, or otherwise attempted to impeach their testimony, but failed to do so or even to try. Advantage (D) offered evidence that every insurance company inquires about prior drug use at some point in the application process. Bias's (P) evidence that some insurance companies existed in 1986 that did not inquire about prior drug use at certain particular stages in the application process does not undermine Advantage's (D) claim that at some point every insurance company did inquire about drug use, particularly where a jumbo policy was involved. Bias's estate (P) failed to name a single particular company or provide other evidence that a single company existed that would have issued a jumbo policy in 1986 without inquiring about an applicant's drug use. Because Bias's estate (P) failed to do more than show that there was "some metaphysical doubt as to the material facts," the district court properly concluded there was no genuine issue of material fact as to the insurability of a drug user. Affirmed.

▶ ANALYSIS

In *Bias*, the court noted that, rather than presenting any evidence or questioning any witnesses, to try to establish a case on non-cocaine use, Bias's estate (P) relied instead "on bare arguments and allegations" or on evidence that did not actually create a genuine issue for trial.

■■■

Quicknotes

MATERIAL FACT A fact without the existence of which a contract would not have been entered.

PRIMA FACIE An action in which the plaintiff introduces sufficient evidence to submit an issue to the judge or jury for determination.

SUMMARY JUDGMENT Judgment rendered by a court in response to a motion by one of the parties, claiming that the lack of a question of material fact in respect to an issue warrants disposition of the issue without consideration by the jury.

■■■

The Trier and the Trial

Quick Reference Rules of Law

McKey v. Fairbairn

Lessee of premises (P) v. Agent of lessor (D)

345 F.2d 739 (D.C. Cir. 1965).

NATURE OF CASE: Appeal from directed verdict and denial of motion to amend.

FACT SUMMARY: Mrs. Littlejohn (P), a tenant, slipped on water that had leaked through the roof of an apartment she rented. The trial court denied her motion to amend her complaint to include certain housing regulations after her counsel had orally agreed with the judge that negligence was her theory of recovery.

🏛 **RULE OF LAW**
A trial judge has broad discretion to exclude evidence supporting a theory of recovery not raised in the complaint.

FACTS: Mrs. Littlejohn (P) notified her landlord (D) of a leak in her apartment. Before repairs could be made, there was a heavy storm that resulted in her bedroom floor becoming wet from the leak in the roof. She twice mopped the room the following morning, but slipped and fell, sustaining certain injuries, when she returned to the bedroom. Mrs. Littlejohn (P) brought this action for damages, and at trial her counsel agreed with the trial judge's assessment of the case as one in negligence. Thereafter, Mrs. Littlejohn (P) moved to amend her complaint to include citations to certain allegedly relevant housing regulations, but the judge denied the motion and directed a verdict for the defendant. Plaintiff appealed.

ISSUE: Has a trial judge broad discretion to exclude evidence supporting a theory of recovery not raised in the complaint?

HOLDING AND DECISION: (Miller, J.) Yes. The questions on appeal are whether a directed verdict was error where evidence of a leak and a promise to repair it was offered and whether denial of the motion to amend to include housing regulations was error. The landlord did not have a duty to make the repairs alleged, so that a directed verdict on the issue of negligence liability was proper. Similarly, it was not error to refuse to allow McKey (P) to change her theory of recovery after the complaint was filed and answered. The trial court has broad discretion in the conduct of a trial, and this discretion was not abused in this case. A trial judge has broad discretion to exclude evidence supporting a theory of recovery not raised in the complaint, as a part of the conduct of the trial. Furthermore, since Mrs. Littlejohn entered a room where she knew there was a slippery wet spot, her own negligence contributed to the accident. Affirmed.

DISSENT: (Fahy, J.) Modification at trial is to be permitted to prevent manifest injustice. We have previously held that a landlord's duty to a tenant is covered in some part by the housing regulations. Modification should be permitted to allow McKey (P) to include the regulations in the complaint as a basis for recovery. Furthermore, the issue of contributory negligence should be initially considered and answered by the district court, not by this court on appeal.

▶ **ANALYSIS**

Under Fed. R. Civ. P. 15, amendment of pleadings after responsive pleadings are served is permitted only by leave of the court or written consent of the adverse party. A party may proceed to trial of issues not raised by pleadings and later amend the pleadings to conform to the evidence, but trial of those unraised issues must be by "express or implied consent of the parties." McKey (P) was outside of all these possibilities in this case.

Quicknotes

AMENDMENT TO PLEADING The modification of a pleading either as a matter of course upon motion to the court or by consent of both parties; a party is entitled to change its pleading once as a matter of course before a responsive pleading has been served.

DIRECTED VERDICT A verdict ordered by the court in a jury trial.

Reid v. San Pedro, Los Angeles & Salt Lake Railroad

Cattle owner (P) v. Railroad company (D)

Utah Sup. Ct., 39 Utah 617, 118 P. 1009 (1911).

NATURE OF CASE: Appeal from award of damages for negligence.

FACT SUMMARY: Reid (P) gave evidence showing that his cow was killed by San Pedro's (D) train either because San Pedro (D) neglected to repair a fence or because Reid (P) neglected to close a gate allowing the cow to get to the tracks.

RULE OF LAW
A plaintiff has the burden of presenting evidence that it is more probable than not that the defendant is liable in order to overcome a motion for a directed verdict for the defendant.

FACTS: Reid (P) was permitted by a landowner to graze certain cows on the landowner's property adjacent to train tracks. One of Reid's (P) cows found its way to the tracks and was struck by one of San Pedro's (D) trains and killed. The cow could have had access to the tracks either by going through a portion of the fence negligently left unrepaired by San Pedro (D) or by going through a gate that could have been negligently left open by Reid (P). There was no direct evidence as to which caused the accident. The jury brought in a verdict for Reid (P) upon which judgment was entered, and San Pedro (D) appealed.

ISSUE: Has a plaintiff the burden of presenting evidence that it is more probable than not that the defendant is liable in order to overcome a motion for a directed verdict for the defendant?

HOLDING AND DECISION: (McCarty, J.) Yes. The evidence presented in this case admits of two readings: one that San Pedro (D) was negligent and one that Reid (P) was negligent. Neither of these propositions is stronger than the other under the facts as known by the court and the jury. Where the undisputed evidence of the plaintiff, from which the existence of an essential fact is sought to be inferred, points with equal force to two things, one of which renders the defendant liable and the other not, the plaintiff must fail. Thus, a plaintiff has the burden of presenting evidence that it is more probable than not that the defendant is liable in order to overcome a motion for a directed verdict for the defendant. In this case, a verdict for San Pedro (D) should have been directed by the trial court. Reversed.

ANALYSIS

As the plaintiff is the master of his lawsuit, it is incumbent upon him to show that the defendant is responsible for whatever injury has been sustained. There must be more than a possibility of the defendant's liability, there must be a probability. Where it is equally possible that defendant is not responsible after the plaintiff has presented all of his evidence, the defendant is entitled to be dismissed from the lawsuit.

Quicknotes

BURDEN OF PERSUASION The duty of a party to introduce evidence to support a fact that is in dispute in an action.

DIRECTED VERDICT A verdict ordered by the court in a jury trial.

RELEVANT EVIDENCE Evidence having any tendency to prove or disprove a disputed fact.

Thompson v. Altheimer & Gray

Employee (P) v. Employer (D)

248 F.3d 621 (7th Cir. 2003).

NATURE OF CASE: Appeal from a defense jury verdict.

FACT SUMMARY: In an employment discrimination case, when the judge refused to strike a juror who stated that the fact she was a business owner "will definitely sway my judgment," the losing party argued that the judge erred in not striking the juror for cause.

> ## 🏛 RULE OF LAW
> A juror must be excused for cause if he holds a belief that would impede him giving due weight to the evidence and following the judge's instructions.

FACTS: Thompson (P) sued her employer, Altheimer & Gray (D), under Title VII of the Civil Rights Act, charging racial discrimination. During voir dire, the juror Leiter stated that she was currently the owner of a business and that, "I feel that as an employer and owner of a business that will definitely sway my judgment in this case." When asked by the judge whether she would be able to apply the law as instructed, she replied: "I think my experience will cloud my judgment, but I can do my best." The judge refused to grant Thompson's (P) attorney's request to strike Leiter for cause, and she remained on the jury. The case was tried, and the jury returned a verdict for Altheimer & Gray (D). Thompson (P) appealed, arguing that Leiter should have been struck for cause.

ISSUE: Must a juror be excused for cause if he holds a belief that would impede him giving due weight to the evidence and following the judge's instructions?

HOLDING AND DECISION: (Posner, J.) Yes. A juror must be excused for cause if he holds a belief that would impede him giving due weight to the evidence and following the judge's instructions. When the juror Leiter said she believed that some people sue their employer just because they have not received a promotion or a raise or some other benefit, she was not manifesting bias. She was simply expressing a prior belief. The question here was not whether Leiter's belief that some claims against employers are spurious was true or false (it was clearly true), but rather whether this belief would somehow impede her in giving due weight to the evidence and following the judge's instructions. In the instant case, that question was not adequately explored by the judge. Had the judge pushed Leiter and had she finally given unequivocal assurances that he deemed credible, his ruling could not be disturbed. But he failed

to do that. Furthermore, the denial of the right to an unbiased tribunal is one of those trial errors that is not excused by being shown to have been harmless. Reversed and remanded.

CONCURRENCE: (Wood, J.) It occasionally happens that not all peremptories are used. If there are left-over peremptories and the plaintiff has failed to convince the court to strike a certain juror for cause, it is at least imaginable that a decision not to use an available peremptory challenge on that juror might amount to a waiver of the right to assert that the juror should not have sat.

▶ ANALYSIS

In *Thompson*, the court stressed that it was pertinent to note that no issue of credibility was presented and no argument that the juror Leiter was not telling the truth. The issue was interpretive: did she manifest a degree of bias such that the judge abused his discretion in failing to strike her for cause.

Quicknotes

CHALLENGE FOR CAUSE Request for removal of a potential juror for a specified cause.

PEREMPTORY CHALLENGE The exclusion by a party to a lawsuit of a prospective juror without the need to specify a particular reason.

VOIR DIRE Examination of potential jurors on a case.

Caperton v. A.T. Massey Coal Co., Inc.

Business associate (P) v. Coal company (D)

556 U.S. 868 (2009).

NATURE OF CASE: Grant of writ of certiorari.

FACT SUMMARY: A judge in a state court who was elected to the bench after receiving $3 million from a donor refused to recuse himself when the court heard a case in which a verdict had been entered against that donor for $50 million. The plaintiff in the case objected that he did not receive a fair trial.

🏛 **RULE OF LAW**

It is unconstitutional for a state court judge to hear a case involving the financial interests of a major backer of the judge's election campaign.

FACTS: Hugh Caperton (P) brought suit against A.T. Massey Coal Co. (Massey) (D) for unlawfully cancelling a contract that bankrupted Caperton (P). A West Virginia jury returned a verdict that found Massey (D) and its affiliates liable for fraudulent misrepresentation, concealment, and tortious interference with existing contractual relations. The jury awarded Caperton (P) the sum of $50 million in compensatory and punitive damages. After the verdict but before the appeal, West Virginia held its 2004 judicial elections, and Don Blankenship, Massey's (D) chairman, chief executive officer, and president, supported Brent Benjamin in the election. He contributed the $1,000 statutory maximum to Benjamin's campaign committee, donated almost $2.5 million to a political organization that supported Benjamin, and just over $500,000 on independent expenditures to support Benjamin. Blankenship's $3 million in contributions were more than the total amount spent by all other Benjamin supporters and three times the amount spent by Benjamin's own committee. Benjamin won the election. Caperton (P) moved to disqualify now-Justice Benjamin under the Due Process Clause and the West Virginia Code of Judicial Conduct, based on the conflict caused by Blankenship's campaign involvement. Justice Benjamin denied the motion. Massey (D) then filed its petition for appeal to challenge the jury verdict. The court of appeals granted review and reversed the $50 million verdict against Massey (D). Justice Benjamin joined the majority opinion. Caperton (P) sought rehearing, and the parties moved for disqualification of three of the five justices who decided the appeal. Justice Benjamin again denied Caperton's (P) recusal motion. The court granted rehearing. Caperton (P) moved a third time for disqualification. Justice Benjamin again refused. A divided court again reversed the jury verdict.

ISSUE: Is it unconstitutional for a state court judge to hear a case involving the financial interests of a major backer of the judge's election campaign?

HOLDING AND DECISION: (Kennedy, J.) Yes. It is unconstitutional for a state court judge to hear a case involving the financial interests of a major backer of the judge's election campaign. The Due Process Clause requires a fair and impartial trial. The leading case on the subject is *Tumey v. Ohio*, 273 U.S. 510 (1927), where it was concluded that the Due Process Clause incorporated the common law rule that a judge must recuse himself when he has "a direct, personal, substantial, pecuniary interest" in a case. Under this rule, personal bias or prejudice "alone" would not be sufficient basis for imposing a constitutional requirement under the Due Process Clause. Over time, the Court has identified additional instances that, as an objective matter, require recusal. These are cases in which the probability of actual bias on the part of the judge is too high to be constitutionally tolerable. For example, where a judge has a financial interest in the outcome of a case, although the interest was less than what would have been considered personal or direct at common law, recusal is required. Similarly, in the criminal contempt context, where a judge had no pecuniary interest in the case but was challenged because of a conflict arising from his participation in an earlier proceeding, recusal was required. The problem in this case arises in the context of judicial elections, a framework not presented in the precedents. Not every campaign contribution by a litigant or attorney creates a probability of bias that requires a judge's recusal, but this is an exceptional case. Here, there is a serious risk of actual bias because a person with a personal stake in the case had a significant and disproportionate influence in placing the judge on the case by raising funds or directing the judge's election campaign when the case was pending or imminent. The inquiry centers on the contribution's relative size in comparison to the total amount of money contributed to the campaign, the total amount spent in the election, and the apparent effect such contribution had on the outcome of the election. Proving what ultimately drives the electorate to choose a particular candidate is a difficult endeavor, but Blankenship's campaign efforts had a significant and disproportionate influence in placing Justice Benjamin on the case. Blankenship contributed some $3 million to unseat the incumbent and replace him with Benjamin.

Continued on next page.

His contributions eclipsed the total amount spent by all other Benjamin supporters and exceeded by 300 percent the amount spent by Benjamin's campaign committee. In the end the people of West Virginia elected him, and they may have done so based on many reasons other than Blankenship's efforts, but whether Blankenship's campaign contributions were a necessary and sufficient cause of Benjamin's victory is not the proper inquiry. The risk that Blankenship's influence engendered actual bias is sufficiently substantial that it "must be forbidden if the guarantee of due process is to be adequately implemented." The temporal relationship between the campaign contributions, the justice's election, and the pendency of the case is also critical. It was reasonably foreseeable, when the campaign contributions were made, that the pending case would be before the newly elected justice. The $50 million adverse jury verdict had been entered before the election, and the Supreme Court of Appeals was the next step once the state trial court dealt with post-trial motions. So it became at once apparent that, absent recusal, Justice Benjamin would review a judgment that cost his biggest donor's company $50 million. Although there is no allegation of a quid pro quo agreement, the fact remains that Blankenship's extraordinary contributions were made at a time when he had a vested stake in the outcome. Just as no man is allowed to be a judge in his own cause, similar fears of bias may arise when—without the consent of the other parties—a man chooses the judge in his own cause. And applying this principle to the judicial election process, there was here a serious, objective risk of actual bias that required Justice Benjamin's recusal. Justice Benjamin did undertake an extensive search for actual bias. But that is just one step in the judicial process. Objective standards may also require recusal whether or not actual bias exists or can be proved. Blankenship's significant and disproportionate influence—coupled with the temporal relationship between the election and the pending case—"offer a possible temptation to the average . . . judge to . . . lead him not to hold the balance nice, clear and true." On these extreme facts the probability of actual bias rises to an unconstitutional level.

DISSENT: (Roberts, C.J.) The majority imprudently expanded the standard for which a judge need recuse himself by merely showing a "probability of bias." The "probability of bias" standard formulated by the majority was excessively vague and discretionary. It fails to provide clear, workable guidance for future cases. At the most basic level, it is unclear whether the new probability of bias standard is somehow limited to financial support in judicial elections, or applies to judicial recusal questions more generally. Forty questions are unanswered by the majority opinion [the casebook excerpt does not list all 40], but these are only a few uncertainties that quickly come to mind.

DISSENT: (Scalia, J.) The majority performed its duties poorly as a clarifying body by making an area of the law vastly more uncertain. That area of law can be raised in all litigated cases in (at least) those 39 states that elect their judges. This course was urged upon us on grounds that it would preserve the public's confidence in the judicial system, but the decision will have the opposite effect. What above all else is eroding public confidence in the judicial system is the perception that litigation is just a game, that the party with the most resourceful lawyer can play it to win, and that our legal proceedings are self-perpetuating but incapable of delivering real-world justice. The majority opinion will reinforce that perception.

▶ ANALYSIS

This case is important for the fact that through it, the Supreme Court set a new standard for judges to recuse themselves from cases, ruling that a state supreme court justice who benefited from $3 million in campaign contributions from a coal executive should have stayed out of a lawsuit involving the executive's company. In light of the fact that many states—39 by last count—currently elect judges to courts, the case will have wide-reaching consequences.

■=■

Quicknotes

DUE PROCESS CLAUSE Clauses found in the Fifth and Fourteenth Amendments to the United States Constitution, providing, that no person shall be deprived of "life, liberty, or property, without due process of law."

QUID PRO QUO What for what; in the contract context used synonymously with consideration to refer to the mutual promises between two parties rendering a contract enforceable.

RECUSAL Procedure whereby a judge is disqualified from hearing a case either on his own behalf, or on the objection of a party, due to some bias or interest on the part of the judge in the subject matter of the suit.

■=■

Pennsylvania Railroad v. Chamberlain

Railroad company (D) v. Estate of brakeman (P)

288 U.S. 333 (1933).

NATURE OF CASE: Appeal of an action for negligent homicide.

FACT SUMMARY: When deceased was killed while routing railroad cars, Chamberlain (P) sued Pennsylvania Railroad (D) for negligently bringing about a collision. Three eyewitnesses testified there was no such collision and one witness gave testimony that would have given equal inferential support for both collision and noncollision.

🏛 RULE OF LAW
Where evidence is so insubstantial that if a verdict is rendered for one of the parties, the other would be entitled to a new trial, it is up to the judge to direct a verdict according to the court's view of all the evidence.

FACTS: Chamberlain (P) sued Pennsylvania Railroad (D) to recover for the death of a brakeman who was killed while routing train cars in a railroad yard. The complaint alleged that certain railroad cars were negligently brought into collision with the cars the deceased was riding on, causing him to fall off and be run over. There was corroborated testimony by three eyewitnesses that there was no such collision. Bainbridge, a witness for Chamberlain (P), testified that a loud crash occurred before the accident. He also stated that he stood about 900 feet away from the body of the deceased, was not paying particular attention, and loud crashes were not an unusual event. The trial court entered a directed verdict for Pennsylvania Railroad (D). Reversed on appeal. Certiorari granted.

ISSUE: Should a judge refrain from ordering a directed verdict where the evidence, taken in toto, would require a new trial to be ordered for one party should the other manage to prevail with the jury?

HOLDING AND DECISION: (Sutherland, J.) No. Where there is a true conflict of testimony, evidence must be left to the jury. Here, there was no such conflict. There was an inference drawn from Bainbridge's testimony that there had been a collision, but the testimony gave equal support to an inference that there was no collision. Argument that a collision took place is mere speculation in light of the witness's limited observations. Bainbridge's testimony was so insubstantial that it did not justify submission to the jury, as there was no evidence that a jury could have properly proceeded

to a verdict for the party offering it as proof. Judgment of appellate court reversed. District court judgment affirmed.

▶ ANALYSIS

This case points up the distinctly minority rule for determining the propriety of a motion for directed verdict. In most jurisdictions, the trial court may look only to the evidence presented by the party against whom a directed verdict is sought to determine whether as a matter of law the evidence is insufficient to support such party's case. In *Chamberlain*, and a minority of jurisdictions, however, the trial court may look to all the evidence presented by both sides to determine whether "reasonable minds could differ" as to the ultimate disposition of the case. Note, of course, that this "minority view" is the majority view for determining the right to a new trial, a fact that gives rise to substantial criticism of the rule as too liberal (since the effect of a new trial is somewhat less drastic than that of a directed verdict).

■=■

Quicknotes

DIRECTED VERDICT A verdict ordered by the court in a jury trial.

■=■

Lind v. Schenley Industries

Sales negotiator (P) v. Employer company (D)

278 F.2d 79 (3d Cir. 1960).

NATURE OF CASE: Appeal from granting of judgment notwithstanding the verdict and, in the alternative, a new trial.

FACT SUMMARY: Although a jury awarded Lind (P) damages in his breach of contract suit against his employer, Schenley Industries, Inc. (D), the trial judge set aside the award as being against the weight of the evidence.

🏛 RULE OF LAW
Where nothing indicates that the jury was not properly presented with correct evidence, the judge may not nullify the jury verdict by granting a new trial so long as the evidence admits of the conclusion made by the jury.

FACTS: Lind (P) sued his employer Schenley Industries, Inc. (Schenley) (D), alleging that Schenley (D) had breached its oral promise to give him an increase in pay and a share of commissions. Lind (P) and his secretary testified to such promises. Schenley's (D) agents denied making the promises. The jury found that a contract was created and awarded damages to Lind (P). The trial judge granted Schenley's (D) motion for judgment notwithstanding the verdict and, alternatively, for a new trial. Lind (P) appealed.

ISSUE: Where nothing indicates that the jury was not properly presented with correct evidence, may the judge nullify the jury verdict by granting a new trial if the evidence admits of the conclusion made by the jury?

HOLDING AND DECISION: (Biggs, C.J.) No. The jury found the testimony of the plaintiff and his secretary credible. The judge disagreed. The evidence given as to what Lind (P) had received as a result of his negotiations demonstrates that the jury's finding was not against the weight of the evidence, however. Furthermore, there was evidence enough to sustain the finding that the contract was not too indefinite to be sustainable. Where nothing indicates that the jury was not properly presented with the correct evidence, the judge may not nullify the jury verdict by granting a new trial if the evidence admits of the conclusion made by the jury. Reversed and remanded.

DISSENT: (Hastie, J.) The judge may not substitute his own verdict for that of the jury. But he may avoid what in his professionally trained and experienced judgment is an unjust verdict by vacating it and causing the matter to be tried again. Here, there was a sharp conflict of testimony as to the offers and promises. It was not an abuse of discretion to grant the new trial.

▶ ANALYSIS

A reversal of an order granting a new trial requires an abuse of discretion by the granting judge. Showing an abuse of discretion is not an easy proposition, but it is possible. Where the new trial is granted despite a logically defensible jury verdict based on properly admitted correct evidence, such an abuse is shown.

■━■

Quicknotes

ABUSE OF DISCRETION A determination by an appellate court that a lower court's decision was based on an error of law.

DIRECTED VERDICT A verdict ordered by the court in a jury trial.

■━■

Peterson v. Wilson

Employee (P) v. Employer (D)

141 F.3d 573 (5th Cir. 1998).

NATURE OF CASE: Appeal from judgment in a retrial of wrongful-termination action.

FACT SUMMARY: The trial court ordered a new trial on its own motion after meeting with a jury after their verdict.

 RULE OF LAW
The admission of juror testimony to impeach a jury verdict is prohibited.

FACTS: Peterson (P) filed suit in district court after he was fired as grant director at Texas Southern University (D). After a trial, a jury awarded Peterson (P) $187,000. The defendants moved for a new trial. Four months later, the district court granted the new trial, but its order revealed that it did so because comments made by the jurors after the verdict indicated that they had disregarded the court's instructions. The case was re-tried and Peterson's (P) claims were rejected by the second jury. Peterson (P) appealed the grant of a new trial.

ISSUE: Is the admission of juror testimony to impeach a jury verdict prohibited?

HOLDING AND DECISION: (Wiener, J.) Yes. The admission of juror testimony to impeach a jury verdict is prohibited. A jury's verdict can be disregarded if it is against the great weight of the evidence. However, in the present case, the district court clearly granted the new trial due to its meeting with jurors following the verdict and the comments made at that time. This post verdict, ex parte meeting was impermissible. Rule 606(b) of the Fed. R. Evid. provides that jurors may not testify as to statements made in deliberations or concerning the mental process of decision making. The only exception is for extraneous and outside influences on the jury. This reflects a conscious decision to disallow juror testimony as to their fidelity to the court's instructions. Given this rule, the court's granting of a new trial in the present case was clearly erroneous. The only reason given for granting the new trial was the comments made by the jurors after the verdict. Therefore, the judgment in the second trial must be vacated and the results of the first trial reinstated. Remanded with instructions.

ANALYSIS

The court also awarded Peterson (P) his costs and attorney's fees incurred in both trials and on appeal. The decision also found that the original verdict was not against the weight of the evidence, even if the district court had used this legal reason for granting the new trial. The exception to the rule in this case is a situation where the jurors are influenced by evidence that is brought illegally into the jury room.

◼◼◼

Quicknotes

EX PARTE A proceeding commenced by one party.

◼◼◼

Appeal

Quick Reference Rules of Law

Aetna Casualty & Surety Co. v. Cunningham

Insurer (P) v. Contractor (D)

224 F.2d 478 (5th Cir. 1955).

NATURE OF CASE: Appeal of breach of trial court judgment.

FACT SUMMARY: [After the insured, a contractor, failed to finish a building project, Aetna Casualty & Surety Co. (P), the insurer, financed the remainder of the project, and then tried to recover from the contractor.]

🏛 RULE OF LAW
A plaintiff who is denied relief to which it claims to be entitled raises contentions of error on appeal.

FACTS: [Cunningham (D), a building contractor, failed to complete a project. Aetna Casualty & Surety Co. (Aetna) (P), the insurer, financed the remainder of the project. Aetna (P) then tried to recover from the contractor based on two theories for recovery: that the terms of the insurance contract permitted such recovery and that the contractor/insured had committed fraud in applying for the policy, and that Aetna's (P) loss was traceable to that fraud. The district court found for Aetna (P) on the contract claim but ruled that the contractor had not committed fraud. Both Aetna (P) and the contractor appealed.]

ISSUE: May a plaintiff who is denied relief to which it claims to be entitled raise contentions of error on appeal?

HOLDING AND DECISION: [Judge not identified in casebook excerpt.] Yes. A plaintiff who is denied relief to which it claims to be entitled raises contentions of error on appeal. To rule on the effect of bankruptcy on a judgment on either claim would be premature, as would a ruling on whether the finding that Cunningham's (D) representations were not fraudulent would be res judicata as to the operation of a discharge in bankruptcy. But since Aetna (D) was denied judgment of the quality to which it laid claim, it is a party aggrieved on appeal When, as a practical matter, the denial of any one claim results in the plaintiff not getting the relief to which it claims to be entitled, whether in the amount or in the quality of the judgment, it has a right to be heard on appeal.

▶ ANALYSIS

This decision is a straightforward illustration of the well-known rule that the plaintiff may appeal on any relevant ground when denied the relief sought, regardless of whether it has to do with the amount or in the nature of the judgment.

■≡■

Quicknotes

RES JUDICATA The rule of law that a final judgment by a court precludes subsequent litigation between the parties regarding the same cause of action.

■≡■

Liberty Mutual Insurance Co. v. Wetzel

Insurer (D) v. Employer insured (P)

424 U.S. 737 (1976).

NATURE OF CASE: Appeal from finding of liability for violation of Title VII of the Civil Rights Act of 1964.

FACT SUMMARY: Wetzel (P) alleged that Liberty Mutual's (D) employee insurance benefits and maternity leave regulations discriminated against women in violation of Title VII of the Civil Rights Act of 1964.

🏛 RULE OF LAW
An interlocutory appeal under Fed. R. Civ. P. Rule 54(b) is limited expressly to multiple-claims actions.

FACTS: Wetzel (P) filed a complaint that asserted that Liberty Mutual's (D) employee insurance benefits and maternity leave regulations discriminated against women in violation of Title VII of the Civil Rights Act of 1964. Wetzel's (P) complaint sought several forms of relief, including monetary damages, attorney fees, and injunctive relief. On January 9, 1974, after finding no issues of material fact in dispute, the district court granted partial summary judgment for Wetzel (P) on the issue of liability only. On February 20, 1974, the district court issued an order of final judgment as to Liberty Mutual's (D) liability, but granted none of the relief requested in Wetzel's (P) complaint. The court of appeals held that it had jurisdiction over Liberty Mutual's (D) appeal under 28 U.S.C. § 1291 and affirmed the judgment of the district court.

ISSUE: Is an interlocutory appeal under Fed. R. Civ. P. 54(b) limited expressly to multiple-claims actions?

HOLDING AND DECISION: (Rehnquist, J.) Yes. Fed. R. Civ. P. 54(b) is limited expressly to multiple-claims actions in which one or more, but less than all, of the multiple claims have been finally decided and are found otherwise to be ready for appeal. Here, Wetzel's (P) complaint set forth a single claim, which advanced a single legal theory that was applied to only one set of facts. Even if the district court's order was a declaratory judgment on the issue of liability, it still left unresolved Wetzel's (P) requests for an injunction, for compensatory and exemplary damages, and for attorney fees. Although it might be argued that the order of the district court, insofar as it failed to include the injunctive relief requested, was an interlocutory order refusing an injunction within the meaning of § 1292(a)(1), even if this would have allowed the obtaining of a review in the court of appeals, there was no denial of any injunction sought. Nor was the order appealable under § 1292(b). There can be no assurance that had the requirements of § 1292(b) been complied with, the court of appeals would have exercised its discretion to entertain the interlocutory appeal. The district court's order is therefore not appealable pursuant to 28 U.S.C. § 1291. Vacated and remanded.

▶ ANALYSIS

The basic rationale for the policy in federal courts of requiring final judgments is one based upon a cost-benefit analysis. If the trial judge turns out to have been correct, the cost of allowing an interlocutory appeal is the cost of an unnecessary extra appeal. Conversely, if the trial judge turns out to have been wrong in his or her judgment, the cost of not allowing an interlocutory appeal is the sum expended for an unnecessary or an unnecessarily long trial. However, because trial judges are affirmed far more often than they are reversed, the federal policy seems to be logical.

Quicknotes

INTERLOCUTORY APPEAL The appeal of an issue that does not resolve the disposition of the case, but is essential to a determination of the parties' legal rights.

Lauro Lines, s.r.l. v. Chasser

Ship company (D) v. Passenger (P)

490 U.S. 495 (1989).

NATURE OF CASE: Interlocutory appeal of a denial of a motion to dismiss action for damages for personal injuries.

FACT SUMMARY: After the district court denied Lauro's (D) motion for dismissal based on a forum-selection clause that purportedly limited Chasser (P) to suing in Naples, Italy, Lauro (D) sought to overturn the denial on interlocutory appeal.

> ## 🏛 RULE OF LAW
> Under the collateral-order doctrine, a prejudgment order may be appealed only when it conclusively determines the disputed question, resolves an important issue completely separable from the merits of the action, and is effectively unreviewable on appeal from a final judgment.

FACTS: Chasser (P) and the other plaintiffs were passengers aboard Lauro's (D) ship, the Achille Lauro, when it was hijacked in the Mediterranean Sea by terrorists. Lauro (D) moved to dismiss Chasser's (P) personal-injury suit on the ground that a forum-selection clause printed on the passenger tickets limited any passenger to suing in Naples, Italy. The district court denied the motion, holding that the ticket did not give passengers reasonable notice that they were giving up the right to sue in the United States. The court of appeals dismissed Lauro's (D) appeal, finding that the district court's order was interlocutory and not appealable. Lauro (D) appealed to the U.S. Supreme Court.

ISSUE: Is a prejudgment order subject to interlocutory appeal when it can be effectively reviewed on appeal from a final judgment?

HOLDING AND DECISION: (Brennan, J.) No. Under the collateral-order doctrine, a prejudgment order may be appealed only when it conclusively determines the disputed question, resolves an important issue completely separable from the merits of the action, and is effectively unreviewable on appeal from a final judgment. An order is "effectively" unreviewable on final judgment when the order involves an asserted right, the practical value of which would be destroyed if it were not vindicated before trial. Thus, interlocutory appeal is allowed when the defendant asserts a right that is not an ultimate right upon which the suit is brought. Here, Lauro (D) only asserted a right not to be sued in a particular forum. This right was not lost. Lauro (D) could assert the forum-selection clause in appealing any unfavorable final judgment. If an appeals court agreed with Lauro's (D) position, it could vacate trial judgment and limit the refiling of the case in Naples. Affirmed.

CONCURRENCE: (Scalia, J.) Implicit in the Court's ruling is that Lauro's (D) right of forum selection is not important enough to require vindication on interlocutory appeal.

▶ ANALYSIS

Where a criminal defendant asserts a right not to be tried an order denying that right is reviewable on interlocutory appeal. In civil cases, a partial list of orders reviewable on interlocutory appeal includes denial of a motion to dismiss based on a claim of absolute or qualified official immunity, an order denying a party leave to proceed in forma pauperis, an order requiring class action defendants to bear the cost of notifying members of the plaintiff class, and an order vacating attachment of a vessel.

■■■

Quicknotes

COLLATERAL ORDER Doctrine pursuant to which an appeal from an interlocutory order may be brought in order to hear and determine claims which are collateral to the merits of the case and which could not be granted adequate review on appeal.

IN FORMA PAUPERIS Permission to proceed with litigation without incurring fees or costs.

INTERLOCUTORY APPEAL The appeal of an issue that does not resolve the disposition of the case, but is essential to a determination of the parties' legal rights.

JUDGMENT ON THE MERITS A determination of the rights of the parties to litigation based on the presentation evidence, barring the party from initiating the same suit again.

■■■

Anderson v. Bessemer City

Sex discrimination claimant (P) v. Municipality (D)

470 U.S. 564 (1985).

NATURE OF CASE: Appeal of finding of discriminatory intent in action brought under Title VII of the Civil Rights Act of 1964.

FACT SUMMARY: In Anderson's (P) action against Bessemer City (D) for discrimination in an action brought under Title VII of the Civil Rights Act of 1964, Anderson (P), a woman applying for a job as a Recreation Director for Bessemer City (D), alleged that she had been denied the position because of her sex, and that the district court's finding of discriminatory intent in Anderson's (P) action was a factual finding that could be overturned on appeal only if it was clearly erroneous.

> ## RULE OF LAW
> Under Fed. R. Civ. P. 52(a), a finding is clearly erroneous only when, although there is evidence to support it, the reviewing court, on the entire evidence, is left with the definite and firm conviction that a mistake has been made.

FACTS: In Anderson's (P) action against Bessemer City (D) for discrimination in an action brought under Title VII of the Civil Rights Act of 1964, Anderson (P), a woman, alleged that she had been denied a position as Recreation Director in a city athletic program because of her sex. After a two-day trial, the court issued a memorandum of decision setting forth its finding that Anderson (P) had been denied the position because of her sex and that male members of the Bessemer City (D) hiring commission for the position had been biased against Anderson (P) because she was a woman. The City (D) appealed and the Fourth Circuit reversed, holding that the lower court's findings were clearly erroneous. Anderson (P) appealed.

ISSUE: Under Fed. R. Civ. P. 52(a), is a finding clearly erroneous only when, although there is evidence to support it, the reviewing court, on the entire evidence, is left with the definite and firm conviction that a mistake has been made?

HOLDING AND DECISION: (White, J.) Yes. Under Fed. R. Civ. P. 52(a), a finding is clearly erroneous only when, although there is evidence to support it, the reviewing court, on the entire evidence, is left with the definite and firm conviction that a mistake has been made. Application of the foregoing principles to the facts of this case lays bare the errors committed. The Fourth Circuit improperly conducted what amounted to a de novo weighing of the evidence in the record. The district court's findings were based on essentially undisputed evidence and from the evidence, the court determined that Anderson's (P) more varied educational and employment background and her extensive experience in variety of civil activities left her better qualified to implement such a rounded program than the other job applicants. Our determination that the findings of the district court regarding Anderson's (P) qualifications, the conduct of her interview, and the bias of the male committee members were not clearly erroneous leads this Court to conclude that the court's finding that Anderson (P) was discriminated against on account of her sex was also not clearly erroneous. Reversed.

▶ ANALYSIS

Anderson v. Bessemer City grows out of a practice that has its roots in the distinction between law and equity. Because cases in equity were considered only on a written record and the appellate court was able to read the record as the trial court, the rule evolved in equity that the appellate court reviewed equity decisions de novo. That standard came to dominate appellate review not just of decisions in equity, but of all decisions by a judge sitting without a jury.

■━■

Quicknotes

DE NOVO The review of a lower court decision by an appellate court, which is hearing the case as if it had not been previously heard and as if no judgment had been rendered.

FED. R. CIV. P. 52(A)(6) Requires that findings of fact not be set aside unless clearly erroneous.

■━■

Harnden v. Jayco, Inc.

Consumer (P) v. Manufacturer (D)

496 F.3d 579 (6th Cir. 2007).

NATURE OF CASE: Appeal of district court's grant of summary judgment to manufacturer.

FACT SUMMARY: Glenn Harnden (P) claimed a recreational vehicle that was manufactured by Jayco, Inc. (D), was defective. He sued Jayco (D), and the district court granted summary judgment for Jayco (D).

🏛 RULE OF LAW

The admission of an expert report is harmless error where the opposing party knew the contents of the report, and remanding the case would result only in a change in format of the report.

FACTS: Glenn Harnden (P) bought a Jayco Eagle Recreational Vehicle. He returned it several times for repair of defects, but the defects were never fixed. He filed a complaint against Jayco Inc. (D), the manufacturer, for breach of contract, violation of the Michigan Consumer Protection Act, breach of written warranty, revocation of acceptance, breach of implied warranty, breach of express warranty, breach of implied warranty of merchantability, and violation of the Michigan Motor Vehicle Service and Repair Act of 2004. An expert report prepared by Randy Zonker, a Jayco (D) employee, determined the problems were only minor and did not stem from the manufacturer, and Harnden (P) did not rebut Zonker's conclusions. The district court granted Jayco (D) summary judgment. On appeal, Harnden's (P) attorney objected to the admission of the expert report because it was not in the form of an affidavit or sworn statement as required by Fed. R. Civ. P. 56(e), and was therefore inadmissible hearsay.

ISSUE: Is the admission of an expert report harmless error where the opposing party knew the contents of the report, and remanding the case would result only in a change in format of the report?

HOLDING AND DECISION: (Martin, J.) Yes. The admission of an expert report is harmless error where the opposing party knew the contents of the report, and remanding the case would result only in a change in format of the report. The admission of Zonker's report is harmless because it does not affect Harnden's (P) substantial rights. Harnden (P) always knew of the contents of the report, and could have rebutted it, but did not. Affirmed.

▶ ANALYSIS

Note that the error committed by the district court may not have been harmless. Consider that Harnden's (P) lawyer may not have expected the district court to consider a report that did not comply with the Federal Rules, and therefore did not prepare rebuttal at that stage. The lawyer might have planned to rebut the report's conclusions once it was properly formatted and admitted into evidence.

■■■

Quicknotes

HARMLESS ERROR An error taking place during trial that does not require the reviewing court to overturn or modify the trial court's judgment in that it did not affect the appellant's substantial rights or the disposition of the action.

■■■

CHAPTER 11

Respect for Judgments

Quick Reference Rules of Law

Frier v. City of Vandalia

Owner of towed car (P) v. Municipality (D)

770 F.2d 699 (7th Cir. 1985).

NATURE OF CASE: Appeal of dismissal of action for deprivation of property without due process under color of law.

FACT SUMMARY: After Frier (P) lost his state court suit against Vandalia (D) for replevin of his car, he then sued Vandalia (D) in federal court under 42 U.S.C. § 1983 for depriving him of his car without due process under color of law.

> ## RULE OF LAW
> Claim preclusion bars a second suit where the first suit arose out of the same transaction.

FACTS: Vandalia (D) police had a garage tow Frier's (P) car because it was parked in traffic. Frier (P) did not receive a citation or a hearing either before the car was towed or after he refused to pay to retrieve it. Frier (P) sued Vandalia (D) and the garage in state court for replevin of his car. After a trial, the court decided that Vandalia (D) had the right to tow Frier's (P) car because it was obstructing traffic. Therefore, the court did not issue the writ of replevin. Frier (P) then filed a 42 U.S.C. § 1983 suit in federal court, seeking equitable relief and compensatory and punitive damages from Vandalia (D) for depriving him of his car without due process under color of law. The district court dismissed Frier's (P) suit for failure to state a claim, and Frier (P) appealed, arguing that he was not precluded from filing a federal suit under a different legal theory than the one he on which he based his state court action.

ISSUE: Does claim preclusion bar a second suit where the first suit arose out of the same transaction?

HOLDING AND DECISION: (Easterbrook, J.) Yes. Claim preclusion bars a second suit where the first suit arose out of the same transaction. Claim preclusion, also called res judicata, is designed to impel parties to consolidate all closely related matters in the same suit. First, this prevents oppression of defendants through multiple cases. Second, when the facts and issues of all theories of liability are closely related, there is no good reason to incur the cost of litigation more than once. Frier (P) could have sued in his state court action for both replevin, to get his car back, and under § 1983, for damages. Both theories alleged the same conduct: that Vandalia (D) towed and detained his cars without lawful process, i.e., without a determination of a parking violation. Thus, claim preclusion bars Frier's (P) federal suit.

The district court, though it properly dismissed the case, should not have reached the merits. Affirmed.

CONCURRENCE: (Swygert, J.) Frier's (P) suit should properly have been dismissed on summary judgment, but not for claim preclusion. Illinois law, applicable in this case, follows the narrower, traditional rule of claim preclusion, not the broader Restatement rule applied by the majority. Under the traditional rule, one suit bars a second where the evidence necessary to sustain a second verdict would have sustained the first, i.e., where the causes of action are based on a common core of operative facts. To prevail on his replevin claim, Frier (P) would have had to prove a superior right to possession of the car, which turned on whether he had parked illegally. However, under § 1983, the legality of Frier's (P) parking was irrelevant. The issues as to § 1983 were whether Frier (P) had notice that he would be towed for parking where he did, and whether he had a fair hearing on the detaining of his car. The fact that Frier (P) could have brought the two causes of action in the same suit is irrelevant under the traditional rule of claim preclusion.

ANALYSIS

Judge Easterbrook and Judge Swygert agree that under the "same transaction" rule Frier's (P) second suit was barred by claim preclusion or res judicata. However, Judge Swygert applied the narrower, traditional, "core of operative facts" rule to reach the opposite result on the claim preclusion issue. The federal courts and most states follow the "same transaction" rule, which is codified in the Restatement (Second) of Judgments § 24 (1982).

Quicknotes

42 U.S.C. § 1983 The Civil Rights Act; usually invoked when a party commences suit based on the alleged state's violation of the party's civil rights.

CLAIM The demand for a right to payment or equitable relief; the fact or facts giving rise to such demand.

RES JUDICATA The rule of law that a final judgment by a court precludes subsequent litigation between the parties regarding the same cause of action.

Searle Brothers v. Searle

Father-son partnership (P) v. Wife (D)

Utah Sup. Ct., 588 P.2d 689 (1978).

NATURE OF CASE: Appeal from decision barring claim of interest in real property.

FACT SUMMARY: Searle Bros. (P) claimed an undivided one-half interest in Slaugh House, which had been awarded to Searle (D) in a divorce proceeding.

🏛 RULE OF LAW
A person is in privity with another if he is so identified in interest with the other that he represents the same legal right.

FACTS: Edlean Searle (D) sued Woodey Searle for divorce. During that proceeding, the court determined that a piece of property known as the "Slaugh House," which was recorded in Woodey's name, was part of the marital property and subsequently awarded the entire property to Edlean Searle (D). Woodey had argued that he had a half interest in the property and that the other half was owned by a partnership with his sons as partners. Searle Bros. (P), the partnership, then sued Edlean Searle (D), claiming an undivided one-half interest in Slaugh House. The trial court held that res judicata and collateral estoppel barred the action by Searle Bros. (P).

ISSUE: Is a person in privity with another if he is so identified in interest with the other that he represents the same legal right?

HOLDING AND DECISION: (Ellett, C.J.) Yes. A divorce decree, like other final judgments, is conclusive as to parties and their privies and operates as a bar to any subsequent action. The legal definition of a person in privity with another is a person so identified in interest with another that he represents the same legal right. This includes a mutual or successive relationship to rights in property. Here, Searle Bros.' (P) interest was neither mutual nor successive. Searle Bros. (P) claims no part of the interest owned by Woodey Searle, but asserts its own, independent, and separate partnership interest in 50 percent of the property involved. Collateral estoppel may not be applied against Searle Bros. (P) because it was not a partner to the first suit, and there is insufficient evidence in the record to show that the interest of the partnership in the Slaugh House was ever litigated. Reversed and remanded.

DISSENT: (Crockett, J.) The doctrine of collateral estoppel should bar the suit by Searle Bros. (P). It is plain that the members of the family were actively involved in the divorce action, which involved whatever interest any of them had in the family assets. Further, Searle Bros.

(P) was fully aware of the adverse claims being asserted to the Slaugh House.

▶ ANALYSIS

It is possible for both res judicata and collateral estoppel to apply here. Res judicata requires that the causes of action be identical, and it is generally assumed that different parties automatically have different causes of action. However, if Searle Bros. (P) were in privity with the parties to the earlier divorce action, the requirements for res judicata are met.

Quicknotes

CLAIM The demand for a right to payment or equitable relief; the fact or facts giving rise to such demand.

COLLATERAL ESTOPPEL A doctrine whereby issues litigated and determined in a prior proceeding are binding upon all subsequent litigation between the parties regarding that issue.

ISSUE A fact or question that is disputed between two or more parties.

RES JUDICATA The rule of law that a final judgment by a court precludes subsequent litigation between the parties regarding the same cause of action.

Taylor v. Sturgell

FOIA requester (P) v. Federal official (D)

553. U.S. 880 (2008).

NATURE OF CASE: Appeal from affirmance of summary judgment for defendant in action under the Freedom of Information Act (FOIA).

FACT SUMMARY: Taylor (P) contended that his Freedom of Information Act (FOIA) suit seeking records from the Federal Aviation Administration (FAA) (D) should not have been dismissed on grounds of claim preclusion—on the theory of "virtual representation"—merely because his friend and close associate, Herrick, had filed a similar suit seeking the same records.

RULE OF LAW
A claim may not be precluded under a doctrine of "virtual representation" where a second claimant brings a suit identical to a first claimant and, although the claimants know each other, there is no legal relationship between them and there is no evidence that the second claimant controlled, financed, participated in, or even had notice of the earlier suit.

FACTS: Herrick, an antique aircraft enthusiast sought to restore a vintage airplane manufactured by the Fairchild Engine and Airplane Corporation (FEAC). He filed a Freedom of Information Act (FOIA) request asking the Federal Aviation Administration (FAA) (D) for copies of technical documents related to the airplane. The FAA (D) denied his request based on FOIA's exemption for trade secrets. Herrick took an administrative appeal, but when Fairchild Corporation (Fairchild) (D), FEAC's successor, objected to the documents' release, the FAA (D) adhered to its original decision. Herrick then filed a FOIA lawsuit to secure the documents, which was dismissed on summary judgment by the district court and later affirmed by the court of appeals. Less than a month after that suit was resolved, Taylor (P), Herrick's friend and an antique aircraft enthusiast himself, made a FOIA request for the same documents Herrick had unsuccessfully sued to obtain. When the FAA (D) failed to respond, Taylor (P) filed suit in federal district court. Holding the suit barred by claim preclusion, the district court granted summary judgment to the FAA (D) and to Fairchild (D), as intervener in Taylor's (P) action. The court acknowledged that Taylor (P) was not a party to Herrick's suit, but held that a nonparty may be bound by a judgment if she was "virtually represented" by a party. The court of appeals affirmed, announcing a five-factor test for "virtual representation." The first two factors of that test—"identity of interests" and "adequate

representation"—are necessary but not sufficient for virtual representation. In addition, at least one of three other factors must be established: "a close relationship between the present party and his putative representative," "substantial participation by the present party in the first case," or "tactical maneuvering on the part of the present party to avoid preclusion by the prior judgment." The court of appeals acknowledged the absence of any indication that Taylor (P) participated in, or even had notice of, Herrick's suit. It nonetheless found the "identity of interests," "adequate representation," and "close relationship" factors satisfied because the two men sought release of the same documents, were "close associates," had discussed working together to restore Herrick's plane, had used the same lawyer to pursue their suits, and Herrick had given Taylor (P) documents Herrick had obtained from the FAA (D) during discovery in his suit. Because these conditions sufficed to establish virtual representation, the court left open the question whether Taylor (P) had engaged in tactical maneuvering to avoid preclusion. The U.S. Supreme Court granted certiorari.

ISSUE: May a claim be precluded under a doctrine of "virtual representation" where a second claimant brings a suit identical to a first claimant and, although the claimants know each other, there is no legal relationship between them and there is no evidence that the second claimant controlled, financed, participated in, or even had notice of the earlier suit?

HOLDING AND DECISION: (Ginsburg, J.) No. A claim may not be precluded under a doctrine of "virtual representation" where a second claimant brings a suit identical to a first claimant and, although the claimants know each other, there is no legal relationship between them and there is no evidence that the second claimant controlled, financed, participated in, or even had notice of the earlier suit. The preclusive effect of a federal-court judgment is determined by federal common law, subject to due process limitations. Extending the preclusive effect of a judgment to a nonparty runs up against the "deep-rooted historic tradition that everyone should have his own day in court." Indicating the strength of that tradition, this Court has often repeated the general rule that "one is not bound by a judgment in personam in a litigation in which he is not designated a party or to which he has not been made a party by service of process." The rule against nonparty preclusion is subject to exceptions, currently grouped into six categories. First,

Continued on next page.

"[a] person who agrees to be bound by the determination of issues in an action between others is bound in accordance with the [agreement's] terms," Restatement (Second) of Judgments § 40. Second, nonparty preclusion may be based on a pre-existing substantive legal relationship between the person to be bound and a party to the judgment, e.g., assignee and assignor. Third, "in certain limited circumstances," a non-party may be bound by a judgment because she was "adequately represented by someone with the same interests who [wa]s a party" to the suit. Fourth, a nonparty is bound by a judgment if he "assume[d] control" over the litigation in which that judgment was rendered. Fifth, a party bound by a judgment may not avoid its preclusive force by relitigating through a proxy. Preclusion is thus in order when a person who did not participate in litigation later brings suit as the designated representative or agent of a person who was a party to the prior adjudication. Sixth, a special statutory scheme otherwise consistent with due process, e.g., bankruptcy proceedings, may "expressly foreclos[e] successive litigation by nonlitigants." Reaching beyond these six categories, the court of appeals recognized a broad "virtual representation" exception to the rule against nonparty preclusion. None of the arguments advanced by that court, the FAA (D), or Fairchild (D) justify such an expansive doctrine. The court of appeals purported to ground its doctrine in this Court's statements that, in some circumstances, a person may be bound by a judgment if she was adequately represented by a party to the proceeding yielding that judgment. But the court of appeals' definition of "adequate representation" strayed from the meaning this Court has attributed to that term. In one case, *Richards v. Jefferson County*, 517 U.S. 793 (1996), the Alabama Supreme Court had held a tax challenge barred by a judgment upholding the same tax in a suit by different taxpayers. This Court reversed, holding that nonparty preclusion was inconsistent with due process where there was no showing (1) that the court in the first suit "took care to protect the interests" of absent parties, or (2) that the parties to the first litigation "understood their suit to be on behalf of absent [parties]." In holding that representation can be "adequate" for purposes of nonparty preclusion even where these two factors are absent, the court of appeals misapplied *Richards*. Fairchild (D) and the FAA (D) ask the Court to abandon altogether the attempt to delineate discrete grounds and clear rules for nonparty preclusion. Instead, they contend, only an equitable and heavily fact-driven inquiry can account for all of the situations in which nonparty preclusion is appropriate. This argument is rejected. First, the balancing test they propose is at odds with the constrained approach advanced by this Court's decisions, which have endeavored to delineate discrete, limited exceptions to the fundamental rule that a litigant is not bound by a judgment to which she was not a party. Second, a party's representation of a

nonparty is "adequate" for preclusion purposes only if, at a minimum: (1) the interests of the nonparty and her representative are aligned, and (2) either the party understood herself to be acting in a representative capacity or the original court took care to protect the nonparty's interests. Adequate representation may also require (3) notice of the original suit to the persons alleged to have been represented. In the class-action context, these limitations are implemented by Fed. R. Civ. P. 23's procedural safeguards. But an expansive virtual representation doctrine would recognize a common-law kind of class action that would lack these protections. Third, a diffuse balancing approach to non-party preclusion would likely complicate the task of district courts faced in the first instance with preclusion questions. Finally, the FAA (D) maintains that nonparty preclusion should apply more broadly in "public-law" litigation than in "private-law" controversies. First, the FAA (D) points to *Richards's* acknowledgment that when a taxpayer challenges "an alleged misuse of public funds" or "other public action," the suit "has only an indirect impact on [the plaintiff's] interests," and "the States have wide latitude to establish procedures [limiting] the number of judicial proceedings that may be entertained." In contrast to the public-law litigation contemplated in *Richards*, however, a successful FOIA action results in a grant of relief to the individual plaintiff, not a decree benefiting the public at large. Furthermore, *Richards* said only that, for the type of public-law claims there envisioned, states were free to adopt procedures limiting repetitive litigation. While it appears equally evident that Congress can adopt such procedures, it hardly follows that this Court should proscribe or confine successive FOIA suits by different requesters. Second, the FAA (D) argues that, because the number of plaintiffs in public-law cases is potentially limitless, it is theoretically possible for several persons to coordinate a series of vexatious repetitive lawsuits. But this risk does not justify departing from the usual nonparty preclusion rules. Stare decisis will allow courts to dispose of repetitive suits in the same circuit, and even when stare decisis is not dispositive, the human inclination not to waste money should discourage suits based on claims or issues already decided. The remaining question is whether the result reached by the courts below can be justified based on one of the six established grounds for nonparty preclusion. With one exception, those grounds plainly have no application here. The FAA (D) and Fairchild (D) argue that Taylor's (P) suit is a collusive attempt to relitigate Herrick's claim. That argument justifies a remand to allow the courts below the opportunity to determine whether the fifth ground for nonparty preclusion—preclusion because a nonparty to earlier litigation has brought suit as an agent of a party bound by the prior adjudication—applies to Taylor's (P)

Continued on next page.

suit. However, courts should be cautious about finding preclusion on the basis of agency. A mere whiff of "tactical maneuvering" will not suffice; instead, principles of agency law indicate that preclusion is appropriate only if the putative agent's conduct of the suit is subject to the control of the party who is bound by the prior adjudication. Finally, the Court rejects Fairchild's (D) suggestion that Taylor (P) must bear the burden of proving he is not acting as Herrick's agent. Claim preclusion is an affirmative defense for the defendant to plead and prove. Vacated and remanded.

▶ ANALYSIS

This case presented an issue of first impression in the sense that the Supreme Court had never before addressed the doctrine of "virtual representation" adopted (in varying forms) by several circuits and relied upon by the district court and court of appeals below. For example, the Eighth Circuit had developed a seven-factor test for virtual representation, which was adopted by the district court in this case. The Eighth Circuit test requires an "identity of interests" between the person to be bound and a party to the judgment. Six additional factors counsel in favor of virtual representation under the Eighth Circuit's test, but are not prerequisites: (1) a "close relationship" between the present party and a party to the judgment alleged to be preclusive; (2) "participation in the prior litigation" by the present party; (3) the present party's "apparent acquiescence" to the preclusive effect of the judgment; (4) "deliberat[e] maneuver[ing]" to avoid the effect of the judgment; (5) adequate representation of the present party by a party to the prior adjudication; and (6) a suit raising a "public law" rather than a "private law" issue. These factors, the court of appeals (D.C. Circuit) in this case observed, "constitute a fluid test with imprecise boundaries" and call for "a broad, case-by-case inquiry." The D.C. Circuit adopted a five-factor test. The Supreme Court resolved these different approaches by rejecting the doctrine of virtual representation altogether, instead relying on well-established principles of due process and claim preclusion.

■■■■

Quicknotes

CLAIM PRECLUSION A procedural rule or order prohibiting the support or opposition to certain claims or defenses.

DUE PROCESS The constitutional mandate requiring the courts to protect and enforce individuals' rights and liberties consistent with prevailing principles of fairness and justice and prohibiting the federal and state governments from such activities that deprive its citizens of life, liberty, or property interest.

INTERVENOR A party, not an initial party to the action, who is admitted to the action in order to assert an interest in the subject matter of a lawsuit.

PARTY Person designated as either the defendant or plaintiff in a lawsuit.

■■■■

Gargallo v. Merrill Lynch, Pierce, Fenner & Smith

Client (P) v. Broker (D)

918 F.2d 658 (6th Cir. 1990).

NATURE OF CASE: Appeal from dismissal of action for securities violations.

FACT SUMMARY: Gargallo's (P) federal court action was dismissed because in a previous state court case, his counterclaim involving the same issues was rejected.

RULE OF LAW

A judgment rendered by a court lacking subject matter jurisdiction does not have claim preclusive effect in subsequent proceedings.

FACTS: Gargallo (P) had a brokerage account with Merrill Lynch (D). When the investments went poorly, Gargallo (P) ended up owing Merrill Lynch (D) $17,000. The broker (D) brought suit in Ohio state court for collection of the debt, and Gargallo (P) filed a counterclaim alleging that the losses were caused by violation of federal securities law. The Ohio court dismissed the counterclaim with prejudice for Gargallo's (P) failure to comply with discovery requests and orders. Gargallo (P) then filed a complaint in U.S. district court. The court dismissed the action on res judicata grounds, finding that the claims were the same as those dismissed by the Ohio court. Gargallo (P) appealed.

ISSUE: Does a judgment rendered by a court lacking subject matter jurisdiction have claim preclusive effect in subsequent proceedings?

HOLDING AND DECISION: (Ryan, J.) No. A judgment rendered by a court lacking subject matter jurisdiction does not have claim preclusive effect in subsequent proceedings. The doctrine of res judicata provides that a final judgment by a court is conclusive of the rights, questions and facts at issue with respect to the parties in all other actions. In the present case, it is clear that Gargallo's (P) federal court complaint alleges the same violations that were alleged in the state court counterclaim. Ordinarily, federal courts are required to give state court judgments the same preclusive effect such judgment would have in a state court. Ohio subscribes to the position that res judicata does not apply where the original court did not have subject matter jurisdiction over the issue. In the present case, Ohio did not have jurisdiction over Gargallo's (P) allegations of securities violations by Merrill Lynch (D). Thus, the dismissal should not have been given preclusive effect in federal district court. [Reversed and remanded.]

ANALYSIS

The decision did not directly address the issue that Gargallo's (P) state court counterclaim was not really decided on the merits. It was dismissed because of failure to abide by discovery requirements. However, it would still have been subject to res judicata if the state court had had subject matter jurisdiction.

Quicknotes

28 U.S.C. § 1738A Federal law governing the enforcement and modification of foreign decrees and the treatment of concurrent proceedings. Only custody determinations made consistent with its provisions are to be given full faith and credit by states. It preempts conflicting state law and requires that a custody determination be made in the child's home state.

JUDGMENT ON THE MERITS A determination of the rights of the parties to litigation based on the presentation evidence, barring the party from initiating the same suit again.

RES JUDICATA The rule of law that a final judgment by a court precludes subsequent litigation between the parties regarding the same cause of action.

SUBJECT MATTER JURISDICTION A court's ability to adjudicate a specific category of cases based on the subject matter of the dispute.

Illinois Central Gulf Railroad v. Parks

Railroad company (D) v. Injured car occupants (P)

Ind. Ct. App., 181 Ind. App. 141, 390 N.E.2d 1078 (1979).

NATURE OF CASE: Interlocutory appeal from denial of motion for summary judgment.

FACT SUMMARY: Parks (P) was injured when his car collided with an Illinois Central Gulf Railroad (D) train.

🏛 RULE OF LAW
The doctrine of estoppel by verdict allows a judgment in a prior action to operate as a complete bar to those facts or issues actually litigated and determined in the prior action.

FACTS: Parks (P) and his wife were injured when their car collided with an Illinois Central Gulf Railroad (Illinois Central) (D) train. Parks's (P) wife recovered $30,000 on her claim for damages for personal injuries, but judgment was rendered for Illinois Central (D) on Parks's (P) own claim for damages for loss of services and loss of consortium. Parks (P) then sued Illinois Central (D) to recover damages for his own injuries. On Illinois Central's (D) motion for summary judgment, the trial court held that Parks's (P) claim was not barred by res judicata, and that the prior action did not collaterally estop Parks (P) on the issue of contributory negligence.

ISSUE: Does the doctrine of estoppel by verdict allow a judgment in a prior action to operate as a complete bar to those facts or issues actually litigated and determined in the prior action?

HOLDING AND DECISION: (Lybrook, J.) Yes. The doctrine of estoppel by verdict allows the judgment in a prior action to operate as an estoppel as to those facts or questions actually litigated and determined in the prior action. Where a prior judgment may have been based upon either or any of two or more distinct facts, a party desiring to plead the judgment as an estoppel by verdict must show the actual basis for the prior judgment. Here, the basis for the prior judgment against Parks (P) could have been predicated on a finding by the jury that either Parks (P) had sustained no damages, or that his own negligence was a proximate cause of his damages. Illinois Central (D) failed to show that the judgment against Parks (P) in the prior action was based upon a finding that Parks (P) was contributorily negligent in the accident. Affirmed.

▶ ANALYSIS

The doctrine of collateral estoppel is reflective of a policy that the needs of judicial finality and efficiency outweigh the possible gains of fairness or accuracy which would result from the continued litigation of an issue that had been decided in prior judicial proceedings. There is a strong policy favoring consistency of judicial rulings in both state and federal courts.

■■■

Quicknotes

COLLATERAL ESTOPPEL A doctrine whereby issues litigated and determined in a prior proceeding are binding upon all subsequent litigation between the parties regarding that issue.

■■■

Parklane Hosiery Co. v. Shore

Hosiery company (D) v. Shareholder (P)

439 U.S. 322 (1979).

NATURE OF CASE: Review of denial of relitigation of issue determined in a separate case.

FACT SUMMARY: Shore (P) sought rescission of a merger on the ground that Parklane Hosiery Co. (Parklane) (D), a party to the merger, had issued a false and misleading proxy statement, and in a separate action filed by the Securities Exchange Commission (SEC), the district court found the proxy statement to be false, so Shore (P) moved for partial summary judgment in this action on that issue, alleging that Parklane (D) was collaterally estopped from relitigating the issue.

RULE OF LAW
A trial judge has broad discretion to permit the offensive use of collateral estoppel to establish an element of a plaintiff's case where it is not unfair to the defendant.

FACTS: Shore (P) brought a shareholder's class action against Parklane Hosiery Co. (Parklane) (D) alleging that Parklane (D) had issued a materially false and misleading proxy statement in violation of §§ 14(a), 10(b), and 20(a) of the Securities Exchange Act. Shore (P) sought rescission of merger to which Parklane (D) was a party because of the proxy statement, which related to the merger. Before trial, however, the Securities Exchange Commission (SEC) filed suit on the same basis seeking injunctive relief. The court in that suit found the statement false and misleading and entered a declaratory judgment to that effect. Shore (P) then moved for partial summary judgment on the issue of falsity, alleging that Parklane (D) was collaterally estopped from relitigating the issue. The district court denied the motion, but the court of appeals reversed. The U.S. Supreme Court granted certiorari.

ISSUE: Has a trial judge broad discretion to permit the offensive use of collateral estoppel to establish an element of a plaintiff's case where it is not unfair to the defendant?

HOLDING AND DECISION: (Stewart, J.) Yes. The defensive use of collateral estoppel to prevent relitigation of issues previously litigated and lost by a plaintiff against another defendant has been upheld by this Court. But the present case involves the offensive use of collateral estoppel to prevent relitigation of issues by a defendant against whom a different plaintiff has obtained a ruling. It is argued that such offensive use will not promote judicial economy because plaintiffs can await a ruling in another matter without intervening, and then be relieved of making proofs if the issue is resolved to their satisfaction, but not be foreclosed from raising it again if it is not. SEC injunction suit, so that this argument is inapplicable. Another argument is that a defendant may have little incentive to defend in an action for small or nominal damages, and should not be subjected to unforeseeable future suits against which he will not be adequately able to defend. But here, Parklane (D) had as strong an incentive offensive use of collateral estoppel to establish an element of a plaintiff's case where it is not unfair to the defendant. Under these circumstances, it is not unfair to use collateral estoppel against Parklane (D), who had a full and fair opportunity to litigate its claims. Preclusion did not violate the Seventh Amendment.

ANALYSIS

In a separate part of the opinion, the Court found that the offensive use of collateral estoppel in this case would violate Parklane's (D) right to a jury trial in the legal action as opposed to the SEC's equitable suit. This Seventh Amendment right did not, however, affect the propriety of use of collateral estoppel offensively where not unfair to the defendant if the jury trial right was not at issue.

■=■

Quicknotes

JOINDER OF PARTIES The joining of parties in one lawsuit.

OFFENSIVE COLLATERAL ESTOPPEL A doctrine that may be invoked by a plaintiff whereby a defendant is prohibited from relitigating issues litigated and determined in a prior proceeding against another plaintiff.

■=■

State Farm Fire & Casualty Co. v. Century Home Components

Insurance company (P) v. Builder of prefab housing (D)

Or. Sup. Ct., 275 Or. 97, 550 P.2d 1185 (1976).

NATURE OF CASE: Appeal from award of damages for negligence.

FACT SUMMARY: State Farm (P) and many others claimed that Century Home (D) had been negligent by allowing a fire to erupt and spread, causing damage to property.

RULE OF LAW
Where prior judicial determinations on a particular matter are inconsistent, the doctrine of collateral estoppel will not bar relitigation of that matter.

FACTS: Over 50 separate actions for damages were filed against Century Home (D) to recover losses from a fire. Three of the actions proceeded separately through trial to final judgment. One judgment was awarded in favor of Century Home (D), and judgment was twice awarded to separate claimants. State Farm (P), who was not a party to any of the previous actions, sought to utilize the prior claimants' judgments to establish conclusively Century Home's (D) negligence and its responsibility for any losses caused by the fire. The trial court held that Century Home (D) was collaterally estopped from any further contesting its liability.

ISSUE: Where prior judicial determinations on a particular matter are inconsistent, does the doctrine of collateral estoppel bar relitigation of that matter?

HOLDING AND DECISION: (Holman, J.) No. In every situation where collateral estoppel is asserted by a person who was neither a party nor in privity with a party to the prior case, it is essential to determine that no unfairness will result to the prior litigant if the estoppel is applied. Where outstanding judicial determinations are inconsistent on the matter sought to be precluded, it would be patently unfair to estop a party by the judgment it lost. The question of whether preclusion would be fair under all the circumstances is independent of, and in addition to, whether a party had a full and fair opportunity to present its case in the action resulting in the adverse judgment. Here, because the prior determinations are basically inconsistent, it would be unfair to preclude Century Home (D) from relitigating the issue of liability. Reversed and remanded.

ANALYSIS

The Restatement position regarding mutuality of estoppel is consistent with the view taken in this case. It allows relitigation of an issue when "the determination relied on as preclusive was itself inconsistent with another determination of the same issue." Restatement of the Law (Second) Judgments (Tent. Draft No. 2 1975). The Restatement would also allow relitigation of an issue in cases where preclusion would complicate the determination of issues in subsequent actions, prejudice the interests of another party, or where the person seeking preclusion could have joined in the initial action.

Quicknotes

COLLATERAL ESTOPPEL A doctrine whereby issues litigated and determined in a prior proceeding are binding upon all subsequent litigation between the parties regarding that issue.

MUTUALITY OF ESTOPPEL Doctrine pursuant to which a court may not consider a judgment final as to one party to a cause of action if it is not final as to the other.

Kovach v. District of Columbia

Ticketed motorist (P) v. District of Columbia (D)

D.C. Ct. App., 805 A.2d 957 (2002).

NATURE OF CASE: Appeal of dismissal of case on res judicata grounds.

FACT SUMMARY: A motorist sued the District of Columbia (D) for forgiving some, but not all, traffic violations recorded by an automatic camera at a stoplight. The trial court ruled that his previous payment of a traffic violation precluded him from contesting the District's (D) subsequent decision to forgive only unpaid fines for violations recorded by the camera.

🏛 RULE OF LAW
Admission of the commission of a violation in an administrative case preclude the relitigation of issues involving the same parties and the same facts, not only as to every ground of recovery or defense actually presented in the action, but also as to every ground which might have been presented.

FACTS: Donald Kovach (P) was among 20,000 motorists who had been issued traffic tickets for running red lights. Many accidentally ran the light, as the camera designed to catch them running the light itself had an automatic red light that confused motorists. The District (D) agreed to dismiss outstanding fines assessed to approximately 2,000 motorists whose infractions were recorded by the camera, but determined that those who had already paid would not be reimbursed. Kovach was among those who paid the fine. He paid it approximately five months before the District (D) decided to remove the camera. He filed suit against the District (D), arguing that the District's (D) decision to forgive some fines and enforce others was facially discriminatory under D.C. statutes and violated the Fifth and Fourteenth Amendments of the Constitution. The trial court ruled that his previous payment of a traffic violation precluded him from contesting the District's (D) subsequent decision to forgive only unpaid fines for violations recorded by the camera.

ISSUE: Does admission of the commission of a violation in an administrative case preclude the relitigation of issues involving the same parties and the same facts, not only as to every ground of recovery or defense actually presented in the action, but also as to every ground which might have been presented?

HOLDING AND DECISION: (Ruiz, J.) Yes. Admission of the commission of a violation in an administrative case precludes the relitigation of issues involving the same parties and the same facts, not only as to

every ground of recovery or defense actually presented in the action, but also as to every ground which might have been presented. The District (D) considers payment of a fine for a traffic violation admission of the commission of the infraction, and those who wish to contest a notice of infraction may do so before a hearing examiner of the Bureau of Traffic Adjudication, and, if appropriate, to an Appeals Board. However, the arguments in Kovach's (P) complaint, based on statutory and constitutional challenges, are distinct from the prior proceeding before the Bureau of Traffic Adjudication (the BTA). And the decision that Kovach (D) is challenging occurred five months after BTA's adjudication, and could not possibly have been raised before the BTA at the time when it adjudicated the traffic ticket. Therefore, res judicata does not bar Kovach's (D) claims. But the trial court's dismissal is nevertheless affirmed because collateral estoppel precludes Kovach (P) from challenging the District's (D) decision as discriminatory as applied to him. Even where res judicata—claim preclusion—is inapplicable, collateral estoppel—issue preclusion—may bar relitigation of the issues settled in a prior action. Kovach (P) had the opportunity to contest the infraction before the BTA but did not. Affirmed.

▶ ANALYSIS

The difference between issue preclusion and claim preclusion is not always easy to identify. One way to initially approach the problem is to think first that issues often arise from claims. Claims can be set forth in broad strokes, but claims consist of issues. In this case, one of the claims—that the District's policy violated the Constitution—was not litigated by the BTA. But the issues that are part of those claims—such as whether the District's policy was discriminatory in its application—was settled, since he admitted to violating the traffic law. Even if the policy was discriminatory, it didn't discriminate against him.

■=■

Quicknotes

COLLATERAL ESTOPPEL A doctrine whereby issues litigated and determined in a prior proceeding are binding upon all subsequent litigation between the parties regarding that issue.

RES JUDICATA The rule of law that a final judgment by a court precludes subsequent litigation between the parties regarding the same cause of action.

■=■

Durfee v. Duke

Landowner (D) v. Title claimant (P)

375 U.S. 106 (1963).

NATURE OF CASE: On writ of certiorari in action to quiet title to land.

FACT SUMMARY: Duke (P), having lost a quiet title action brought in the Nebraska court by Durfee (D), brought an additional quiet title action regarding the same land in a Missouri court.

🏛 RULE OF LAW
The principles of res judicata and full faith and credit preclude relitigation of judgments of a foreign state when the parties have appeared and have fully and fairly litigated the issues.

FACTS: Durfee (D) brought an action against Duke (P) in a Nebraska court to quiet title to land situated on the Missouri River at the Missouri-Nebraska boundary line. The Nebraska court had subject matter jurisdiction only if the land was in Nebraska. Duke (P) appeared in the Nebraska court and finally litigated the issues, including the court's jurisdiction. Both the Nebraska trial and appellate courts found for Durfee (D) and held that the Nebraska court had subject matter jurisdiction based on their finding that the land was in Nebraska. Duke (P) then brought this action in a Missouri court to quiet title on the same land. Because of diversity of citizenship, the action was removed to the federal district court. That court held that, although the disputed land was in Missouri, since the Nebraska litigation had adjudicated and determined all the issues, the judgment of the Nebraska court was res judicata and binding. Duke (P) argued that the Nebraska judgment was not conclusive on the merits in the Missouri court since Nebraska had no jurisdiction over Missouri land. The appellate court reversed, holding that the court was not obliged to give full faith and credit to the Nebraska judgment and that res judicata was inapplicable because the controversy involved land and the Missouri court was therefore free to retry the issue of the Nebraska court's jurisdiction over the subject matter.

ISSUE: Once a matter has been fully and fairly litigated and judicially determined, does the principle of res judicata preclude the same issue being retried by the same parties in another state?

HOLDING AND DECISION: (Stewart, J.) Yes. The constitutional command of full faith and credit requires that judicial proceedings shall have the same full faith and credit in every court with the United States as they have by law or usage in the courts of the state from which they are taken. Full faith and credit as well as the principle of res judicata therefore preclude relitigation of judgments of a foreign state when the parties have appeared and have fully and fairly litigated the issues. Here, it is not questioned that the Nebraska courts would give full res judicata effect to the Nebraska judgment quieting title in Durfee (D) and therefore the Missouri court was limited to inquiring only whether the jurisdictional issues had been fully and fairly litigated by the parties and finally determined in the Nebraska courts. The underlying rationale is the doctrine of jurisdictional finality that holds that one trial of an issue is enough. The principles of res judicata apply to questions of jurisdiction of the subject matter as well as to other issues. Also public policy demands that there be an end to litigations, that those who have voluntarily, fully, and fairly contested an issue should be bound by the result. This rule applies to real as well as personal property. While there are the exceptions of federal preemption and sovereign immunity, these overriding considerations are not present here. The judgment of the court of appeals is reversed and that of the district court is affirmed.

CONCURRENCE: (Black, J.) The dispute in this case is as to whether the tract of land in question is in Nebraska or in Missouri. The Nebraska Supreme Court has held that it is in that state and the majority today has agreed that the determination in that suit bars a second suit brought in Missouri. I concur in the holding, but with the understanding that the Nebraska decision would be binding in the event of an authoritative determination by an original suit between the two states or by state compact.

▶ ANALYSIS

Following the principle of collateral attack, a judgment may always be attacked either in the state where rendered, or in any other state or forum, on the basis of lack of jurisdiction. Lack of subject matter jurisdiction is never waived and hence a collateral attack may be made for the first time when the judgment is accorded res judicata effect in some other action. However, collateral attack is available only to a party who did not appear in the original action. No such attack is permitted by a party who raised and litigated the jurisdictional defect in the original action (or merely appeared and therefore could have raised it). In such a case, the

Continued on next page.

first court's findings as to its jurisdiction—no matter how erroneous—are themselves entitled to res judicata and cannot be relitigated.

∎══∎

Quicknotes

ACTION TO QUIET TITLE Equitable action to resolve conflicting claims to an interest in real property.

COLLATERAL ATTACK A proceeding initiated in order to challenge the integrity of a previous judgment.

FULL FAITH AND CREDIT Doctrine that a judgment by a court of one state shall be given the same effect in another state.

ISSUE A fact or question that is disputed between two or more parties.

RES JUDICATA The rule of law that a final judgment by a court precludes subsequent litigation between the parties regarding the same cause of action.

SUBJECT MATTER JURISDICTION The authority of the court to hear and decide actions involving a particular type of issue or subject.

∎══∎

United States v. Beggerly

Federal government (D) v. Alleged property owner (P)

524 U.S. 38 (1998).

NATURE OF CASE: Appeal from dismissal of action to set aside settlement in prior quiet title litigation.

FACT SUMMARY: Beggerly (P) sought to set aside an earlier judgment based on a settlement.

🏛 RULE OF LAW
Independent actions pursuant to Fed. R. Civ. P. 60(b) are reserved for cases of injustice sufficiently gross to demand departure from adherence to the doctrine of res judicata.

FACTS: In 1979, the United States (D) brought a quiet title action in Mississippi against Beggerly (P) over certain real property. The issue was whether the land in question had been deeded prior to the date of the Louisiana Purchase in 1803. If not, the United States (D) would own it and not have to purchase it from Beggerly (P). During discovery, Beggerly (P) sought proof of title. A search by government officials of public records revealed nothing that proved a land grant prior to 1803. On the eve of trial, the case was settled for a modest sum and judgment entered based on the agreement. However, Beggerly (P) continued to search for information and in 1991, a specialist claimed to have found a grant in 1781. Beggerly (P) then filed a complaint seeking to set aside the settlement and award damages. The district court dismissed the case on jurisdictional grounds but the court of appeals reversed, deciding that it qualified as an independent action under Fed. R. Civ. P. 60(b).

ISSUE: Are independent actions pursuant to Rule 60(b) reserved for cases of injustice sufficiently gross to demand departure from adherence to the doctrine of res judicata?

HOLDING AND DECISION: (Rehnquist, C.J.) Yes. Independent actions pursuant to Rule 60(b) are reserved for cases of injustice sufficiently gross to demand departure from adherence to the doctrine of res judicata. Prior to the adoption of the Federal Rules of Civil Procedure, the availability of relief from a judgment turned on whether the court was still in the same term in which the challenged judgment was entered. The 1946 amendment to Fed. R. Civ. P. 60 made clear that all old forms of relief from a judgment were abolished except for the independent action. However, an independent action is only available to prevent a grave miscarriage of justice. In the present case, it is obvious that Beggerly's (P) allegations do not come close to meeting this standard. Beggerly (P) only alleges that the government (D) failed to thoroughly search its record. It would surely result in no grave injustice to allow the settlement and judgment in the prior litigation to stand. Therefore, the court of appeals is reversed and the case remanded.

▌ANALYSIS

The decision noted that the alleged failure to furnish relevant information could possibly fit under Fed. R. Civ. P. 60(b)(3). This subsection provides for a one-year limit on motions. Given that the time limit had long expired, the court declined to fully rule on this possibility.

■=■

Quicknotes

ACTION TO QUIET TITLE Equitable action to resolve conflicting claims to an interest in real property.

RES JUDICATA The rule of law that a final judgment by a court precludes subsequent litigation between the parties regarding the same cause of action.

■=■

Quick Reference Rules of Law

Plant v. Blazer Financial Services

Borrower (P) v. Lender (D)

598 F.2d 1357 (5th Cir. 1979).

NATURE OF CASE: Appeal from ruling finding a counterclaim compulsory.

FACT SUMMARY: Plant (P) was a debtor of Blazer Financial Services (Blazer) (D) who sued Blazer (D) for violations of the Truth-in-Lending Act, and Blazer (D) asserted a counterclaim on the debt owing which Plant (P) sought to dismiss.

🏛 RULE OF LAW
A claim for the amount of a debt owed pursuant to a transaction that is the subject of a truth-in-lending suit brought in federal court is a compulsory counterclaim of such suit.

FACTS: Plant (P) executed a note for $2,520 to be paid to Blazer (D) in monthly installments. No payments were made. Plant (P) brought suit in federal court alleging violations of the Truth-in-Lending Act by Blazer (D) for failure to disclose a limitation on an after-acquired security interest. Blazer (D) sought to interpose a counterclaim for the amount of the note, which Plant (P) challenged as not compulsory and an improper permissive counterclaim, as no diversity or federal question existed. The district court ruled the counterclaim compulsory, and Plant (P) appealed.

ISSUE: Is a claim for the amount of debt owed pursuant to a transaction that is the subject of a truth-in-lending suit brought in federal court a compulsory counterclaim?

HOLDING AND DECISION: (Roney, J.) Yes. Fed. R. Civ. P. Rule 13(a) provides that a counterclaim is compulsory if it "arises out of the transaction or occurrence" which is the subject matter of the plaintiff's claim. Four inquiries are designed to provide an answer: (1) Are the issues of fact and law the same? (2) Would res judicata bar a subsequent suit on the counterclaim? (3) Is the same evidence involved? (4) Is the counterclaim logically related to the main claim? All need not be satisfied. Under the last or logical relation test, it is clear that the same operative facts give rise to both claims here. A claim for the amount of a debt owed pursuant to a transaction that is the subject of a truth-in-lending suit brought in federal court is a compulsory counterclaim of such suit. Other district courts are in accord. Had Congress intended to insulate truth-in-lending recoveries from counterclaims of creditors, it could have done so. Affirmed.

▶ ANALYSIS

A compulsory counterclaim falls under a federal court's ancillary jurisdiction. Unlike a permissive counterclaim, it needs no independent basis for jurisdiction. The policy of avoiding multiple litigations is served by allowing courts to resolve all matters that are substantially enough related to an action properly brought.

■■■

Quicknotes

ANCILLARY JURISDICTION Authority of a federal court to hear and determine issues related to a case over which it has jurisdiction, but over which it would not have jurisdiction if such claims were brought independently.

COMPULSORY COUNTERCLAIM An independent cause of action brought by a defendant to a lawsuit that arises out of the same transaction or occurrence that is the subject matter of the plaintiff's claim.

FED. R. CIV. P. 13(A) Lays out the requirements for a compulsory counterclaim.

RES JUDICATA The rule of law that a final judgment by a court precludes subsequent litigation between the parties regarding the same cause of action.

■■■

Mosley v. General Motors Corp.

Class-action plaintiffs (P) v. Car company (D)

497 F.2d 1330 (8th Cir. 1974).

NATURE OF CASE: Appeal from order requiring severance of joint action.

FACT SUMMARY: Mosley (P) and nine other plaintiffs brought this class action against General Motors Corp. (D) for various acts of race and sex discrimination, and the district court ordered the ten plaintiffs to bring ten separate actions due to the wide variety of the claims and the unmanageability of the joint proceeding.

🏛 RULE OF LAW
Permissive joinder of parties is to be broadly granted under Fed. R. Civ. P. 20 where each party seeks relief arising out of the same transaction or series of transactions and a common question of fact or law will arise in the action.

FACTS: Mosley (P) and nine other plaintiffs brought this class action against General Motors Corp. (GM) (D) alleging various different acts that in some cases they contended constituted racial discrimination and in others sex discrimination. They filed complaints individually with the Equal Employment Opportunity Commission (EEOC), and the EEOC notified each of their right to bring a civil action in federal court. At that point the plaintiffs joined in bringing the class action. The district court ordered that each plaintiff bring a separate action, separately filed, due to the differing types of claims alleged and the unmanageability of the joint proceeding. The judge found that there was no right to relief arising out of the same transaction or series of transactions or a common question of fact or law as required by Fed. R. Civ. P. 20. Mosley (P) appealed.

ISSUE: Is permissive joinder to be broadly granted under Fed. R. Civ. P. 20 where each party seeks relief arising out of the same transaction or series of transactions and a common question of fact or law will arise in the action?

HOLDING AND DECISION: (Ross, J.) Yes. The purpose of Fed. R. Civ. P. 20 is to promote trial convenience and expedite the final determination of disputes. The rules permit the trial judge, however, to order separate trials within his discretion if such an order will prevent delay or prejudice. Reversal of such an order depends upon an abuse of that discretion. In this case, a series of "logically related" events occurred, which has been held to constitute a single series of transactions as required. Furthermore, the rights asserted depend on a common question of law. The district court abused

its discretion, therefore, in ordering the separate trials. Permissive joinder is to be broadly granted under Fed. R. Civ. P. 20 where each party seeks relief arising out of the same transaction or series of transactions and a common question of fact or law will arise in the action. Reversed and remanded.

▶ ANALYSIS

It is not often easy to determine what is a single series of transactions when distinct events have taken place. However, a series of employment or advancement decisions together appearing like a policy of discrimination is the kind of matter that Fed. R. Civ. P. 20 seeks to have determined in one action. It is when the rights of the parties suffer at the expense of judicial economy that Fed. R. Civ. P. 20(b) can be involved to require separate trials, rather than when the judge finds the case "unmanageable."

Quicknotes

FED. R. CIV. P. 20 Provides that parties requesting relief for injuries arising from the same transaction or common question of law or fact be permitted to consolidate their actions into a single action.

PERMISSIVE JOINDER The joining of parties or claims in a single suit if the claims against the parties arise from the same transaction or occurrence or involve common issues of law or fact; such joinder is not mandatory.

Price v. CTB, Inc.

Chicken farmer (P) v. Construction contractor (D)

168 F. Supp. 2d 1299 (M.D. Ala. 2001).

NATURE OF CASE: Motion to dismiss an impleaded party.

FACT SUMMARY: When Price (P) sued Latco (D) for faulty construction of a chicken house, Latco (D), in turn, impleaded ITW (D), the manufacturer of the nails, on theories of statutory and common law indemnity.

RULE OF LAW

A defendant may assert a claim against anyone not a party to the original action if that third party's liability is in some way dependent upon the outcome of the original action.

FACTS: Price (P), a chicken farmer, hired Latco (D) to build a chicken house. Alleging defective construction, Price (P) sued CTB (D), which equips poultry houses, and Latco (D) who was the original defendant in the underlying suit concerning the quality of construction workmanship. Latco (D), in turn, moved to implead ITW (D), alleging that ITW (D), a nail manufacturer, defectively designed the nails used in the construction. The specific causes of action against ITW (D) included (1) breach of warranty, (2) Alabama's extended manufacturer's liability doctrine, and (3) common-law indemnity. ITW (D) moved that it be dismissed from the suit on the grounds that it had been improperly impleaded under Fed. R. Civ. P. Rule 14.

ISSUE: May a defendant assert a claim against anyone not a party to the original action if that third party's liability is in some way dependent upon the outcome of the original action?

HOLDING AND DECISION: (De Ment, J.) Yes. A defendant may assert a claim against anyone not a party to the original action if that third party's liability is in some way dependent upon the outcome of the original action. Under the doctrine of implied contractual indemnity, Alabama courts recognize that a manufacturer of a product has impliedly agreed to indemnify the seller when (1) the seller is without fault, (2) the manufacturer is responsible, and (3) the seller has been required to pay a monetary judgment. Here, under Latco's (D) theory, should it be found liable for its construction of the chicken houses, it can demonstrate that the true fault lies with the nail guns and the nails manufactured by ITW (D). Accordingly, Alabama law provides Latco (D) a cause of action under common-law indemnity against ITW (D). Although the doctrine permits recovery only when the party to be indemnified is without

fault, whether such a factual scenario will be proven at trial is irrelevant for present purposes. The only issue presently is whether there is a legal basis to implead ITW (D), not whether ITW (D) is, in fact, liable to Latco (D). Since Fed. R. Civ. P. 14 permits Latco (D) to implead any party who "may be liable," it follows that the court must permit development of the factual record so the extent of that liability may be determined. Furthermore, it is well established that a properly impleaded claim may serve as an anchor for separate and independent claims under Rule 18(a). In short, Latco (D) has properly impleaded ITW (D) under Rule 14(a). ITW's (D) motion to dismiss is denied.

▶ ANALYSIS

In *Price*, the court noted that there is a limitation on the general rule of permitting a defendant to assert a claim against anyone not a party to the original action if that third party's liability is in some way dependent upon the outcome of the original action. Even though it may arise out of the same general set of facts as the main claim, a third party claim will not be permitted when it is based upon a separate and independent claim. Rather, the third party liability must in some way be derivative of the original claim; a third party may be impleaded only when the original defendant is trying to pass all or part of the liability onto that third party.

■■■

Quicknotes

FED. R. CIV. P. 14 Permits the impleader of a party who is or may be liable in order to determine the rights of all parties in one proceeding.

IMPLEADER Procedure by which a third party, who may be liable for all or part of liability, is joined to an action so that all issues may be resolved in a single suit.

INDEMNITY The duty of a party to compensate another for damages sustained.

■■■

Kroger v. Omaha Public Power District

Administratrix (P) v. Power company (D)

523 F.2d 161 (8th Cir. 1975).

NATURE OF CASE: Action to join a party to a lawsuit.

FACT SUMMARY: James Kroger was accidentally electrocuted while working. Geraldine Kroger (P), administratrix of his estate, brought suit based on diversity jurisdiction for damages resulting from his wrongful death.

> 🏛 **RULE OF LAW**
> Liability for negligence cannot be imposed without first establishing that a duty was owed to the plaintiff.

FACTS: James Kroger was accidentally electrocuted while working. He had been employed by Paxton & Vierling Steel Company. While helping to move a large steel tank by a crane with a 60-foot boom, the boom came close enough to high-tension lines, and an arc of electricity killed Kroger. Geraldine Kroger (P), administratrix of his estate, brought suit based on diversity jurisdiction for damages resulting from his wrongful death.

ISSUE: Can liability for negligence be imposed without first establishing that a duty was owed to the plaintiff?

HOLDING AND DECISION: (Nangle, J.) [No. Liability for negligence cannot be imposed without first establishing that a duty was owed to the plaintiff. Ownership of the transmission lines lay indisputably with Paxton & Vierling, not Omaha Public Power District (OPPD). OPPD had no duty to maintain the lines, OPPD had not been requested to discontinue the flow of electricity on the date of the accident, and OPPD had not been put on notice that a crane was being operated in the vicinity of the lines. As a result, there was no duty owed by OPPD to Kroger. As a matter of law, OPPD did not owe any duty to Kroger because OPPD did not own the transmission lines, and OPPD did not have a duty to maintain or a right of control over the lines involved.]

▶ ANALYSIS

The court focused on four criteria to determine whether a duty of due care was owed by OPPD to Kroger: ownership of the lines, maintenance of the lines, control over the flow of electricity through the lines, and knowledge of the use of steel equipment in the vicinity of the lines. Because OPPD didn't own or maintain the lines, and

because it had no knowledge of construction in the area of the lines, which would have required the company to discontinue the flow of electricity, there was no duty owed to Kroger. See *Owen Equipment & Erection Co. v. Kroger*, 437 U.S. 365 (1978).

Owen Equipment & Erection Co. v. Kroger

Crane company (D) v. Wife of electrocuted decedent (P)

437 U.S. 365 (1978).

NATURE OF CASE: Action for damages for wrongful death.

FACT SUMMARY: Kroger (P) brought a wrongful death action in federal court against a defendant of diverse citizenship and then amended her complaint to include an impleaded third-party defendant, Owen Equipment & Erection Co. (D), even though they were citizens of the same state.

🏛 RULE OF LAW
In a diversity case, the federal court does not have ancillary jurisdiction over the plaintiff's claims against a third-party defendant who is a citizen of the same state.

FACTS: Kroger's (P) husband was electrocuted when the boom of a steel crane owned and operated by Owen Equipment & Erection Co. (Owen) (D), and next to which he was walking, came too close to a high tension electric power line of the Omaha Public Power District (OPPD). Kroger (P) brought a wrongful death action against OPPD in federal court in Nebraska, she being a resident of Iowa. However, OPPD filed a third-party complaint against Owen (D), alleging its negligence had caused the electrocution. Eventually, OPPD's motion for summary judgment was granted, and Owen (D) was the only defendant left in the case. During trial, it was discovered that Owen (D), a Nebraska corporation, had its principal place of business in Iowa and was therefore a citizen of the same state as Kroger (P). The district court denied Owen's (D) motion to dismiss the complaint for lack of jurisdiction, and the jury returned a verdict in favor of Kroger (P). The court of appeals affirmed.

ISSUE: Can a federal court exercise ancillary jurisdiction over a plaintiff's claims against a third-party defendant who is a citizen of the same state in a diversity case?

HOLDING AND DECISION: (Stewart, J.) No. The concept of ancillary jurisdiction is not so broad as to permit a federal court in a diversity case to exercise jurisdiction over the plaintiff's claims against a third-party defendant who is a citizen of the same state. 28 U.S.C. § 1332(a)(1) requires complete diversity of citizenship. To allow ancillary jurisdiction in a case like this would be to allow circumvention of that requirement by the simple expedient of suing only those defendants who were of diverse citizenship and waiting for them to implead nondiverse defendants. Reversed.

DISSENT: (White, J.) Section 1332 requires complete diversity only between the plaintiff and those parties he actually brings into the suit, which would not include Owen (D) in this case. Beyond that, I would hold the district court has the power to entertain all claims among the parties arising from the same nucleus of operative fact as the plaintiff's original, jurisdiction-conferring claim against the original defendant. Thus, ancillary jurisdiction existed in this case.

▌ ANALYSIS

Fed. R. Civ. P. 14 permits ancillary jurisdiction. In amending it, the Advisory Committee stated that any attempt by a plaintiff to amend his complaint to assert a claim against an impleaded third party would be unavailing, by majority view, where the third party could not have been joined by the plaintiff originally due to jurisdictional limitations. Congress reenacted § 1332 without relevant change and with knowledge of the aforementioned view. The majority opinion took this as evidence of congressional approval of that view.

▪▭▪

Quicknotes

28 U.S.C. § 1332 Governs the requirements for diversity jurisdiction.

ANCILLARY JURISDICTION Authority of a federal court to hear and determine issues related to a case over which it has jurisdiction, but over which it would not have jurisdiction if such claims were brought independently.

FED. R. CIV. P. 14 Permits the impleader of a party who is or may be liable in order to determine the rights of all parties in one proceeding.

IMPLEADER Procedure by which a third party, who may be liable for all or part of liability, is joined to an action so that all issues may be resolved in a single suit.

▪▭▪

Temple v. Synthes Corp.

Medical implant user (P) v. Implant manufacturer (D)

498 U.S. 5, *reh'g. denied*, 498 U.S. 1092 (1990).

NATURE OF CASE: Appeal of dismissal with prejudice of action for damages for products liability, medical malpractice, and negligence.

FACT SUMMARY: Temple's (P) federal suit against Synthes Corp. (D), the manufacturer of a plate implanted in Temple's (P) back, was dismissed when Temple (P) failed to join the doctor and the hospital responsible for installing the plate.

🏛 RULE OF LAW
Joint tortfeasors are not necessary parties under Fed. R. Civ. P. 19.

FACTS: A plate and screw device implanted in Temple's (P) back malfunctioned. Temple (P) filed a federal court products liability action against Synthes Corp. (D), the manufacturer of the device. Temple (P) also filed a state-court medical-malpractice and negligence action against the doctor who implanted the device and the hospital where the operation was performed. Synthes (D) filed a motion to dismiss the federal lawsuit under Fed. R. Civ. P. 19 for Temple's (P) failure to join necessary parties. The district court agreed that the doctor and the hospital were necessary parties and gave Temple (P) 20 days to join them. When Temple (P) did not, the court dismissed the suit with prejudice. The court of appeals affirmed, finding that Rule 19 allowed the district court to order joinder in the interest of complete, consistent, and efficient settlement of controversies. It further found that overlapping, separate lawsuits would have prejudiced Synthes (D) because Synthes (D) might claim the device was not defective but that the doctor and the hospital were negligent, and the doctor and the hospital might claim the opposite. Temple (P) appealed, arguing that joint tortfeasors are not necessary parties under Rule 19.

ISSUE: Are joint tortfeasors necessary parties under Fed. R. Civ. P. 19?

HOLDING AND DECISION: (Per curiam) No. Joint tortfeasors are not necessary parties under Fed. R. Civ. P. 19. It has long been the rule that joint tortfeasors need not be named as defendants in a single lawsuit. Rule 19 does not change that principle. The Advisory Committee Notes to Rule 19(a) state that a tortfeasor with the usual joint and several liability is merely a permissive party. There is a public interest in avoiding multiple lawsuits. However, since the requirements of Rule 19(a) have not been met, the district court had no authority to order dismissal. Reversed and remanded.

▶ ANALYSIS

The function of compulsory joinder codified in Fed. R. Civ. P. 19 is to bring all affected parties into the same lawsuit. Joinder is often required where the suit involves jointly held rights or liabilities, where more than one party claims the same property, or where granting relief necessarily would affect the rights of parties not in the lawsuit. Though there is a strong interest in "complete, consistent, and efficient settlement of controversies," compulsory joinder is limited. There is a strong tradition of allowing the parties themselves to determine who shall be a party, what claims shall be litigated, and what litigation strategies shall be followed.

■══■

Quicknotes

COMPULSORY JOINDER The joining of parties to a lawsuit that is mandatory if complete relief cannot be afforded to the parties in his absence or his absence will result in injustice.

FED. R. CIV. P. 19 Sets forth the rules governing joinder.

JOINDER The joining of claims or parties in one lawsuit.

JOINT TORTFEASORS Two or more parties that either act in concert, or whose individual acts combine to cause a single injury, rendering them jointly and severally liable for damages incurred.

NECESSARY PARTIES Parties whose joining in a lawsuit is essential to the disposition of the action.

■══■

Helzberg's Diamond Shops v. Valley West Des Moines Shopping Center

Jewelry stores (P) v. Shopping center (D)

564 F.2d 816 (8th Cir. 1977).

NATURE OF CASE: Appeal from denial of motion to dismiss for failure to join an indispensable party.

FACT SUMMARY: Helzberg's Diamond Shops (Helzberg's) (P) brought this suit to enjoin Valley West Des Moines Shopping Center (Valley West) (D), Helzberg's (P) commercial landlord, from breaching their lease agreement by leasing more than two full-line jewelry stores in the mall where Helzberg's (P) leasehold was located, and Valley West (D) unsuccessfully moved to dismiss on the ground that Helzberg's (P) failed to join the full-line jewelry store tenant, Lord's.

🏛 RULE OF LAW
A tenant under a lease that violates a clause in another tenant's lease from a common landlord is not an indispensable party under Fed. R. Civ. P. 19 to a suit by such other tenant against that landlord.

FACTS: Helzberg's Diamond Shops (Helzberg's) (P), a full-line jewelry store, leased space in Valley West Des Moines Shopping Center (Valley West) (D) shopping center to operate their store. The lease agreement provided that no more than two such stores would be allowed to rent space other than Helzberg's (P) in the mall. Valley West (D), however, leased space to a third such store, Lord's. Helzberg's (P) brought this action to enjoin such a lease, and Valley West (D) moved to dismiss on the ground that Lord's was not joined and was an indispensable party. Helzberg's (P) brought suit in district court in Missouri and could not obtain personal jurisdiction over Lord's, which had no Missouri contacts. The district court denied Valley West's (D) motion, and Valley West (D) appealed.

ISSUE: Is a tenant under a lease that violates a clause in another tenant's lease from a common landlord an indispensable party under Fed. Civ. P. 19 to a suit brought by such other tenant against that landlord?

HOLDING AND DECISION: (Alsop, J.) No. A tenant under a lease that violates a clause in another tenant's lease is not an indispensable party under Fed. R. Civ. P. 19 to a suit brought by such other tenant against their common landlord. Fed. R. Civ. P. 19 defines an indispensable party as one in whose absence complete relief cannot be accorded, or claims an interest related to the subject of the action and whose absence will impair or impede his ability to protect that interest or force him to risk multiple or inconsistent obligations. Valley West (D) contends that Lord's and Valley West's (D) rights under their contract cannot be adjudicated in Lord's absence. However, the determination that may result in this action is that Valley West (D) may be forced to terminate that contract, in which case Lord's will still be empowered to assert its rights under the contract for that eventuality. The claim that Valley West (D) may be subjected then to inconsistent obligations following another contract action also fails. Valley West's (D) inconsistent obligations will result from their voluntary execution of two lease agreements with inconsistent obligations required under them. The litigation here can proceed without Lord's, which is not an indispensable party under these circumstances. Affirmed.

▶ ANALYSIS

In federal practice, the court will balance the prejudice to an absent party against the desirability of ruling on a meritorious claim. The judge can shape the relief granted under his equitable powers so as to avoid any such prejudice so long as he renders an effective judgment.

■═■

Quicknotes

COMPULSORY JOINDER The joining of parties to a lawsuit that is mandatory if complete relief cannot be afforded to the parties in his absence or his absence will result in injustice.

FED. R. CIV. P. 19 Sets forth the rules governing joinder.

INDISPENSABLE PARTY Parties whose joining in a lawsuit is essential for the adequate disposition of the action and without whom the action cannot proceed.

■═■

Natural Resources Defense Council v. United States Nuclear Regulatory Commission

Federal regulatory agency (D) v. Federal commission (P)

578 F.2d 1341 (10th Cir. 1978).

NATURE OF CASE: Appeal of denial of motion to intervene.

FACT SUMMARY: The American Mining Congress (AMC) and Kerr-McGee (KM) appealed the denial of their motion to intervene in an action brought by the Natural Resources Defense Council (NRDC) (P) against the Nuclear Regulatory Commission (NRC) (D) seeking a declaration that state-granted nuclear power operation licenses are subject to the requirement of filing an environmental impact statement and seeking an injunction of the grant of one such license by the New Mexico Environmental Improvement Agency (NMEIA).

RULE OF LAW

A party may intervene in an action under Federal Rule of Civil Procedure 24(a)(2) if he has an interest upon which the disposition of that action will have a significant legal effect.

FACTS: The Nuclear Regulatory Commission (NRC) (D) is permitted by federal law to give the several states the power to grant licenses to operate nuclear power facilities. The NRC (D) is empowered to grant such licenses subject to a requirement that such "major federal action" be preceded by the preparation of an environmental impact statement. The NRC (D) entered into an agreement with the New Mexico Environmental Improvement Agency (NMEIA) permitting it to issue a license, which it did, to United Nuclear without preparing an impact statement. The Natural Resources Defense Council (NRDC) (P) brought this action seeking a declaration that state-granted licenses are the product of "major federal action" and subject to the statement requirement and seeking an injunction against the issuance of the license. United Nuclear intervened without objection. KM, a potential recipient of an NMEIA license, and AMC, a public interest group, sought to intervene, but their motions were denied. Both appealed.

ISSUE: May a party intervene in an action under Fed. R. Civ. P. 24(a)(2) if he has an interest upon which the disposition of that action will have a significant legal effect?

HOLDING AND DECISION: (Doyle, J.) Yes. Fed. R. Civ. P. 24(a) gives a party the right to intervene when he has a sufficiently protectable interest related to the property or transaction that is the subject of the action and the disposition will "as a practical matter, impair or impede his ability to protect that interest." The argument that the effect upon the movant's right must be a res judicata effect is unpersuasive. The effect must "as a practical matter" impair or impede the ability to protect the right. A party may thus intervene in an action under Fed. R. Civ. P. 24(a)(2) if he has an interest upon which the disposition of that action will have a significant legal effect. It need not be a strictly legal effect. KM and AMC each have rights, not protected by other parties to the litigation, which will be thus effected, and they must be allowed to intervene. Reversed and remanded.

ANALYSIS

Fed. R. Civ. P. 24(a) covers the intervention of right, while Rule 24(b) sets forth criteria for permissive intervention. Intervention is permissive if there is a common question of law or fact or if a statute gives a conditional right to intervene. In either case, an intervenor has the same status in the litigation as an original party, but he cannot raise any new issues. Ancillary jurisdiction attaches over the intervenor.

Quicknotes

FED. R. CIV. P. 24 Governs permissive intervention and intervention as a matter of right.

INTERVENTION The method by which a party, not an initial party to the action, is admitted to the action in order to assert an interest in the subject matter of a lawsuit.

Martin v. Wilks

Firefighters (P) v. Court (D)

490 U.S. 755 (1989).

NATURE OF CASE: Review of reversal of dismissal of reverse-discrimination action.

FACT SUMMARY: Several white firefighters challenged affirmative action plans mandated by a consent decree that was entered in an action of which they had knowledge but had not intervened.

🏛 RULE OF LAW
A party may not be bound by a judgment rendered in an action in which he was not a party, even if he had knowledge of the action.

FACTS: As part of a discrimination action, a consent decree was rendered between the City of Birmingham, Alabama, and a class of Black firefighters. As part of the decree, the City instituted an affirmative action program. Subsequent to this, a group of white firefighters filed a reverse-discrimination action. The district court dismissed, holding that because the white firefighters had notice of the prior action but had elected not to intervene, the matter was res judicata as to them. The Eleventh Circuit reversed, and the U.S. Supreme Court granted review.

ISSUE: May a party be bound by a judgment rendered in an action in which he was not a party, if he had knowledge of the action?

HOLDING AND DECISION: (Rehnquist, C.J.) No. A party may not be bound by a judgment rendered in an action in which he was not a party, even if he had knowledge of the action. It is a principle of general application that one is not bound by an in personam judgment in a litigation in which he is not designated as a party or has not been made a party by service of process. The argument asserted by those defending the consent decree is that by knowing about the underlying action and failing to intervene, the plaintiffs herein waived that objection to being bound. This is incorrect. A party seeking a judgment binding on another cannot obligate that person to intervene; he must be joined. This was the position taken by the Eleventh Circuit, and it was correct in so doing. Affirmed.

DISSENT: (Stevens, J.) In no sense were the white firefighters herein "bound" by the consent decree; rather it was the City that was so bound. The district court properly dismissed the action because the City was fulfilling its legal obligations, not because the white firefighters were somehow bound by the consent decree.

▶ ANALYSIS

Joinder is governed by Fed. R. Civ. P. 19. The rule distinguishes between parties that should be joined and parties that must be joined. Parties may be joined either as defendants or as involuntary plaintiffs.

Quicknotes

COMPULSORY JOINDER The joining of parties to a lawsuit that is mandatory if complete relief cannot be afforded to the parties in his absence or his absence will result in injustice.

FED. R. CIV. P. 19 Sets forth the rules governing joinder.

INTERVENTION The method by which a party, not an initial party to the action, is admitted to the action in order to assert an interest in the subject matter of a lawsuit.

PERMISSIVE JOINDER The joining of parties or claims in a single suit if the claims against the parties arise from the same transaction or occurrence or involve common issues of law or fact; such joinder is not mandatory.

RES JUDICATA The rule of law that a final judgment by a court precludes subsequent litigation between the parties regarding the same cause of action.

Paragon Molding, Ltd. v. Safeco Insurance Company

Insured (P) v. Creditors (D)

2010 WL 2386355 (S.D. Ohio 2010).

NATURE OF CASE: Action in interpleader.

FACT SUMMARY: After a fire at one of Paragon Molding's (P) facilities, an insurer deposited funds with the court. All persons and corporations with claims against Paragon Molding (P) were joined as defendants and required to interplead.

🏛 RULE OF LAW
In determining the manner in which interpleaded funds should be distributed, the district court sits as a court of equity, possessing the remedial flexibility to do complete equity between the parties.

FACTS: A fire at the Paragon Molding, Ltd. (Paragon) (P) facility caused damage to the real estate and the inventory for its molding and game calls business. As a result, Paragon (P) filed suit against American Economy Insurance Company (AEIC), claiming that AEIC wrongfully withheld proceeds from a fire insurance policy from Paragon (P). AEIC was prepared to pay, but first required Paragon's (P) creditors to come forward and state their claims. AEIC deposited $1,334,812.98 in fire insurance proceeds with the court to settle the debts. Among the parties that intervened, alleging claims to the insurance proceeds, were Paragon (P); Miller Industries, owner of the real estate occupied by Paragon (P); the Alex N. Sill Company, which helped Paragon (P) prepare the fire insurance claim; Roy Rhodes and Jimmie Rhodes, who had non-realty assets in Paragon (P) that were destroyed in the fire; and JPMorgan Chase Bank, for various loans to Paragon (P).

ISSUE: In determining the manner in which interpleaded funds should be distributed, does the district court sit as a court of equity, possessing the remedial flexibility to do complete equity between the parties?

HOLDING AND DECISION: (Rice, J.) Yes. In determining the manner in which interpleaded funds should be distributed, the district court sits as a court of equity, possessing the remedial flexibility to do complete equity between the parties. Under the Federal Rules of Civil Procedure, persons with claims that may expose a plaintiff to double or multiple liability may be joined as defendants and required to interplead. In this case at request of various parties, the subject insurance proceeds were deposited and all parties with a claim to those proceeds filed a claim with the court. The case will proceed in the nature of interpleader unless there is objection by any of the parties. Assuming the parties are in agreement as to the nature of this case, AEIC need not be a party in this litigation, since its original dispute with Paragon (P) has now been resolved, and since it has now deposited the fire insurance proceeds with the court. Parties that disagree with the court's conclusion that AEIC should now be dismissed from this litigation must show cause as to its reasons therefor. Further, an interpleader plaintiff is the "stakeholder" that holds title to the fund in dispute. In this case, the stakeholder that holds title to the fund in dispute is Paragon. Paragon (P) is, thus, the only proper plaintiff. All other parties are claimants to the stake or party-defendants. Priority of distribution in interpleader actions goes to those claimants who have a claim in the specific *res* held by the Court, rather than having general, unrelated claims against the stakeholder. Therefore, the parties must specify to what extent they have a claim in the specific *res* at issue or, if not, what, if anything, entitles each of them to priority of payment over other claimants, together with citations of relevant authority. Finally, 28 U.S.C. § 1335 requires the participation of at least two adverse claimants of diverse citizenship in order for a court to have jurisdiction over an interpleader action. According to the pleadings in this case, Paragon (P) is a citizen of the State of Ohio. In order for the Court to confirm that it has jurisdiction over the present interpleader action, the parties must file an amendment to their pleadings (not an amended pleading) to include a short and plain statement as to jurisdiction.

▶ ANALYSIS

This case illustrates the nature of interpleader and the steps in an action that typically occur. The judge will oversee the deposit and distribution of funds, requiring agreement that the distribution will be a final judgment on the matter, thus foreclosing additional liability of the plaintiff.

Quicknotes

INTERPLEADER An equitable proceeding whereby a person holding property which is subject to the claims of multiple parties may require such parties to resolve the matter through litigation.

RES Thing; subject matter of a dispute to establish rights therein.

Hansberry v. Lee

Black land purchaser (D) v. Party to covenant (P)

11 U.S. 32 (1940).

NATURE OF CASE: A class action to enforce a racially restrictive covenant.

FACT SUMMARY: Lee (P) sought to enjoin a sale of land to Hansberry (D) on the grounds that the sale violated a racially restrictive covenant.

🏛 RULE OF LAW
There must be adequate representation of the members of a class action or the judgment is not binding on the parties not adequately represented.

FACTS: Hansberry (D), a Black, purchased land from a party who had signed a restrictive covenant forbidding the sale of the land to Blacks. Lee (P), one of the parties who signed the covenant, sought to have the sale enjoined because it breached the covenant. Lee (P) contended that the validity of the covenant was established in a prior case in which one of the parties was a class of landowners involved with the covenant. To be valid, 95 percent of the landowners had to sign the covenant, and the trial court in the prior case held that 95 percent of the landowners had signed the covenant. That case was appealed, and the Illinois Supreme Court upheld the decision, even though they found that 95 percent of the landowners had not signed the covenant, but they held that since it was a class action, all members of the class would be bound by the decision of the court. Hansberry (D) claimed that he and the party selling him the house were not bound by the res judicata effect of the prior decision, as they were not parties to the litigation. The lower court held that the decision of the Illinois Supreme Court would have to be challenged directly in order that it be set aside or reversed. Otherwise, their decision was still binding. The case was appealed to the U.S. Supreme Court.

ISSUE: For a judgment in a class action to be binding, must all of the members of the class be adequately represented by parties with similar interests?

HOLDING AND DECISION: (Stone, J.) Yes. It is not necessary that all members of a class be present as parties to the litigation to be bound by the judgment if they are adequately represented by parties who are present. In regular cases, to be bound by the judgment the party must receive notice and an opportunity to be heard. If due process is not afforded the individual, then the judgment is not binding. The class action is an exception to the general rule. Because of the numbers involved in class actions, it is enough if the party is adequately represented by a member of the class with a similar interest. Hansberry (D) was not

adequately represented by the class of landowners. Their interests were not similar enough to even be considered members of the same class. Lee (P) and the landowners were trying to restrict Blacks from buying any of the land, and Hansberry (D) was a Black attempting to purchase land. When there is such a conflicting interest between members of a class, there is most likely not adequate representation of one of the members of the class. There must be a similarity of interest before there can even be a class. Since there was no similarity of interests between Lee (P) and Hansberry (D), Hansberry (D) could not be considered a member of the class and so the prior judgment was not binding on Hansberry (D). Hansberry (D) was not afforded due process because of the lack of adequate representation. The judgment is reversed.

▶ ANALYSIS

Fed. R. Civ. P. 23(c)(3) requires that the court describe those whom the court finds to be members of the class. The court is to note those to whom notice was provided and also those who had not requested exclusion. These members are considered members of the class and are bound by the decision of the court whether it is in their favor or not. The federal rules allow a member of the class to request exclusion from the class, and that party will not be bound by the decision of the court. Since a party must receive notice of the class action before he can request exclusion from the class, the court must determine if a party received sufficient notice of the action or if sufficient effort was made to notify him of the action. The rules state if the court finds that the party did have sufficient notice and was considered a member of the class, he is bound by the decision.

■=■

Quicknotes

CLASS ACTION A suit commenced by a representative on behalf of an ascertainable group that is too large to appear in court, who shares a commonality of interests and who will benefit from a successful result.

COVENANT A written promise to do, or to refrain from doing, a particular activity.

FED. R. CIV. P. 23 Sets forth the requirements in order to maintain a class-action suit.

■=■

Phillips Petroleum v. Shutts

Gas and oil company (D) v. Class of lessees (P)

472 U.S. 797 (1985).

NATURE OF CASE: Appeal of a judgment in a class-action suit.

FACT SUMMARY: Shutts (P) filed a class-action suit against Phillips Petroleum (D) for allegedly underpaying royalties on gas leases.

🏛 RULE OF LAW
A state may exercise jurisdiction over absent plaintiffs in a classification suit even if the plaintiffs have no contacts with that state.

FACTS: Phillips Petroleum (Phillips) (D) had gas and mineral leases with numerous individuals. Royalties were based on the selling price of the final product. When prices were raised, Phillips (D) would often pay royalties at a lower price. Shutts (P) filed a class-action suit on behalf of over 33,000 individuals, seeking damages. A Kansas court certified the class. Letters were sent to all members of the plaintiff class. A plaintiff had the right to opt out of the class or be bound by the judgment. About 3,000 opted out. A judgment for the plaintiffs was entered. The Kansas Supreme Court rejected an appeal by Phillips (D) claiming that Kansas could not exercise jurisdiction over plaintiffs not residents of Kansas. Phillips (D) appealed to the U.S. Supreme Court.

ISSUE: May a state exercise jurisdiction over absent plaintiffs in a class-action suit, if the plaintiffs have no contacts with that state?

HOLDING AND DECISION: (Rehnquist, J.) Yes. A state may exercise jurisdiction over absent plaintiffs in a class-action suit even if the plaintiffs have no contacts with that state. The "minimum contacts" rule is a matter of personal liberty, not state sovereignty. It exists to protect defendants from being hauled into a distant forum unfairly. A plaintiff in a class-action suit is in a much different position. He is in no danger of a loss of freedom or assets and, in fact, can sit back and let others do the work for him. His ability to opt out of the class further protects him; he is not forced to enter a class unwillingly. Affirmed in part, reversed in part, and remanded.

▌ANALYSIS

The Court stated in this opinion that minimum contacts is an issue of liberty, not sovereignty. This issue has been touched upon since *Pennoyer v. Neff*, 95 U.S. 714 (1877). The Court here held that the opt-out procedure was a sufficient protection of personal liberty.

Quicknotes

CLASS ACTION A suit commenced by a representative on behalf of an ascertainable group that is too large to appear in court, who shares a commonality of interests and who will benefit from a successful result.

MINIMUM CONTACTS The minimum degree of contact necessary in order to sustain a cause of action within a particular forum, consistent with the requirements of due process.

Wal-Mart Stores, Inc. v. Dukes

Retail giant (D) v. Female employees (P)

131 S. Ct. 2541 (2011).

NATURE OF CASE: Class action based on gender discrimination.

FACT SUMMARY: A small group of women filed a gender discrimination claim against Wal-Mart Stores, Inc. (D). A class was certified, and the original small group of women who filed the claims wanted to represent the class. The class was the largest in history.

RULE OF LAW

(1) A class consisting of more than one million women employed by a single employer nationwide cannot be certified as a class if they do not meet the "commonality" threshold for class certification under Fed. R. Civ. P. 23(a)(2) because they cannot demonstrate all class members were subject to the same discriminatory employment policy.

(2) Claims for monetary relief may not be certified under Fed. R. Civ. P. 23(b)(2) where the monetary relief is not incidental to the injunctive or declaratory relief.

FACTS: Betty Dukes (P), a Wal-Mart "greeter" at a Pittsburg, Calif., store, and five other women filed a class-action lawsuit in which they alleged that the company's nationwide policies resulted in lower pay for women than men in comparable positions and longer wait for management promotions than men. The U.S. District Court for the Northern District of California certified the class, finding Plaintiffs satisfied the requirements of Rules 23(a)(2) and 23(b)(2). The certified class was estimated to include than 1.5 million women, all women employed by Wal-Mart nationwide at any time after December 26, 1998, making this the largest class action lawsuit in U.S. history. Wal-Mart (D) argued that the court should require employees to file on an individual basis, contending that class actions of this size—formed under Rule 23(b) of the Federal Rules of Civil Procedure—are inherently unmanageable and unduly costly. The U.S. Court of Appeals for the Ninth Circuit upheld the class certification three times.

ISSUE:

(1) Can a class consisting of more than one million women employed by a single employer nationwide be certified as a class if they do not meet the "commonality" threshold for class certification under Fed. R. Civ. P. 23(a)(2) because they cannot demonstrate all class members were subject to the same discriminatory employment policy?

(2) May claims for monetary relief be certified under Fed. R. Civ. P. 23(b)(2) where the monetary relief is not incidental to the injunctive or declaratory relief?

HOLDING AND DECISION: (Scalia, J.)

(1) No. A class consisting of more than one million women employed by a single employer nationwide cannot be certified as a class if they do not meet the "commonality" threshold for class certification under Fed. R. Civ. P. 23(a)(2) because they cannot demonstrate all class members were subject to the same discriminatory employment policy. The class action is "an exception to the usual rule that litigation is conducted by and on behalf of the individual named parties only." In order to justify a departure from that rule, "a class representative must be part of the class and 'possess the same interest and suffer the same injury' as the class members." Rule 23(a) ensures that the named plaintiffs are appropriate representatives of the class whose claims they wish to litigate. The Rule's four requirements—numerosity, commonality, typicality, and adequate representation—effectively "limit the class claims to those fairly encompassed by the named plaintiff's claims." Proof of commonality—the second of the Rule's four requirements—necessarily overlaps with the group's argument that Wal-Mart (D) engages in a pattern or practice of discrimination. Under Title VII, the central inquiry involves the reason for a particular employment decision, and the plaintiffs wish to sue for millions of employment decisions at once. Without something holding together the alleged reasons for those employment decisions, it would be impossible to say that examination of all the class members' claims will produce a common answer to the crucial discrimination question. The testimony of the plaintiffs' social science expert who claimed that Wal-Mart's (D) culture was susceptible to gender bias is unpersuasive. The testimony is useless to the question of whether the plaintiffs could prove a general policy of discrimination. Also rejected was the use of aggregate statistical analyses and the mere existence of gender disparities in pay, promotion, or representation to meet the commonality burden. Instead, to show commonality, a plaintiff would at least need to demonstrate store-by-store disparities. Third, affidavits from 120 individuals, or one out of every 12,500 class members, did not constitute "significant proof" that Wal-Mart (D) operates under a general policy of discrimination. The members of

the plaintiffs' group held many different jobs, at different levels of Wal-Mart's (D) hierarchy, for variable lengths of time, in 3,400 stores, across 50 states, with many different supervisors (male and female), subject to a variety of regional policies that all differed. Some thrived while others did not. They have little in common but their sex and this lawsuit.

(2) No. Claims for monetary relief may not be certified under Fed. R. Civ. P. 23(b)(2) where the monetary relief is not incidental to the injunctive or declaratory relief. After satisfying the elements of Rule 23(a), the proposed class must satisfy at least one of the three requirements listed in Rule 23(b). The plaintiffs sought certification under Rule 23(b)(2), which applies when "the party opposing the class has acted or refused to act on grounds that apply generally to the class, so that final injunctive relief or corresponding declaratory relief is appropriate respecting the class as a whole." But Rule 23(b)(2) applies only when a single injunction or declaratory judgment would provide relief to each member of the class. It does not authorize class certification when each individual class member would be entitled to a different injunction or declaratory judgment against the defendant. Similarly, it does not authorize class certification when each class member would be entitled to an individualized award of monetary damages. The "predominance test" established by the Ninth Circuit, which permitted the certification of claims for monetary damages as long as claims for injunctive relief "predominated" over the claims for monetary damages, is rejected. Rather, the "incidental damages" test, which permits certification of claims for monetary relief as long as that relief "flow[s] directly from liability to the class as a whole," which "should not require additional hearings," is more appropriate. The adoption of a bright-line rule prohibiting all money damages from ever being certified under Rule 23(b)(2) is not considered here. "The judgment of the Court of Appeals is reversed."

CONCURRENCE AND DISSENT: (Ginsburg, J.) The class should not have been certified under Fed. R. Civ. P. 23(b)(2), because the plaintiffs, alleging discrimination in violation of Title VII, seek monetary relief that is not merely incidental to any injunctive or declaratory relief that might be available. But a class of this type may be certifiable under Rule 23(b)(3), if the plaintiffs show that common class questions "predominate" over issues affecting individuals, such as qualification for, and the amount of, backpay or compensatory damages, and that a class action is "superior" to other modes of adjudication. Whether the class the plaintiffs describe meets the specific requirements of Rule 23(b)(3) is not before the Court, and that matter should be reserved for consideration and decision on remand. But the majority disqualifies the class under 23(a)(2), holding that the plaintiffs cannot cross the "commonality" line, and by doing so imports into the Rule 23(a) determination concerns properly addressed in a Rule 23(b)(3) assessment. The majority errs in importing a "dissimilarities" notion suited to Rule 23(b)(3) into the Rule 23(a) commonality inquiry.

▶ *ANALYSIS*

This is a landmark case that was thoroughly analyzed in the media when it was released. Many criticized the decision as inappropriately and unfairly raising the bar for certification to the detriment of those with valid Title VII claims. District courts will now be required to scrutinize closely all alleged common questions of law and fact to determine if the proposed common questions generate common answers that are apt to drive resolution in each case. It will not be sufficient for plaintiffs to allege a "general policy" without proving the existence of the policy and its impact on each class member.

■■■

Quicknotes

CLASS ACTION A suit commenced by a representative on behalf of an ascertainable group that is too large to appear in court, who shares a commonality of interests and who will benefit from a successful result.

CLASS CERTIFICATION Certification by a court's granting of a motion to allow individual litigants to join as one plaintiff in a class action against the defendant.

■■■

Amchem Products, Inc. v. Windsor

Asbestos producer (D) v. Class-action plaintiffs (P)

521 U.S. 591 (1997).

NATURE OF CASE: Appeal from reversal of class certification in mass tort action.

FACT SUMMARY: The district court certified a class (P) of persons exposed to asbestos products in order to effect a settlement of the case.

> 🏛 **RULE OF LAW**
> Fed. R. Civ. P. 23 requirements for class certification must be met even if the certification is for settlement only.

FACTS: All of the asbestos exposure cases pending in federal courts were transferred and consolidated for pretrial proceedings to a single district court. Following this consolidation, the parties began settlement negotiations. The defendants' steering committee (D) made an offer to settle all pending and future asbestos cases by providing a fund from which to pay claims. Eventually, a settlement was reached for pending cases. A second settlement for potential plaintiffs was then reached. The parties then sought certification of this class of potential plaintiffs for purposes of settlement only. Nine lead plaintiffs were named who were designed to be representative of a class of all persons and family members who had been exposed to asbestos products but had not yet filed suit. The district court approved the settlement, certified the class (P), and enjoined class members from filing additional suits. Objectors raised numerous challenges to the settlement, claiming that it unfairly disadvantaged those without current problems. The court of appeals reversed the certification on the grounds that Fed. R. Civ. P. 23 requirements were not met. The defendants appealed.

ISSUE: Must Fed. R. Civ. P. 23 requirements for class certification be met even if the certification is for settlement only?

HOLDING AND DECISION: (Ginsburg, J.) Yes. Fed. R. Civ. P. 23 requirements for class certification must be met even if the certification is for settlement only. Rule 23, authorizing class actions, has several requirements that must be satisfied. These standards are designed to protect absent class members. They may not be disregarded simply because a court believes that a settlement is fair. First of all, common questions of law or fact must predominate over questions affecting individual members. The district court's reliance on the claimants' interest in a compensation scheme does not meet this requirement. A compensation scheme is a

matter for legislative consideration. Secondly, the named parties in a class action must fairly and adequately protect the interests of the class. The district court failed to break the class into subclasses. Thus, the named parties had diverse medical conditions and diverse interests that could cause conflicts of interest. Furthermore, there are impediments to the provision of adequate notice because there are persons in the class who may not even know of their exposure to asbestos yet. The only proper accommodation that should be made to settlement-only class certification is that the problems of trial administration should be ignored. Accordingly, in the present case, the class was improperly certified because the requirements of Rule 23 were not satisfied. Affirmed.

CONCURRENCE AND DISSENT: (Breyer, J.) The need for settlement in mass tort cases is greater than the majority suggests. Also, settlement-related issues should be given more weight for purposes of determining whether common issues predominate. The settlement is something that should help the class meet the Rule 23 requirements.

▶ **ANALYSIS**

Settlement classes have become more and more common since the advent of Rule 23, which does not make provision for such classes. Many commentators have called for revision to Rule 23 to address the reality of settlement classes. However, others have objected on the basis that settlement classes invite collusion among class counsel and the defense.

■▬■

Quicknotes

FED. R. CIV. P. 23 Sets forth the requirements in order to maintain a class-action suit.

SETTLEMENT An agreement entered into by the parties to a civil lawsuit agreeing upon the determination of rights and issues between them, thus disposing of the need for judicial determination.

■▬■

Glossary

Common Latin Words and Phrases Encountered in the Law

A FORTIORI: Because one fact exists or has been proven, therefore a second fact that is related to the first fact must also exist.

A PRIORI: From the cause to the effect. A term of logic used to denote that when one generally accepted truth is shown to be a cause, another particular effect must necessarily follow.

AB INITIO: From the beginning; a condition which has existed throughout, as in a marriage which was void ab initio.

ACTUS REUS: The wrongful act; in criminal law, such action sufficient to trigger criminal liability.

AD VALOREM: According to value; an ad valorem tax is imposed upon an item located within the taxing jurisdiction calculated by the value of such item.

AMICUS CURIAE: Friend of the court. Its most common usage takes the form of an amicus curiae brief, filed by a person who is not a party to an action but is nonetheless allowed to offer an argument supporting his legal interests.

ARGUENDO: In arguing. A statement, possibly hypothetical, made for the purpose of argument, is one made arguendo.

BILL QUIA TIMET: A bill to quiet title (establish ownership) to real property.

BONA FIDE: True, honest, or genuine. May refer to a person's legal position based on good faith or lacking notice of fraud (such as a bona fide purchaser for value) or to the authenticity of a particular document (such as a bona fide last will and testament).

CAUSA MORTIS: With approaching death in mind. A gift causa mortis is a gift given by a party who feels certain that death is imminent.

CAVEAT EMPTOR: Let the buyer beware. This maxim is reflected in the rule of law that a buyer purchases at his own risk because it is his responsibility to examine, judge, test, and otherwise inspect what he is buying.

CERTIORARI: A writ of review. Petitions for review of a case by the United States Supreme Court are most often done by means of a writ of certiorari.

CONTRA: On the other hand. Opposite. Contrary to.

CORAM NOBIS: Before us; writs of error directed to the court that originally rendered the judgment.

CORAM VOBIS: Before you; writs of error directed by an appellate court to a lower court to correct a factual error.

CORPUS DELICTI: The body of the crime; the requisite elements of a crime amounting to objective proof that a crime has been committed.

CUM TESTAMENTO ANNEXO, ADMINISTRATOR (ADMINISTRATOR C.T.A.): With will annexed; an administrator c.t.a. settles an estate pursuant to a will in which he is not appointed.

DE BONIS NON, ADMINISTRATOR (ADMINISTRATOR D.B.N.): Of goods not administered; an administrator d.b.n. settles a partially settled estate.

DE FACTO: In fact; in reality; actually. Existing in fact but not officially approved or engendered.

DE JURE: By right; lawful. Describes a condition that is legitimate "as a matter of law," in contrast to the term "de facto," which connotes something existing in fact but not legally sanctioned or authorized. For example, de facto segregation refers to segregation brought about by housing patterns, etc., whereas de jure segregation refers to segregation created by law.

DE MINIMIS: Of minimal importance; insignificant; a trifle; not worth bothering about.

DE NOVO: Anew; a second time; afresh. A trial de novo is a new trial held at the appellate level as if the case originated there and the trial at a lower level had not taken place.

DICTA: Generally used as an abbreviated form of obiter dicta, a term describing those portions of a judicial opinion incidental or not necessary to resolution of the specific question before the court. Such nonessential statements and remarks are not considered to be binding precedent.

DUCES TECUM: Refers to a particular type of writ or subpoena requesting a party or organization to produce certain documents in their possession.

EN BANC: Full bench. Where a court sits with all justices present rather than the usual quorum.

EX PARTE: For one side or one party only. An ex parte proceeding is one undertaken for the benefit of only one party, without notice to, or an appearance by, an adverse party.

EX POST FACTO: After the fact. An ex post facto law is a law that retroactively changes the consequences of a prior act.

EX REL.: Abbreviated form of the term "ex relatione," meaning upon relation or information. When the state brings an action in which it has no interest against an individual at the instigation of one who has a private interest in the matter.

FORUM NON CONVENIENS: Inconvenient forum. Although a court may have jurisdiction over the case, the action should be tried in a more conveniently located court, one to which parties and witnesses may more easily travel, for example.

GUARDIAN AD LITEM: A guardian of an infant as to litigation, appointed to represent the infant and pursue his/her rights.

HABEAS CORPUS: You have the body. The modern writ of habeas corpus is a writ directing that a person (body) being detained (such as a prisoner) be brought before the court so that the legality of his detention can be judicially ascertained.

IN CAMERA: In private, in chambers. When a hearing is held before a judge in his chambers or when all spectators are excluded from the courtroom.

IN FORMA PAUPERIS: In the manner of a pauper. A party who proceeds in forma pauperis because of his poverty is one who is allowed to bring suit without liability for costs.

INFRA: Below, under. A word referring the reader to a later part of a book. (The opposite of supra.)

IN LOCO PARENTIS: In the place of a parent.

IN PARI DELICTO: Equally wrong; a court of equity will not grant requested relief to an applicant who is in pari delicto, or as much at fault in the transactions giving rise to the controversy as is the opponent of the applicant.

IN PARI MATERIA: On like subject matter or upon the same matter. Statutes relating to the same person or things are said to be in pari materia. It is a general rule of statutory construction that such statutes should be construed together, i.e., looked at as if they together constituted one law.

IN PERSONAM: Against the person. Jurisdiction over the person of an individual.

IN RE: In the matter of. Used to designate a proceeding involving an estate or other property.

IN REM: A term that signifies an action against the res, or thing. An action in rem is basically one that is taken directly against property, as distinguished from an action in personam, i.e., against the person.

INTER ALIA: Among other things. Used to show that the whole of a statement, pleading, list, statute, etc., has not been set forth in its entirety.

INTER PARTES: Between the parties. May refer to contracts, conveyances or other transactions having legal significance.

INTER VIVOS: Between the living. An inter vivos gift is a gift made by a living grantor, as distinguished from bequests contained in a will, which pass upon the death of the testator.

IPSO FACTO: By the mere fact itself.

JUS: Law or the entire body of law.

LEX LOCI: The law of the place; the notion that the rights of parties to a legal proceeding are governed by the law of the place where those rights arose.

MALUM IN SE: Evil or wrong in and of itself; inherently wrong. This term describes an act that is wrong by its very nature, as opposed to one which would not be wrong but for the fact that there is a specific legal prohibition against it (malum prohibitum).

MALUM PROHIBITUM: Wrong because prohibited, but not inherently evil. Used to describe something that is wrong because it is expressly forbidden by law but that is not in and of itself evil, e.g., speeding.

MANDAMUS: We command. A writ directing an official to take a certain action.

MENS REA: A guilty mind; a criminal intent. A term used to signify the mental state that accompanies a crime or other prohibited act. Some crimes require only a general mens rea (general intent to do the prohibited act), but others, like assault with intent to murder, require the existence of a specific mens rea.

MODUS OPERANDI: Method of operating; generally refers to the manner or style of a criminal in committing crimes, admissible in appropriate cases as evidence of the identity of a defendant.

NEXUS: A connection to.

NISI PRIUS: A court of first impression. A nisi prius court is one where issues of fact are tried before a judge or jury.

N.O.V. (NON OBSTANTE VEREDICTO): Notwithstanding the verdict. A judgment n.o.v. is a judgment given in favor of one party despite the fact that a verdict was returned in favor of the other party, the justification being that the verdict either had no reasonable support in fact or was contrary to law.

NUNC PRO TUNC: Now for then. This phrase refers to actions that may be taken and will then have full retroactive effect.

PENDENTE LITE: Pending the suit; pending litigation under way.

PER CAPITA: By head; beneficiaries of an estate, if they take in equal shares, take per capita.

PER CURIAM: By the court; signifies an opinion ostensibly written "by the whole court" and with no identified author.

PER SE: By itself, in itself; inherently.

PER STIRPES: By representation. Used primarily in the law of wills to describe the method of distribution where a person, generally because of death, is unable to take that which is left to him by the will of another, and therefore his heirs divide such property between them rather than take under the will individually.

PRIMA FACIE: On its face, at first sight. A prima facie case is one that is sufficient on its face, meaning that the evidence supporting it is adequate to establish the case until contradicted or overcome by other evidence.

PRO TANTO: For so much; as far as it goes. Often used in eminent domain cases when a property owner receives partial payment for his land without prejudice to his right to bring suit for the full amount he claims his land to be worth.

QUANTUM MERUIT: As much as he deserves. Refers to recovery based on the doctrine of unjust enrichment in those cases in which a party has rendered valuable services or furnished materials that were accepted and enjoyed by another under circumstances that would reasonably notify the recipient that the rendering party expected to be paid. In essence, the law implies a contract to pay the reasonable value of the services or materials furnished.

QUASI: Almost like; as if; nearly. This term is essentially used to signify that one subject or thing is almost analogous to another but that material differences between them do exist. For example, a quasi-criminal proceeding is one that is not strictly criminal but shares enough of the same characteristics to require some of the same safeguards (e.g., procedural due process must be followed in a parole hearing).

QUID PRO QUO: Something for something. In contract law, the consideration, something of value, passed between the parties to render the contract binding.

RES GESTAE: Things done; in evidence law, this principle justifies the admission of a statement that would otherwise be hearsay when it is made so closely to the event in question as to be said to be a part of it, or with such spontaneity as not to have the possibility of falsehood.

RES IPSA LOQUITUR: The thing speaks for itself. This doctrine gives rise to a rebuttable presumption of negligence when the instrumentality causing the injury was within the exclusive control of the defendant, and the injury was one that does not normally occur unless a person has been negligent.

RES JUDICATA: A matter adjudged. Doctrine which provides that once a court of competent jurisdiction has rendered a final judgment or decree on the merits, that judgment or decree is conclusive upon the parties to the case and prevents them from engaging in any other litigation on the points and issues determined therein.

RESPONDEAT SUPERIOR: Let the master reply. This doctrine holds the master liable for the wrongful acts of his servant (or the principal for his agent) in those cases in which the servant (or agent) was acting within the scope of his authority at the time of the injury.

STARE DECISIS: To stand by or adhere to that which has been decided. The common law doctrine of stare decisis attempts to give security and certainty to the law by following the policy that once a principle of law as applicable to a certain set of facts has been set forth in a decision, it forms a precedent which will subsequently be followed, even though a different decision might be made were it the first time the question had arisen. Of course, stare decisis is not an inviolable principle and is departed from in instances where there is good cause (e.g., considerations of public policy led the Supreme Court to disregard prior decisions sanctioning segregation).

SUPRA: Above. A word referring a reader to an earlier part of a book.

ULTRA VIRES: Beyond the power. This phrase is most commonly used to refer to actions taken by a corporation that are beyond the power or legal authority of the corporation.

Addendum of French Derivatives

IN PAIS: Not pursuant to legal proceedings.

CHATTEL: Tangible personal property.

CY PRES: Doctrine permitting courts to apply trust funds to purposes not expressed in the trust but necessary to carry out the settlor's intent.

PER AUTRE VIE: For another's life; during another's life. In property law, an estate may be granted that will terminate upon the death of someone other than the grantee.

PROFIT A PRENDRE: A license to remove minerals or other produce from land.

VOIR DIRE: Process of questioning jurors as to their predispositions about the case or parties to a proceeding in order to identify those jurors displaying bias or prejudice.

Casenote® Legal Briefs